Serenity found

Other Titles in the Smart Pop Series

Taking the Red Pill
Seven Seasons of Buffy
Five Seasons of Angel
What Would Sipowicz Do?
Stepping through the Stargate
The Anthology at the End of the Universe
Finding Serenity
The War of the Worlds
Alias Assumed
Navigating the Golden Compass
Farscape Forever!
Flirting with Pride and Prejudice
Revisiting Narnia
Totally Charmed
King Kong Is Back!
Mapping the World of the Sorcerer's Apprentice
The Unauthorized X-Men
The Man from Krypton
Welcome to Wisteria Lane
Star Wars on Trial
The Battle for Azeroth
Boarding the Enterprise
Getting Lost
James Bond in the 21st Century
So Say We All
Investigating CSI
Literary Cash
Webslinger
Halo Effect
Neptune Noir
Coffee at Luke's
Perfectly Plum

More Unauthorized Essays on
Joss Whedon's *Firefly* Universe

EDITED BY

JANE ESPENSON

WITH

LEAH WILSON

BENBELLA BOOKS, INC.
Dallas, Texas

BenBella Books, Inc.
6440 N. Central Expy., Suite 617
Dallas, TX 75206
Send feedback to feedback@benbellabooks.com.

Printed in the United States of America
10 9 8 7 6 5 4 3 2 1

Library of Congress Cataloging-in-Publication Data is available for this title.

Proofreading by Emily Chauvier and Jennifer Canzoneri
Cover design by Todd Michael Bushman
Text design and composition by Laura Watkins
Printed by Bang Printing

Distributed by Independent Publishers Group
To order call (800) 888-4741
www.ipgbook.com

For special sales contact Yara Abuata at yara@benbellabooks.com

Contents

Introduction 1
JANE ESPENSON

Catching Up with the Future 5
ORSON SCOTT CARD

Mars Needs Women 15
MAGGIE BURNS

Girls, Guns, Gags 27
NATALIE HAYNES

River Tam and the Weaponized Women of the Whedonverse 37
MICHAEL MARANO

I, Malcolm 49
NATHAN FILLION

Freedom in an Unfree World 55
P. GARDNER GOLDSMITH

A Tale of Two Heroes 67
SHANNA SWENDSON

The Good Book 79
ERIC GREENE

Mal Contents 95
ALEX BLEDSOE

Curse Your Sudden but Inevitable Betrayal 107
LANI DIANE RICH

Mutant Enemy U 117
LONI PERISTERE

Geeks of the World, Unite! 131
NATASHA GIARDINA

The Alliance's War on Science 141
KEN WHARTON

The Virtual 'Verse 151
COREY BRIDGES

***Firefly* and Story Structure, Advanced** 161
GEOFF KLOCK

Cut 'Em Off at the Horsehead Nebula! 175
BRUCE BETHKE

The Bonnie Brown Flag 187
EVELYN VAUGHN

Signal to Noise 203
JACOB CLIFTON

Acknowledgments 217

Introduction

Everyone has Moments of Serenity. Here are four of mine:

August 2002: I'm walking though an elaborately decorated back lot street at Universal Studios. Mal is there, and Kaylee and Wash and Zoe and Jayne, and even Badger and his fine hat. There are girls behind glass windows, one of them sweating in a pink layer-cake dress. The place is teeming with extras and strange-looking set dressing. Huge electric fans are blowing, and crew members release bits of brightly colored paper in front of them, decorating even the air. There might be chickens. It is the most exotic, most alien, most thoroughly imagined set I think I've ever been on. It is absolutely magical.

September 2004: I spend the day on the set of the movie *Serenity*. I get to walk through the ship once more, recreated here, bigger and better, on a different soundstage across town from its original home. It's easy to imagine it might have flown here. This is, I believe, the last day of principal photography. I know it is the day that River kicks Reaver ass. I get to watch multiple takes of the fight. Over and over she kicks and ducks and whirls. It is a blur of balletic violence.

September 2005: There is a red-carpet premiere for *Serenity* here in Los Angeles. The fans are here too, some inside the theater, others crowded just outside. Any of us fortunate enough to have been connected to the movie or to the series in some way are recognized as we walk into the event across an actual Hollywood red carpet. Joss-driven projects inspire a certain cult-of-the-writer, and we are hooted at and flash-bulbed at almost as vigorously as the stars.

February 2007: I am invited to WonderCon in San Francisco to speak on a panel about gender roles in science fiction, and to sign copies of whatever people want me to sign: *Firefly* scripts, artwork of Kaylee in that layer-cake dress, and lots of copies of *Finding Serenity*, the precursor to this book. People walk the convention floor dressed as Mal and Jayne. Almost five years after my one singular episode of *Firefly* was filmed, the world Joss created is still spinning.

So why is *Firefly* (note that I will use "*Firefly*" and "*Serenity*" interchangeably to refer to this particular Jossiverse as a whole) still inspiring this kind of interest and devotion so long after it began, so long after it ended? Why are there buyers for a book such as this one? Why are there contributors, for that matter? Other series, even ones with more viewers, even ones with much longer histories, don't get this kind of treatment. There are, as far as I know, very few books filled with essays like this:

> *"Stabler Than What?" A look at* Law and Order: SVU's *Detective Elliot Stabler, this essay suggests that the character symbolizes the International Monetary Fund in a way that should be read more as cautionary tale than Hero's Journey.*

No, you just don't get much of that kind of thing.

Part of the reason, of course, is that science fiction is a genre that naturally invites analysis. Sci-fi tends to work through metaphor. Some Other-World is intended to represent our own world through some sort of mapping. The details of the correspondences are not stated explicitly; that work is left to the viewers. This encourages participation, which leads viewers to feel proprietary. It also fosters debate: points of view, passionately contested. In other words, metaphor leads to books of essays. Go metaphor!

And *Firefly* isn't just sci-fi. It is also, in its own way, a Western. Westerns are the other major genre that tends to work through metaphor. Traditional movie Westerns used the wide-open other worldliness of the American frontier to stand for everything from the quest for personal freedom, to general continental expansion, to Vietnam.

But this is not the complete answer to the question. There's something else that made *Firefly* special.

Here is a Pre-*Serenity* moment: When I was fairly new to television writing, I attended the Writers' Guild Awards one year. Someone won a WGA award for writing an episode of *ER*. She got up on the stage, clutched the award, and thanked "The Creator." It was only a few sentences later that I realized she was referring to Michael Crichton. She hadn't intended to be humorous; the phrasing was totally ingenuous. It was also very apt.

When a creator is also a showrunner he or she really is the god of the show. Joss Whedon, the god of Serenity, is that missing element, the key to the lasting appeal, the lasting lure, of *Firefly*.

Joss had other brainchildren before *Firefly*. I was lucky enough to work with him for five years at *Buffy the Vampire Slayer*, and to write two freelance scripts under his direction at *Angel*. I was able to observe some of what makes Joss's storytelling so powerful.

Any new writer on a Joss Whedon show learns early on that the way *not* to sell Joss on an idea for an episode of television is to try to sell him on a cool monster, a cool visual, or a cool moment. There always has to be a real reason to tell the story. There has to be a truth exposed through the story. Either a truth about the world, or a truth about a character. Or, ideally, both. Joss's takes on gender, the nature of heroism, and the role of religion cannot be separated from the ways he writes his people. This insistence on having a reason to tell the story means that Joss's stories are striving in a very real way to communicate content beyond just a stream of well-imagined fictional events. They set out to do more than simply keep the audience tuned in through the commercial breaks.

Which brings us to the other secret ingredient: Joss's attitude toward the viewers. I don't recall Joss ever talking about "the audience" as a separate identity with an agenda separate or lesser (or greater, for that matter) than his own. He writes what interests him, what he would want to see. This is why when Joss writes a surprise it genuinely surprises, why his shocking revelations shock us, why his jokes make us laugh. It's not just that he assumes that you, the viewers, are as smart as him. He assumes, in a way, that you *are* him. And that he is you.

Not every writer does this. They assume that there is a chance that the viewer is distracted, or very young, or unsophisticated. They try to accommodate. Joss doesn't give you an inch. He demands attention and intelligence and he rewards it.

So, after all that . . . what better way could there be, really, to invite analysis? Create a world that floats on a layer of metaphor, drench it in big ideas about the world, fill it with real people, and then absolutely demand intelligence of your viewers.

Welcome to Serenity.

Jane Espenson — Los Angeles, 2007

We've all assembled here today because of a shared interest in Firefly. *(Unless your interest is actually fireflies. Sorry, you have purchased this book in error.) But how does* Firefly *fit into the pantheon of sci-fi greats? There can be no doubt that Orson Scott Card knows his sci-fi, and here he explains what it is that makes the* Firefly *universe special, literary, modern, and smart. He also makes the point that good writers are inspired by good writing. Indeed. Read this and be inspired.*

Catching Up with the Future

ORSON SCOTT CARD

It was 25 May 1977. A work day, supposedly. But it was the opening day of *Star Wars*.

Jay Parry and Lane Johnson and I were editors at a magazine in Salt Lake City. We were conscientious employees. We worked hard. We often worked late. We gave an honest day's work for each day's paltry pay.

We were also novice science fiction writers. We would spend our lunch hours down in the miserable cafeteria in our building, drinking generic soda pop (you couldn't guess the flavor if someone hid the can), and talking about our ideas for sci-fi stories that we would sell, launching brilliant careers that would turn us into the Heinleins, Asimovs, Ellisons, Silverbergs, or Nivens of our generation.

So when Lane suggested that we take a "long lunch" and see *Star Wars*, it actually caused a moral quandary.

A brief one.

(I suspect that Jay told our boss what we were doing and got tacit permission. He's a better man than I am, and always was. But maybe not, in which case that was certainly the most wicked thing Jay ever did in his life, and his conscience is still bothering him about it, and it is so wrong of me to tell.)

When the time rolled around, we were out the door and walking down the street to one of those grand old theaters—the kind with only one screen and a very large seating capacity. With an actual stage, where you could imagine someone actually performing a play. (I have to describe it, because the youthful readers of this book have probably never seen theaters like that. For that matter, most of the youthful readers have probably never walked to a theater, unless you count the trip from the parking lot to the box office.)

There had been a lot of hype about *Star Wars*. The screenings for the press had resulted in cover stories in magazines and full-page spreads in newspapers, with reviewers talking as if George Lucas had just invented the moving picture.

I had missed most of that, being such a conscientious, hard-working, and newly married guy. (Eight days by actual count, and no, it didn't cross my mind to take my wife to the movie—why would *she* want to see a sci-fi film? You have to understand that up to that moment, sci-fi films were generally—and more or less correctly—perceived as a branch of the horror film genre. *2001: A Space Odyssey* had been one of a kind.) Who had time to notice the newspapers and magazines?

So it was without any particular expectations that I sat down with Lane and Jay and watched those massive letters crawl up the screen. And crawl and crawl and crawl.

Then the massive ship came into view and I felt a tingle under my skin. This did not look like the standard rocket ships from old sci-fi films. Nor did it look like the realistic, utilitarian, minimalist spaceships of *2001* or the real space program.

This was a ship that was more like an old-time surface battleship, except that there was no hull—the bottom bristled with structures just like the top and sides. And, like an aircraft carrier surrounded by gnat-like planes, the big ship dwarfed the fighters swarming around it.

The tingling continued as I saw robots that looked like nothing I'd seen before—or, when they did, they at least didn't *talk* like they had before. When we met aliens, they were a potpourri of every alien ever imagined in science fiction. (We recognized many of them—the wookie was an obvious borrowing from Larry Niven's Kzin, for instance.)

This was the science fiction of my earliest imagining. This was space adventure, a kind of storytelling that had been missing from the movies for a long time.

And at the end, when my friends and I walked out of the theater, we were floating. What a great experience.

But it took about three minutes for somebody to say to me, "Don't you wish you could write something like that?"

I'm afraid I laughed in the person's face; Lane and Jay laughed too. We all knew the same thing: No writer of science fiction stories in 1977 would aspire to write something as childish as *Star Wars*.

The movie experience was great. The story was fun. But in the world of print, that level of storytelling had "1935" written all over it. In print, science fiction had come a long, long way since then. It was still possible to write wonderful adventures—Larry Niven was proving that with every book—but they had to be *way* smarter than *Star Wars*.

In print science fiction, the science had to be at least remotely plausible; *Star Wars* had real howlers, like treating "parsec" as a measure of time rather than distance, and fighters that moved aerodynamically in space, complete with impossible whooshing sounds. And light sabers? What a hoot. No self-respecting science fiction writer would dare to use something so unnecessary and improbable—but it made a great *visual*.

Star Wars amounted to a swords-and-sorcery fantasy, except in space instead of in a medieval kingdom, and not a particularly clever or emotionally engaging one at that. And "the Force"—can you imagine something so silly? In *print* science fiction we would have recognized that instantly as either magic or religion; nothing to do with science fiction.

But that's how things were back then—and still are, mostly, today. Film science fiction was firmly rooted in the era of lurid adventure writing—which wasn't a bad thing, as long as you understood that print science fiction had long since grown up into a multi-faceted genre in which you could have writerly stories like Harlan Ellison's and Samuel R. Delany's, or thoughtful anthropological science fiction like Ursula K. LeGuin's and James Blish's, or gung-ho, hard-science competent-man stories in the tradition of Asimov and Heinlein, Clarke and Niven.

But sci-fi films were stuck at the level of *Lost in Space* and *Star Trek* on TV: aliens who all spoke English, ray guns, spaceships that looked like living rooms with odd furniture (because that was the kind of set that was cheap to build), with magic technology and stories that could always be resolved by courage and brawn and a thimbleful of brains.

Above all, sci-fi films and television shows had *no characters whatsoever.* Oh, they had people wearing costumes and saying lines, but once you had stated their role, there was nothing more to say. On *Star Trek*, what were the crew of the *Enterprise* after you set aside their ethnicity and their job description on the ship? Nothing. And as for Spock, he was a one-note character. (He gave the illusion of being an interesting character because he was played by the one excellent actor in the series.)

(I realize, of course, that saying these things will result in Trekkers burning me in effigy, but it's simply true. We know what film and television characterization looks like—finally—and it simply was not present, was not even attempted, in *Star Trek*—or, I must add, any of its spin-offs and sequel series. It simply wasn't part of the formula as it is today in, say, *Lost* and *Medium*.)

As far as I knew, the only science fiction film that showed any awareness of where print science fiction was up to 1977 had been *2001: A Space Odyssey*.

I had enjoyed *2001* very much—it had accomplished the formidable task of making movement in space look real. It certainly did a better job than *Star Wars* of getting space and technology right. But it also moved at an excruciatingly slow pace—a deliberate and, I think, correct choice for the story that was being told.

It was a very cerebral story, and it collapsed into deliberate incoherence at the end—with Kubrick in charge, it was always going to be about the director, not the story. Arthur C. Clarke's novel was, as a story, much better. It was as if Kubrick decided that he would make a film that *looked* like it knew about good science fiction, but he had to prove that as an auteur, he was above mere storytelling.

2001 hadn't changed film sci-fi that much, because it was regarded as a fluke, a one-shot. *Star Wars*, however, remade the landscape, especially when the first two sequels showed that the phenomenal ticket sales could be repeated.

What happened then? In screen sci-fi, we simply got more *Star Wars* imitations. *Battlestar Galactica* on television—it was hilarious when Lucas sued Glen Larson for infringing on *Star Wars*, since everything in *Star Wars* was stolen from print science fiction, directly or indirectly, and I hadn't noticed Lucas paying anybody for the privilege of using their ideas.

And in film, we had some great movies—the Alien franchise, and Terminator franchise. But those were both throwbacks to sci-fi as monster movies.

Starman was a powerful exception—a very personal story, which made a serious effort to be both smart and character-driven. But it was also not a blockbuster success, barely making back its budget in domestic box office. It was not the beginning of a trend.

Blade Runner also tried, and it was a good movie, too. In truth *Blade Runner* and *Starman* succeeded in bringing 1950s science fiction to the screen. It was an enormous step forward, but screen sci-fi still lagged behind print science fiction by a generation.

In film, the serious money went into big blockbusters. Even when, like the Lynch *Dune*, they were ghastly failures, nobody noticed that the actual stories of first-rate science fiction were usually butchered and made incoherent or tedious or ridiculous when they were adapted to the blockbuster formula.

Hollywood knew what sci-fi film was supposed to be, and whenever serious money was involved, they made sure that it never became anything else.

Without Hollywood ever noticing, however, film and television sci-fi began to serve the longtime social function of print sci-fi, as the scripture of our culture's public religion. Now that we no longer admit to sharing the Judeo-Christian tradition as our common heritage, it is in science fiction that we find our parables, doctrines, dogmas, homilies, and faith-promoting Sunday school stories, along with, now and then, serious examinations of important moral issues and existential questions. Am I the only one who noticed that *2001*, *Star Trek*, and *Star Wars* (which together moved film sci-fi out of the horror-film ghetto toward mainstream respectability) all had mystical and moral lessons that had far more to do with Sunday school than science? They completely replaced the public hunger that used to be satisfied with epics like *The Ten Commandments* and *Ben-Hur*.

Meanwhile, *Star Wars* and *Star Trek* were also dealing a crippling blow to print science fiction.

People wanted more movies than Hollywood could afford to produce. Those for whom *Star Trek* and *Star Wars* had become either their church or their social group could not wait. They wrote their own "fan fiction," which the studios finally stopped trying to suppress, instead replacing it with dozens, then hundreds of professionally written work-for-hire novels that began to crowd out original science fiction in the bookstores.

People reading *Star Trek* and *Star Wars* novels are getting the *opposite* of the experience readers of the genre always looked for. The science fiction genre, in print, had always been about having new experiences. There were series and sequels, of course, but the best writers prided themselves on having each entrant in a series be quite different from the others. And, unlike the mystery genre, the sci-fi genre allowed writers of successful series to do completely unrelated books—and the readers would follow along.

The writers tried to come up with genuinely new ideas with each book. When Frederik Pohl wrote *Man-Plus* and *Gateway* in the mid-1970s, it was hard to tell that this was the same writer who had done his earlier work. Not that it was necessarily better; rather he was developing ideas that had simply not been available in the 1950s.

Whereas with media tie-in novels, readers are disappointed if they don't get *exactly* the same experience they had before. The story is cosmetically different, but it takes readers to the same place; that's why they buy it.

It is an exercise in familiarity.

So not only was film and television sci-fi mired in an old-fashioned kind of story, it had become so financially and culturally successful that it was driving *real* science fiction into a corner, both in print and in film.

And I was waiting.

For what? I wasn't sure. But I'd know it when I saw it.

I wanted film sci-fi that had the characterization of good science fiction. It didn't have to be obsessive, but I needed to have a sense that these people had a life before they arrived in their spaceship, and that their personal relationships were changing over time.

I didn't want stories that hinged on getting away from monsters or on becoming an adept of some mystical religion; I didn't want them to feel like the characters were moving through space in order to have adventures. I wanted the characters to have individual motives and purposes; I wanted the stories to take place in real-seeming cultures that might actually exist.

And then I gave up.

Oh, I still went to sci-fi films, and enjoyed some of them. The feature film *Stargate* was fun, though it was really more *Indiana Jones* than genuine sci-fi.

I loved Charlie Kaufman's *Being John Malkovich* and *The Eternal Sunshine of the Spotless Mind*—these were truly in the spirit of the best of print science fiction, and if they had been published as novels or short stories in the sci-fi genre, they would have been hailed in the years they came out as showing the voice of an excellent new writer.

But Kaufman's stories weren't set in space. They weren't even considered sci-fi films.

On television, I knew Straczynski was doing interesting things with *Babylon 5*, and people kept telling me that this or that series was the "good" *Star Trek*. But I just couldn't engage. The people were still their jobs. It was still sci-fi that would not have been interesting if it came out in print.

And then . . .

And then I saw *Firefly*.

Years late. It had already been canceled. Like many viewers, I only caught up with it because I was forced to by insistent people that I couldn't ignore. "But television sci-fi is boring," I said. "Life is too short to waste any more of it on this stuff."

Then, at last, I started watching *Firefly* and within ten minutes I knew: The writer of this series had actually read a book, and instead of copying it, like everybody else doing film sci-fi, he had understood what science fiction is for and how it's done, and he had created something *new*.

Oh, it superficially looks like *Star Trek*—if it hadn't sounded familiar in a pitch meeting, it would never have made it to the screen at all. In the pitch meeting, while it's possible no one said the words *Star Trek*, you know that the studio executives were hearing the word constantly. Let's see, a ship that goes from planet to planet and has adventures. The lead is the captain. The ship is always on the verge of falling apart and a mechanic magically fixes it just in time. The captain takes his crew to the surface and meets people in different cultures and fights and barely makes it back to the ship and. . . . Okay, sounds exactly like *Star Trek*, only different enough that Paramount won't sue us. Go ahead.

But the differences were more than cosmetic. This wasn't *Wagon Train* in space. The characters had a history. They were different from each other. They did way more (and less) than their jobs. They didn't always like each other, didn't always trust each other.

The cultures they ran into were always human (no aliens, did you notice?) and they functioned like real human societies. The characters they picked up had real problems (or plausible nefarious plans).

Best of all, it was a witty show. Not just a show trying to be witty, but a show in which the characters' one-liners were actually funny and true to character. Not since *The Dick Van Dyke Show*'s sessions in the comedy-writers' room had I seen writing this clever.

Television does force a shape onto every TV series; you can only bend the rules so far. *Firefly* was still a TV series. But within that frame, Joss Whedon had brought, not just the appearance of recent print sci-fi, but the fact of it: He was writing characters who had not existed before, and putting them into situations that, if they had been in short stories submitted to magazines or anthologies, would certainly have sold and been published.

He and his writing staff were creating stories every bit as current and credible as the science fiction of Charlie Kaufman—only *Firefly* was set in space so that viewers *knew* they were getting sci-fi.

And by the time I saw it, it was already dead.

But you know the saga of how *Serenity* arose from the ashes of *Firefly*. You also know the problems faced by the script. This movie had to reach an audience that was *not* already familiar with the TV series. Therefore it had to ignore much of the character development that had already taken place in the series. Most particularly, the relationship between the doctor and the captain was dropped back to a level of suspicion and hostility that denied the experiences they had shared.

So what? The movie was meant to be a new start. It hit the ground running, gave the series's fans a dollop of what we had come to expect, and then took us into brand new territory.

The story of *Serenity* was smart, hard science fiction. Not only were the regular cast still good strong characters, the new characters—Mr. Universe and the assassin—were fascinating, surprising, quirky. The plot actually hinged on a moral decision *made by the bad guy*. Who does *that*?

In most film sci-fi, as with *Star Wars*, serious sci-fi readers have to squint or hold their noses now and then to pretend that the story isn't really this dumb. But that didn't happen with *Serenity*. Not once. Whereas many sci-fi films and TV shows seem to be going out of their way to find new kinds of stupidity—about science, about human nature, about formulaic storytelling—*Serenity* never made me wince.

Joss Whedon, like Charlie Kaufman, is a new breed of film sci-fi writer: He knows how to read, he knows how to think, he knows how to create new milieux, believable characters, smart technology, plausible cultures, and great dramatic and comic scenes and dialogue.

Of course, *Serenity* did about as well, financially, as *Starman*. So I fear that it will be another flash in the pan. Except . . . except. . . .

Now that they've seen what sci-fi *can* be on the screen, isn't it just possible that a new generation of writers will take the same kind of care to create scripts that aspire to this new standard? Even if *Serenity* didn't wow the executives, won't the writers insist that the script isn't done unless it has real characters and relationships, great dialogue, and stories that make sense?

Of course, a writer like that will quickly get fired and replaced with somebody who'll give the executives a script that follows the lame film-school formulas that don't work and never have.

But what if the replacement writer *also* takes some pride in his work? What if you can't get anybody to deliberately write bad sci-fi any more?

George Lucas's awful *Star Wars* prequels in recent years are an embarrassment. The religious *Star Wars* fans still go, and many can't tell the difference.

But the writers can. It's just possible that *Firefly* and *Serenity* have pulled the whole sci-fi film genre up to a level where it is possible for science fiction as good as the best of contemporary print sci-fi to be put on the screen.

I sure hope so, because I have a script right here. . . .

Orson Scott Card, the author of *Ender's Game*, *Ender's Shadow*, *Magic Street*, and *Enchantment*, is a distinguished professor of writing and literature at Southern Virginia University.

I've remarked before that when some viewers see giant spaceships hover into view, they fear that giant ideas are right behind them. Over the years, science fiction has become linked with the idea of "message" in much the same way that rare ground beef has become linked with the idea of "E. coli." Burns makes a great case for characters—messy, human, relatable, and even sometimes female characters—as the remedy to this unfortunate situation.

Mars Needs Women
How a Dress, a Cake, and a Goofy Hat Will Save Science Fiction

MAGGIE BURNS

Science fiction is broken. Like poetry and art music, science fiction threatens to spin itself into a self-referential genre so disconnected from everything else that only initiates can find value in it, a tiny irrelevant genre jealously guarded by hard-core fans. So much insider knowledge accrues about each created universe that it pushes away the newcomer. A genre that fired the imaginations of those who actually got humanity into space is reduced to teddy bear aliens, macho swagger, and jiggle. Those of us who love sci-fi are so hungry for it that we will devour nearly anything, which only serves to keep the standards low and the scenarios familiar.

What is the cure for sci-fi's problems? A goofy knitted hat. A frilly dress. A birthday cake. You and me, and people we know, in space: *Firefly*.

Sci-fi at its best has higher goals than any other genre. Its creators bring us hope, fear, and truth. Hope in sci-fi shows us what we can be, what we could be if we lived up to our potential. Fear plays out in warnings about our present and future. Of these three, fear appears most often, since it encompasses all of the dystopian fiction: extrapolations of society's flaws taken to their logical extremes, dark explorations of human nature, terrifying insights into the ugly side of our societies. This type of sci-fi also brings us aliens, which have been standing in for our fears and our flaws in various forms since they first appeared in literature.

But the highest goal of science fiction is to tell us the truth about ourselves. We find it in every sci-fi work that ever tried to say: "This is how it is. Don't pretend, don't turn away, don't lie. This is who you are. This is what we are." Seeking truth is the strongest and the bravest course, the hardest fiction to write, the most difficult to fall in love with, because it holds an honest mirror to humanity. We never want to look that clearly at our own reflections. Is that a blemish coming on? Does this dress make me look like the privileged product of a globally exploitative oligarchy? Why, yes, actually, it does. Turn that mirror to face the wall.

Firefly sets out to tell larger truths through fiction, just as sci-fi tackles larger social and socio-economic issues than most other genres. *Firefly* is not merely telling entertaining stories, though it does that exceptionally well. It's not simply creating a vivid and gorgeously textured universe, one that is completely believable. It's not just a fun ride with space cowboys and excellent cussing in Mandarin.

Firefly is all those things, but like the finest print sci-fi, from *A Canticle for Leibowitz* to *The Martian Chronicles* to *The Dispossessed*—and unlike the vast majority of sci-fi on television—it also sets out to show us our world through a created one. Like the best sci-fi novels, *Firefly* does this by being honest in its depiction of the breadth of life, in its inclusions and exclusions, in its reflections of class and gender and economics. The only sci-fi television show that has ever dared to tell the truth like this was *Farscape*, which only got away with it because every character except the hero was an alien. *Farscape* showed us messy, gross, violent, crazy alien life in Technicolor: old women who make soup that you don't want to look at too closely, young women with good hearts and damaged souls, insecure warrior men who need friends, alien warrior women who discover they can be more—people we know in our own lives, but never see represented in sci-fi TV. Sci-fi television only allows this much reality, this much painful insight, only hits this close to the bone, when the characters are aliens. Until *Firefly*, we never saw so much reality played out with people. No aliens in *Firefly*. And no easy answers. There are plenty of monsters, but they all take human form, just like in our world.

Firefly reaches us in a way we can accept by giving us a world that draws us in, using touchstones that tell us: This is the real world. This is a recognizable 'verse, where we could live. The show does not use any of the easier sci-fi tropes: no aliens to embody our difficult or less palatable traits, no black-and-white hero, and most of all, no simple world consisting primarily of militaristic men. This world includes women of all kinds, rich and poor, strong and weak, brave and scared. This is so rare in science fiction that it's completely revolutionary. Who lives in a world with so few women? Who lives so far removed from the messy realities of life? Modern sci-fi television has its roots in a genre historically so sexist that women and the messy realities of life are identical, both eradicated from all those sparkling spaceship interiors, except for the occasional beautiful scientist's daughter who needs to be rescued.

One of the biggest weaknesses of sci-fi television is its insistence on framing so many narratives within that same sparkling, orderly, male-dominated militarized hegemony. From *Star Trek* to *Stargate SG-1*, the universe appears through this lens. Whether it's *Star Trek*'s Federation, or *Stargate*'s recognizable U.S. Air Force—right down to guest appearances by each Air Force Chief of Staff—this framework dominates television science fiction. The militaristic framework is off-putting, whether you have a military background or not. If you do, it's always inaccurate and irritating, especially when lives are thrown away without comment. If you don't have a military background, it's alienating, familiar only through all of its sci-fi forebears. The trope is self-referential and lacks any visceral link to a familiar reality. Ultimately the military framework is a narrative cheat, a shorthand, without depth of thought or character resonance at all.

Powerful and cruel but faceless bureaucracies fronted by militaries made up of marching automatons are the dullest cheap trick of sci-fi. *Firefly* mercifully kept these people in the distant background, where we like our governments to be. When we did see representatives, the soldiers were wearing absurd purple armor and the officers appeared to be jackbooted hotel staff. Even the scariest villains seemed to be taking time from their office jobs to scrub the bathroom, with their black suits and blue rubber gloves, though their mysterious blue baton of infinite nosebleeds was quite effectively terrifying. The true villains of *Firefly* were far more frightening, because they were recognizable from our daily lives. They included ethical dilemmas, conflicting loyalties, putting food on the table. Financial survival, taking care of family. Trying to stay safe. Trying to keep flying.

Faceless bureaucracies, expendable military forces, demonized villains, God-like aliens: these will kill a genre that has infinite potential, because they dangerously limit the ways we allow ourselves to imagine. They exchange endless imaginative possibilities for a vending machine array of choices. As much as I love the decade of *Stargate SG-1*, it has done more than any other show to reinforce the prevailing male-dominated militaristic and oppositional human/alien tendency in science fiction. Humanity's problem is ultimately humanity, after all. Sci-fi does not need to eradicate reality as we know it to speak the truth. Instead, it needs to embrace the familiar, as *Firefly* does. The people we know, the things they use. These draw us into a fictional world on such a deep level that we accept the truth of it without question.

Firefly is the only sci-fi show ever to feature the kind of people I went to high school with, the people who aren't usually represented in fiction except as cannon fodder. Take Jayne, the mercenary muscle on the ship. I went to high school with approximately one thousand Jaynes, wearing that same green coat, so Jayne embodies truth to me. He wasn't great at school, was deeply loyal to his friends and family, liked trucks and guns and beer and women he could understand. Anything else was suspicious. When you see someone so completely true on screen, how can you react with anything but pleasure, no matter what kind of untrustworthy horndog bonehead he is? The truth in the character of Jayne says to me that people matter, as they are, with all of their flaws and idiocies. We're all in this together.

Take Kaylee, a genius mechanic from a podunk moon, the sweetest person you'll ever meet. I went to high school with a thousand Kaylees, too, though they were busy fighting for survival, because the lives of the rural poor are scary and harsh, with narrow boundaries and a limited choice of futures. But they had Kaylee's heart, that fragile fear that people were looking down on them, that they weren't good enough or pretty enough or smart enough. I recognized Kaylee. Kaylee is true. Follow the truth of that character logically and you understand the heart of the show.

Kaylee can fix nearly anything, sees the good in everyone, can't handle a gun. (Though I bet she'd be able to field strip one in no time flat, plus fix that sticky chambering mechanism that always jams when the humidity is high.) Kaylee was the beating heart of the show as she tended the beating heart of *Serenity*. When have you ever seen anyone like her on a spaceship before? You see capable and tough women, women who are essentially men, and not just regular men like you and I know, but a Navy SEAL in a D-cup woman suit, with twelve advanced degrees and not one single trait that we would recognize as belonging to a female human. Fantasy women. Projections of idiotic ideals.

Is anyone surprised that sci-fi appeals to relatively few women, when these are the characters out there to identify with? I adore the admirable Samantha Carter of *Stargate SG-1*, for instance, but she is just not representative of most women I've ever met—at least outside of Caltech. Which leads back to the original problem. Yes, Samantha Carter is pretty much the image of my brilliant sister, who got her Ph.D. at Caltech—but that's still not a way into the fiction for the rest of us. I admire Samantha Carter, I even know people exactly like her, but she's not me, and in her world, there's no place for me. She's a militarized superhero. There's no place for librarians or liberal arts types or your mom or the woman who works in the bakery down the street in almost any sci-fi universe. That omission commits two crimes: it makes the created world not true, and it alienates a vast segment of the audience. So much of sci-fi is guilty of these crimes.

Except for *Firefly*. *Firefly* has Kaylee, who in "Shindig" saw that big frilly pink and white ruffly dress in the window of a shop and fell in love with it. Kaylee breaks your heart, because Mal made a rude comment about her and the dress—how she would have been like a sheep walking on its hind legs—and Kaylee, who loves everyone, wouldn't speak to Mal again until he showed up with the dress for her. It was a powerful, human moment. Mal needed Kaylee dressed up and on his arm to go to a fancy party. And our Kaylee was beside herself with delight. This is someone we know.

Kaylee breaks your heart again because a gaggle of mean girls mocked her dress. Looking at them, you have to agree, their dresses are gorgeous and subtle, especially that gold one with the sort of cutaway jacket worn by the queen bitch. Wait, do you realize what just happened? We're talking about dresses in sci-fi. We're talking about mean girls at a party. We're talking about girl stuff. Which is an essential part of life for half of the human race.

I've never actually had front row seats for a supernova, been involved in a spaceship dogfight, used warp drive, had dinner with a Cylon (that I know of), or watched a planet explode from orbit. But I do know a thing or two about mean girls at parties, and how terrible you feel when they are horrible to you. And how great was it when the nice man with the sash came over and told off the mean girls? And how fun was it when all the boys wanted to talk to Kaylee because she knew all about spaceship engines? Vindication!

It's not real—it's not truth—unless you include the mean girls at the party as well as the part about how the singularity is about to explode, weapons at maximum, fire! You're not telling the truth if you leave out Kaylee, or Zoe, or Inara, or crazy barefoot River tearing labels off all the cans or rubbing soup in people's hair. It's not true, if they're not there. It can't be. No matter what story you're trying to tell about humanity and its problems, your fiction will never ring true without the people and things that tie it to a reality we recognize and feel on a visceral level.

In "Out of Gas," Kaylee baked a cake for Simon for his birthday. Like the dress, it's far more than just an object out of Planet Stereotypical Femininity, stuck in frame to give texture to the world. That would be a cheat. We've all seen that in sci-fi. Colonel Caltech shows a slightly feminine side and then gets defensive about it to the rest of the crew, all men, who snicker at her ("Look, she's wearing a dress!") in a deeply ugly way that plays into the fallacy that women can't be strong and effective in traditionally male milieus without giving up everything that we associate with the feminine. Everyone on *Firefly* completely disproved that idiotic fallacy—like real people, who disprove it daily.

Who would you rather stare down at the end of a barrel, Mal or Zoe? Mal, obviously, because he'd blink, and then bash you in the head and leave you there to come back and bite him in the ass another day. But

Zoe would blow your head off without thinking twice or breathing hard. Yet Zoe also has a wonderfully true traditionally feminine side. She wants a dress with some slink. She was married to a kind and gentle man. The closest *Firefly* comes to a superhero is Zoe, who is saved from becoming a knee-jerk feminist cliché by her genuine layers and depth.

The birthday cake Kaylee baked in "Out of Gas" is much more than a simple realistic touch. To begin with, Kaylee had a crush on Simon and everyone knew it, except maybe Simon, which lends a deliciously true texture to the proceedings. The scene in the kitchen played out in such a lovely way, everyone gathered at the table together. We didn't get to see that very often on *Firefly*, so every time it happened was precious. The crew had come together from the most disparate walks of life, from all classes, a man of the cloth and a prostitute, fighters and professed wimps, a couple of geniuses and a mercenary lunkhead. The family gathered over dinner and settled down to birthday cake together, though later in the episode everyone but Mal abandoned the ship, only to return at the end, united again.

Would it mean as much without the cake? There's a mess hall scene in *Alien* that I think of, whenever food shows up in sci-fi. Goop for dinner, blue milk, everyone acting like a bunch of guys, even the women. The food is deliberately alienating, not your mother's macaroni and cheese or anything we recognize, a choice which further equates the abandoned normal world of grass and air with women, family, home, playing into the feminine equivalent of emasculation that I object to so strongly. Food can still be food as we know it, in space. Woman can still be women as we know them. Sci-fi seems to be the last bastion of the absurdly archaic idea that a woman must give up all of the traditional trappings of femininity to be strong. That the politically correct representation of a woman must absolutely not include any of those traditional trappings or it somehow belittles women. That food can't be apples and chicken or we won't believe that we're on an alien planet. That women can't be recognizably women or we won't know we're in space. That it's not the future unless we eradicate the messy realities of life.

Why does sci-fi cling to this so strongly? We know perfectly well it's not true. We all know dozens of fierce, strong women who enjoy the whole range of human endeavors without losing one molecule of their strength. To propose otherwise, as so much sci-fi does incessantly, is to deny the richness and texture of humanity, to set a story in a shallow world populated by cardboard heroes. Is my sister less of a brilliant scientist because she knits booties for her co-workers when they have babies? That sounds completely insane, yet it's exactly what most sci-fi tries to force you to believe. Were all those heroes really hatched out of incubation chambers? Who changed their space diapers? Who grew the cotton and wove the cloth? You look closely and it all falls apart. Worse, removing the whole range of women and all of the messy realities of life impoverishes the landscape so badly that it's nearly impossible to tell a decent story. It takes almost all of the colors out of the paintbox and leaves you with a muddy olive drab.

Consider Jayne's mother, who sent him a wonderfully goofy knitted wool hat in "The Message." Orange and yellow bulky wool, with rust-colored earflaps and a big pompom on top. If you weren't in love with Jayne already, for being 100 percent himself, then watching him open up his mother's present and immediately put it on would have made you fall in love. Wash made fun of him instantly: "Man walks down the street wearing that hat, people know he's not afraid of anything." To which our Jayne replied, "Damn straight," because he didn't quite get the meaning and took it as a compliment to himself instead of an insult to the hat. (Luckily for Wash, I'm thinking.) That was a gorgeous scene.

Jayne's hat played all throughout "The Message." He took it off as a sign of respect for the dead, when the crew was listening to Tracey's message asking Mal and Zoe to take him back home to his folks on St. Albans. Womack, the Fed who chased them down, told Jayne that the hat made him look like an idiot. Jayne took it off again in respect for the dead when Mal and Zoe carried Tracey's body down *Serenity*'s ramp to the waiting family.

Jayne's hat didn't really even mean anything in "The Message." It was just a hat, doing hat things. But like the cake and the frilly dress, Jayne's hat signifies an entire wealth of background to this universe, where mothers still knit hats for their grown sons, where sons unconditionally love the hats their mothers send them. Where a mechanical genius can fall in love with an unfashionable ruffled dress and wear it to a party, so that you're just dying with embarrassment for her in front of the mean rich girls in their expensive, tailored gowns. Where the same genius mechanic can take a break from fixing a spaceship engine and bake a cake for the cute doctor she has a crush on. Each of these things grounds the fiction in a vital, recognizable, complex, dirty universe. Each of these things is far more than just a thing.

Firefly does some lovely work with people and objects, playing with the shifting boundaries between them. Villains like Adelai Niska and Rance Burgess and Jubal Early turn people into things, treat people as objects. But when the transformation goes the other direction, as with the dress, the hat, and the cake, it's exactly what we do in our lives every day in order to belong to a world in which physical objects are our interface: we imbue objects with meaning. A dress means something—it's never just a dress. In fiction, a cigar is never just a cigar. Nothing in sci-fi is ever free of valence, weight, meaning.

A gun is a tree branch is a gun. River became *Serenity* itself, in the addled mind of Early, the bounty hunter in "Objects in Space" who, more than anyone in the series, read things as people and people as things. "Ain't nothing more than a body to me," he said to Kaylee, as he calmly threatened her with rape, turning our beloved Kaylee into an object and his own body into a weapon. Turning people into objects is the worst crime you can commit; its obverse, making objects take on the hearts and meanings of the people around you, that's quintessentially human, one of our highest accomplishments. Objects are what we use to read the world and how we make the world reflect ourselves back to us. Objects are where we put our hearts outside of us, in gifts, in memories, in meaning. The biggest object of all, *Serenity*, is far more than a ship: it's a home, a family, a place to belong.

The crew of *Serenity* lived in space, yes, but it was space that was familiar. It's home, just somewhere else. *Firefly* is people we know, with relationships and objects we can understand. In the pilot episode alone we saw easily a couple dozen things we'd never seen in space before: the spaceship's captain peeing then washing his hands; a recognizable Christian preacher with a Bible; a pretty girl with a dirty face and no education running the engine room; veterans of a lost war who had to live with that loss and that mockery every day; the painful daily effects of class differences; a realistic gunshot wound, with blood and pain and someone going into shock; men and women who cared about each other as friends, without any sexual overtones; horses and cowboy hats; people who were barely scraping by and needed every bit of cash they could get their hands on, just to survive. Didn't you always wonder about the bathrooms on the *Enterprise*? *Serenity* herself felt so much more real than any spaceship we've seen. There were dirty dishes and mended clothes, comfortable couches and weird art, birthday cake and strawberries. People ate apples. It's the present, in the future. Imaginative fiction about the future makes no sense to us at all unless we can imagine ourselves in it.

What's wrong with science fiction? Try to get someone who doesn't like science fiction to watch *Firefly*. If they won't, it's because they've seen too many shows along the lines of the various Star Treks, where women and men are interchangeable, or *Stargate SG-1*, a show which I love dearly despite all of its flaws. These types of shows push people away with military uniforms and guns and firefights, with aliens who are ever so slightly—but ever so importantly—different from us. Maybe they cannot use contractions; maybe they have glowy eyes or a little prosthetic on their foreheads, or slightly strange ears. These signals tell us that we're dealing with an easy world, familiar tropes, a sanitized, polarized reality: the usual. And because of this constant use of the easy way out in sci-fi television, people who would love *Firefly* if they watched it will flinch when you suggest they try some. That's a loss, both to them and to the genre, because sci-fi is consistently poorer for the lack of a more varied audience and a more varied range of experiences among its creators. It doesn't have to be like this. Science fiction can be infinitely better. It can be more.

The cure for science fiction can be found in *Firefly*, where realistic men and women rise above the kinds of nightmare realities we've all faced, in order to solve their small problems, and from there, the big ones. Antiseptic rumbling spaceship troop carriers full of space Nazis are not going anywhere, and that's perfectly fine, as long as there's someone in the picture, somewhere, who feels like someone you know. Someone wearing a goofy knitted hat from his mom, or someone proudly presenting a lopsided birthday cake, or someone who falls in love with a great big frilly confection of a dress.

MAGGIE BURNS is an aspiring television writer and novelist living in Los Angeles. Educated at Oberlin College and Penn State University, she very nearly completed a Ph.D. in comparative literature, in the course of which she learned an awful lot of ancient, medieval, and modern languages, as well as how to write for television. She has taught literature and writing at the University of Pennsylvania, Temple University, and Willamette University. A lifelong musician and omnivorous reader, she writes incessantly, knits, quilts, repairs engines, watches a lot of quality television, works at a major studio, and climbs Mt. Hollywood as often as possible.

Haynes here gives Firefly *its due as a feminist work. Along the wa[illegible] exposes a truth about Joss's writing that is sometimes, astonishingly, mis[illegible] Joss writes people, not just women. (In fact, everyone gets to be people, eve[illegible] if they're not human.) Sometimes in all the emphasis on the new and excit[illegible]ing way he writes women as people, we forget that he writes men as people too. In a Joss story, everyone gets to be funny, real, human, damaged, good and bad, loving-or-not, and satisfyingly complex.*

Girls, Guns, Gags

Why the Future Belongs to the Funny

NATALIE HAYNES

Earlier this year, I read an essay on *Firefly* which suggested that the show was a feminist step down from *Buffy the Vampire Slayer*, because it inhabited the more misogynistic world of gun-fights at the Last Chance Saloon—because women weren't physically as strong as men, so they could only really beat them by using feminine wiles, and occasionally, heaven forbid, their beauty and guile.

This simply goes to prove that no matter how much time, money, and effort you throw into an education system, stupidity, arrogance, and a total failure to grasp the basic tenets of feminism will nonetheless thrive like rats in a fetid storm drain. So, let me explain: the power structure in *Buffy* was pyramidal—at the bottom were innocent people, above them was a race of fewer but physically much stronger vampires, and above them was one (or were two) slayers, strongest and fewest of all. The power structure in *Firefly* was quite different, because everyone was human. No pointy ears, no stick-on proboscides, no extra arms. Some of the men were stronger than some of the women, but by no means all: as Wash told Saffron, Zoe could kill him with her little finger.

To even things up, though, most of the fighting wasn't hand-to-hand combat, as this was the future, not medieval times. It involved guns, and

, which seemed to show little interest in the chro-
of the person handling them. We are left in no
weaponry exactly as well as Mal—she was, after
…n he chose to take on a job. And we saw exactly why
…ories" when she walked fearlessly into her enemy's ship and
…t blanch as he hacked off her captain's left ear and handed it to her. A squeamish shriek would have been a perfectly reasonable reaction, but she merely thanked him, wrapped it in cloth, and as soon as she could, told Simon to pack it in ice. If someone were to feel the need to separate me from my left ear, or even my right, Zoe is precisely the person I'd want taking care of it. Sure, she called Mal "Sir" (and really, who wouldn't?), but that wasn't to do with gender, it was because he was her sergeant in the army and then became her boss. She still ignored his orders when she thought them ill-advised, and he acknowledged that he owed his life to her independence in "Out of Gas."

And while Kaylee couldn't shoot to kill, even in a crisis, nor could Simon, as Shepherd Book rather unchristianly pointed out. Mal would ride in to rescue the best little whorehouse in the 'verse, but it was Inara who had to teach him to fence overnight so that he wasn't killed in a duel. The power of the men in *Firefly* was matched exactly by that of the women—Simon may have been a brilliant doctor, but Kaylee had the same flair for mechanics as he had for anatomy. And though the crew got into plenty of scrapes where Simon's medical help was invaluable, before they took him and River onboard they had been flying quite successfully without a doctor. They couldn't even take off until Kaylee fixed up *Serenity*. Also, did I mention that River could kill you using just her brain?

It is undoubtedly the case that the women in *Firefly* were beautiful, and that you would have to be tied to a tree not to follow most of them home. But it's worth bearing in mind that this is television, so the men were pretty cute too. You show me a woman who wouldn't crawl across broken glass to kiss Nathan Fillion chastely on the mouth, and I'll show you Helen Keller. Inara was a vision of loveliness, but she was also the only one who could out-smart Saffron, the anti-Inara. And River was the one who out-smarted Jubal Early—she was psychic, she was a genius, and she convinced the universe's creepiest bounty-hunter that she'd turned into a ship. That is, indisputably, a good day at the office.

But the real gender-leveler in *Firefly* wasn't guns, or even brains, it was jokes. The show was, just as *Buffy* was, a comedy and a drama, and it had girls in it, saying funny things. In case you were wondering, this happens almost never. Think about the celebrated comedies of the past few years, and then think about the roles women played in them. *There's Something About Mary* starred Cameron Diaz, but did she get to make jokes? Nope, she got to be a joke—she's beautiful and sweet, so she gets to put spunk in her hair unknowingly. Feel free to insert your own Hitchcockian misogynist subtext about despoiling perfect blondes—I don't have the energy. Diaz gets to do something less grimy but essentially similar in the *Charlie's Angels* movies—she's now a beautiful, sweet genius who can kick-box, but luckily she's still a klutz, and answers the door in her knickers, because she hasn't realized the postman is perving over her. Sandra Bullock is always described as a comic actress, which she is in the action-movie *Speed* where she gets to say smart, funny things. But put her in a comedy, *Miss Congeniality* (yes, just a comedy for the purposes of this essay, I know, I know), and she immediately gets to say nothing funny at all. On the plus side, she does fall over a lot, and sometimes she gets to do it with gusto.

Girls do occasionally get to be both pretty and funny in all-girl films (Lindsey Lohan gets the odd joke in *Mean Girls* and *Freaky Friday*), but not too often. Hollywood tends to be happier when there is someone beautiful being pretty and ditzy, and someone less beautiful (in their rather asinine interpretation of beauty) to play funny. Case in point—*The Truth About Cats and Dogs*, a re-working of *Cyrano De Bergerac* where Uma Thurman is the dumb beauty and the funny is provided by Janeane Garofalo, beautiful by any sensible measure but here playing the smart-mouthed plain chick. (Having said that, of course, most people standing next to Uma Thurman would look like they were having a bad hair day.)

When *Buffy* first began, people were rightly blown away by how smart it was, how neatly the narratives played out, how high the emotional stakes were, how cool the fighting looked, how great the effects were. They were also witnessing something extraordinary—a heroine who was beautiful, smart, tough, and, above all, funny. Instead of standing in the corner while boys did the fighting, Buffy was the warrior girl. And instead of watching boys make jokes, she did that bit too. Actually, everyone in *Buffy* was funny. Willow was geek funny, Xander was skater funny, Cordelia was bitchy funny, Giles was Brit funny, and Buffy was a mix: sometimes she was dumb funny, because she hadn't done her homework and didn't know enough; sometimes she was smart-mouth funny, because she was about to slay a vampire and she was cocky; sometimes she was grown-up funny, because Dawn was driving her nuts; and sometimes she was bitchy funny, too—who could forget her famous comeback to Darla, when asked if she knew what the saddest thing in the world was: "That hair on top of that outfit?" (*BtVS*, "Angel" 1-7).

Buffy blazed an important trail here—the *Scream* franchise has been so wide-reaching, it's easy to forget that horror used to be utterly po-faced (obviously, I am omitting the seemingly unintentional humor of such delights as *Dr Terror's House of Horrors*, where Michael Gough manages to humiliate and terrorize Christopher Lee using only his amputated hand and a chimpanzee who paints. Or indeed *From Hell It Came*, where an evil tree stump, hell-bent on revenge, persecutes innocent islanders with death on its mind, or at least its grain). But when the *Buffy* movie came out in 1992, several years before Drew Barrymore gave it everything in her fifteen minutes of *Scream*, the rules were changed, because there were jokes. People finally realized that horror was more horrifying if you liked the characters you were watching, so that you cared if they died. It was much easier to like characters who made you laugh than ones who screamed a bit, and cried. And when the *Buffy* TV series began, things became all the scarier and the stakes grew higher, because the characters were now in your home, every week. They were also consistently funny, which is why we grew to love characters we didn't initially even like—Cordelia, Anya, Spike, Andrew.

So it came as no surprise when *Firefly* followed the same rules—it was a Western, it was sci-fi, but the characters were clever and smart-mouthed. Again, this is pretty rare—with the exception of the radiantly funny Douglas Adams, there aren't many jokes in the future. It's usually a post-apocalyptic universe, there have often been wars, everyone has a spaceship, some people have tentacles, but people rarely say anything funny. I've made my living from jokes for a long time, so I probably like 'em more than most, but they seem to me to fulfill a basic sociological need. Look in the Lonely Hearts section of any newspaper, gloat for a moment, then look again—everyone wants a good sense of humor. If we want it from our sexual partners, it stands to reason that we want it from our culture. This goes across the board—we want to sleep with someone beautiful, so film stars are usually pretty cute. (This thesis probably doesn't work if you belong to a fetish subgroup, though. If you want to have sex with someone who has a glass eye, for example, then culturally you're pretty much limited to perving over Columbo.)

A real weakness of sci-fi, for me, has been that much as I love spaceships, laser guns, and doors that slide upwards, I find it difficult to retain interest in characters with little emotional range beyond angry, frightened, or triumphant. If they don't say anything funny, how am I supposed to know if I'd like them? And if I don't know if I'd like them, why would I care if they live to fight another day, or die a lonely carbonized space-death (Tim Robbins, *Mission to Mars*)? I have the same problem with Westerns. There's some great dialogue in *Butch Cassidy and the Sundance Kid*, but it's an exception. Have you ever heard John Wayne laugh? Engage in some witty badinage? His shooting is indisputably sharp, but his wit seems kind of blunt (in the interests of balance, I should point out here that I am useless with a lasso). I acknowledge that Lee Marvin raises the game in *Cat Ballou*, as does Gene Wilder in *Blazing Saddles*, but a metal-nosed villain or shaky-handed sharp-shooter is a rare comic turn in a genre filled with worthy two-dimensional goodies, nasty two-dimensional baddies, and some only reasonably pretty cows.

Firefly was a real eye-opener—the characters spoke quickly and often acerbically, finally laying to rest the inexplicable theory that anyone in the future (or in Middle Earth, now I come to think of it) must speak at roughly the same pace as someone who has had to re-learn language after a particularly virulent stroke. Like anyone else who'd first seen Nathan Fillion as the frankly terrifying Caleb in season seven of *Buffy*, I was blown away by the casual way he smashed one-liners out of the park. And as soon as Wash appeared in a Hawaiian shirt, I felt I'd found out what happened to Xander when he grew up.

Firefly's was a much more difficult setting than *Buffy*'s—a high school offers endless opportunities to subvert stereotypes that we all already know: the bitchy fashion queen, the geeky girl genius, the not-so-academic boy with a skateboard. But *Firefly* dropped us straight into a world we didn't know at all—it was the future, we were in space, and the last time we saw the captain (in countries other than the U.S. and Canada, *Firefly* didn't show on television at all, but was available only on belated DVD), he was a mean, mean preacher with big scary eyes, who channelled evil and hit girls.

The *Firefly* crew weren't people we already knew: a tomboy girl mechanic who hankered for a beautiful dress; an uptight doctor who gave up everything to save his sister; a crazy, damaged teenager; an ex-soldier; an eerily beautiful courtesan. The way in to the characters, and thus the program, was through the funny. Simon could so easily have been sanctimonious—he gave up his promising future to rescue his sister from a vicious regime, he was highly educated, often disapproving, and from a different social class from the others. Yet his dry wit, even when faced with the horrors of Jubal Early, threatening to rape Kaylee unless Simon gave up his sister, sold him to us completely. "Come on out, River, the nice man wants to kidnap you," he observed as Early held a gun to his head ("Objects in Space").

Jayne had only the shakiest grasp of morality, but we never lost faith in him as a man, because his blunt jokes kept us on his side, often in the face of all the other evidence. "You got a wife? All I got's that dumb-ass stick, sounds like it's raining. How come you got a wife?" he demanded in "Our Mrs. Reynolds." And it was hard not to like a man who refused to help strangers until told they're hookers: "Don't know these folks, don't much care to," he stated. "They're whores," said Mal, striding past. "I'm in," Jayne concluded, without missing a beat ("Heart of Gold").

River was probably the toughest sell of all—a crazy chick is never that much fun, not even in *Hamlet*. Only River *was* fun, firstly because she could sharp shoot using maths and a gun, and secondly because she made the occasional perfectly timed crack. In "Trash," Simon explained to Jayne that in spite of Jayne's betrayal of them in the hospital on Ariel, which nearly cost them their freedom and their lives, he would nonetheless honor the doctor-patient relationship, and Jayne would always be safe in the infirmary. "I don't know what you've done, I don't know what you're planning on doing, but I'm trusting you just the same. Because I don't see this working any other way." It was hard for us not to feel there was something left unsaid. Whereupon River put her head around the door and delivered the killer punch: "Also, I can kill you with my brain." It's the use of the word "also" that makes that joke great. And who could have failed to love her terror at Shepherd Book's untamed hair? She hid and refused to come out, even after Zoe (with an admirably straight face) promised her that the hair was gone. "It will still be there," she stated, unmoving. "Waiting" ("Jaynestown").

As for Mal Reynolds, the captain we had to love for the show to succeed, he was another character who could easily have been tricky for an audience to reach—a former soldier, battle-weary and disenchanted with the Alliance regime. Like most cynics, he was a broken romantic: a man who fought for what he believed in, but who believed in the losing side. He was a man who faced pretty much every situation with a world-weary sardonic crack; it's hard (for many reasons) not to think about him in the opening scenes of "Trash," sitting in the desert, naked and stranded, saying, "Yeah, that went well." And once again, this was our way into a character who may rob and occasionally kill, but whose ethics were completely humane, in spite of (or perhaps because of) his lawless existence.

Perhaps the most extraordinary episode of *Firefly* was the genuinely horrifying "War Stories." As Mal and Wash were tortured surely beyond reason, Mal was still, inevitably, making jokes. And Wash realized immediately on leaving the torture chamber exactly what Mal had been doing: "He's crazy. He wouldn't break, Zoe. He kept me from . . . I wouldn't have made it. . . ." The real Mal Reynolds was the one who was still looking out for his crew, even while he was in agony, and that's why we love him. But we also like him, because he looked out for Wash by making cheap gags about his wife.

So, the jokes made *Firefly*. We were taken into a world we didn't know, with unfamiliar characters speaking a combination of old-fashioned slang and sporadic Chinese. We never questioned why we should be following them, because we were on their side from the very beginning, and that's because we liked them and would have bought them a drink. Finally, there was payback for all those times when someone with a stick-on nose, often green, was talking gibberish, with subtitles like an art-house movie, only not in a village in northern Spain but on a moon in some solar system I couldn't have cared about less.

The even-handed distribution of jokes also made all but the most willfully dense of us realize that we were hanging out in a feminist universe—just like in *Buffy*, everyone got to be funny, and the smart women usually got the best gags. Look at Zoe: a beautiful warrior, fiercely professional, utterly deadpan. Buffy herself couldn't have done a better job of taking out the ranting doctor on Ariel, who was just about to report Mal to the authorities and blow their cover. She came up behind him, placed the CPR paddles on his back, and blasted him with electricity, then watched him slump to the floor, and said, calmly, "Clear" ("Ariel").

Also, the jokes weren't at the expense of gender (see sitcoms, passim, for gags on why men are useless and women are uptight. Then watch *Arrested Development*, and see how it should be done, with jokes about individuals, instead of about stereotypes. Then write to an appropriate TV executive, and threaten to kill their pets for canceling it). Making someone laugh is an exercise of power—for just a second, you have total control over someone else's emotional state. Giving that power to female characters is a much greater emancipation than physical strength or bigger guns.

I wonder if Buffy is, in many ways, a sociological millstone around the neck of her creator. We'd become so used to girls being victims of vampires, right from when *Dracula* was first published, and then suddenly here was a chick who didn't scream and run away. Hell, she could take 'em in a fight. It was hard not to stand up and cheer at the fact that finally girls were being offered a role model who didn't swoon and wait for a boy to sort things out for her, but took the fight right to her enemies. The only trouble with this is that then, when you go on to create something less overtly feminist, with a male lead rather than a female one and with no superpowers for girls, then some of your audience, if they're not paying attention, can feel like you've betrayed them. But here's the thing—equality means equality of everything. It doesn't mean being the same as each other, but it does mean having the same opportunities as each other. If a girl always has to be in charge, all the time, then she isn't equal at all—she's superior. That's why we needed to see that Buffy couldn't win every fight, couldn't save her mother, couldn't beat Glory without sacrificing herself.

In *Buffy* the alpha character was female, and in *Firefly* he was male—that seems pretty much equal to me. They're both ensemble pieces, so that's what we should be considering. Jayne was the brawn of *Firefly* (he does have a girl's name, though, so make of that what you will. I like to see it as a nod to Johnny Cash's "A Boy Named Sue," but then, I can see nods to that anywhere), but Zoe was the brains. When Mal and Wash were taken prisoner in "War Stories," she didn't hesitate, she came up with a plan and carried it out to perfection. She tried negotiation, and got half of what she wanted, so then she returned, using force—she is both a consummate soldier and diplomat. In many ways, she is a greater feminist icon than Buffy: it's easy to wish to be a girl with super strength, but it's harder to achieve. Zoe is what Condoleezza Rice would be, if she were in the future and had a better boss—smart, brave, and compassionate, with really nice outfits.

Wash flew the ship like a dream, but without Kaylee, he would have had nothing to fly. It's worth bearing in mind that most people can drive, but very few of us can fix a car. In "Shindig," Kaylee was made conscious of the fact that her beautiful, longed-for dress was not the height of fashion—she was belittled by bitchy women, who were threatened by the presence of an outsider. In a matter of minutes, however, she was the center of attention for all the men in the room, not because she had the minxiest dress or the sluttiest habits, but because she knew loads of cool stuff about engines, which was far more interesting than stuff about frocks.

The way I feel about Zoe and Kaylee is exactly the same as the way I feel about Hermione in *Harry Potter*—at last, a girl in popular culture who worries about more than the occasional broken nail. And *Harry Potter* too has been taken to task for shoddy feminism: Harry and Ron have adventures, Hermione sits reading books. This kind of thing makes me feel like crying—just because Hermione isn't good at Quidditch doesn't mean she's less of a person. It just means she's less of a Quidditch player. Ah, says the meta-feminist, but Quidditch is important, and she can't play because she's just a girl. Gah, say I, punching the meta-feminist in the head, and thus proving that violence is, in fact, the answer. Ginny can play Quidditch, and she is also just a girl. She's way better at it than Ron, who gets all nervous, and Hermione is better than both of them at other stuff, like spells, which are pretty key, this being a world of magic and all.

This is how feminism is supposed to work—women aren't better than men at everything, they're better at some things and less good at others, and thus they are equals. This is illustrated by the fact that they talk to each other like equals—teasing, mocking, and cracking jokes, acknowledging each other's strengths and weaknesses with humor and generosity, and occasionally outright spite. That's what you got in *Firefly*. Yes, Mal could have taken Saffron in a fist-fight. And she could have taken him in a battle of wits—not because she had feminine wiles, but because she was willing to take advantage of his humanity. And Mal knew that; that's why he had Inara on his team. He won in the end, just like Buffy, not by being the strongest individual, but by having the strongest gang. They were bound together by affection, and that's why jokes were the key. Lucky *Firefly* only ran for half a season, or I might have got the idea that everything could be this good.

NATALIE HAYNES is a comedian and writer. Her first stand-up show was nominated for a Perrier Best Newcomer Award at the Edinburgh Fringe Festival in 2002. Her first novel, *The Great Escape*, is published in September 2007, and she writes regularly for *The Times*. She reviews theater, film, books, and television for *BBC Newsnight Review*.

In this piece I believe that Marano correctly identifies a genuinely Jossian theme; nothing shows up this pervasively in one writer's work without it having a real significance. When you trace a character's arc, it's natural to look ahead to see where they end up. In this piece, Marano looks backward to see how some of Joss's most memorable women began their journeys. What he finds there is truly interesting.

River Tam and the Weaponized Women of the Whedonverse

MICHAEL MARANO

Joss Whedon shares a lot in common with the Greek god Hephaestus—and I don't mean that he's a hairy, ugly dude conceived by his mom through parthenogenesis in a fit of jealous pique and thrown off Olympus with such force that he fell for nine days.[1] Hephaestus was the armorer of the gods. He made Zeus's thunderbolts and scepter, Athena's shields, Eros's arrows, Achilles's armor, and Helios's chariot. But there's a certain blurring of Hephaestus's specialization, if you rummage through *The Iliad*. In Book Eighteen, Hephaestus is shown not only as a manufacturer of weapons, but of women, having created two artificial maidens made of gold as his workshop help who are as smart and skilled as any living girl.

I bring this up because the idea of a woman as created by a weapon-maker within Patriarchal contexts is a recurring motif in the worlds imagined by Joss Whedon, the so-called "Whedonverse."[2] It's a motif, perhaps

[1] I find no evidence in his biography to support such a background, even on Wikipedia.
[2] Disclosure time. Years back, I wrote a horror novel called *Dawn Song*. In it, the demon Belial crafts a succubus, whom he sends from Hell to our world as part of his eons-long war for supremacy of Hell with his enemy Leviathan. I created a story in which a woman is crafted to be a weapon. Just bringing this up, in case anyone thinks I'm pulling a "kettle calling the pot black" on Whedon.

better defined as "the woman as weapon," that reaches its apotheosis with the developmental journey of River in *Firefly* and *Serenity*. I say it reaches its apotheosis, because as I write this, she's the most recent example of this trend; there could be more in Whedon's future work that are more apotheosis-y. But for now, let's take a look at River's creation and development as a weapon—as the creation of weapon-makers—by first taking a look at a few of her antecedents. The motif of the woman-as-weapon is a fairly complicated one, with a number of disparate elements, and by looking at Whedon's other lethal women, we can see how these elements converge into the figure of River.[3] While these characters have been developed by a number of writers, directors, and actors working with Whedon, it's Whedon's guiding vision that has shaped that development. These characters are reflective of his vision and thus can be thought of as existing within a single body of work.

ALIEN: RESURRECTION

Alien: Resurrection may not usually be considered part of the Whedonverse, but Whedon's script for the 1997 sequel is rife with the woman-as-weapon theme as it would develop over the course of his future work. First, there's the cloned Ripley (number eight in the series of clones), scraped together from DNA remnants of the original Ripley by a secret military cabal headed by General Perez. In the previous movies, the Alien itself was sought after by the evil Weylan Yutani company for development as a weapon. In *Alien: Resurrection*, part of that development is a manufactured Ripley, who is, to a certain extent, weaponized as a human/Alien hybrid, with enhanced abilities and mildly acidic blood. Ripley is a commodity (referred to in the movie as a "meat by-product"), existing in a twilight state between being an independent person and a lethal device. Part of her journey to humanity entails her confronting a lab full of proto-Ripleys, botched clones with too many Alien characteristics to be useful commodities, which she destroys (or, rather, euthanizes) with a flamethrower . . . an act which prompts Ron Perlman's character Johner to mutter: "Must be a chick thing."

[3] Aren't you glad I used "converge" into River, instead of "flow"?

And it is a "chick thing," in that it is a *human* thing she does. Her euthanizing the botched clones is a crucial decision she makes on her journey throughout the film to be human, to define herself as her own person independent of her origins as she rejects her status as a weapon created by a Patriarchal authority. Part of that journey is subverting her potential as a weapon, reclaiming her artificially heightened abilities and her acidic blood to destroy the Alien threat to humanity.

To a lesser degree, the android Call, played by everyone's favorite shoplifter Winona Ryder, is also a weapon. True, as an android manufactured on a planet of androids, she's not created as a weapon. But she's used by the crew of the *Betty* (and isn't the *Betty*, old beat-up ship that she is with a crew full of scruffy misfits, a proto-*Serenity*?) in a tactical way. Her very body is used as an interface with the "Father" computer of the military ship *Auriga*, so that it can be crashed into Earth and end the Alien menace—though it's done with her permission. Like Ripley, her humanity is defined by her human choices, including her stated mission as an android to save a dumb Xenomorph-cloning humanity from itself, even though said choices involve the use of her manufactured body in a tactical way.

Buffy the Vampire Slayer and *Angel*

Well, where to begin with Buffy and all her attendant mythology? How about with the very First Slayer?

The First Slayer was a girl who was weaponized by three shaman Shadow-Men in the distant past to fight demons and vampires, the implication being that, like the cloned Ripley, the girl was partly infused with the essence of the demonic agencies she would eventually fight on the Shadow-Men's behalf. Again, the needs of Patriarchal authority are fulfilled by making a woman a lethal object. The First Slayer had no Watcher. She could not develop any further as a person beyond her function as a weapon, and was exiled from her community even as she served it.

Buffy, though she was born and not made with the potential to be lethal, was a continuation of this "woman as created weapon" legacy. The Patriarchal legacy of the Shadow-Men had been supplanted by the Watchers

Council, which saw to it that the Slayer, as a weapon, was used and developed in ways acceptable to the decrees of this new Patriarchal authority. (And yes, there were women on the Council, but the tweedy Eurocentric ambience of the organization reeked of an English Men's Club.)

As with Ripley and Call, Buffy asserted her primacy as a human being over her status as a lethal tool through her human choices, standing up to the Watchers Council, most dramatically so during her conflict with Glorificus.

But within the subset of the Whedonverse that is the *Buffy*verse, Buffy is by no means the only woman-as-weapon.

There's also Anya, everybody's favorite Vengeance Demon, alias Aud and Anyanka. Anya was "elevated" to the status of Vengeance Demon by her Patron, D'Hoffryn, who used her and her fellow female Vengeance Demons to further his ends. The Vengeance Demons were, essentially, D'Hoffryn's arsenal.[4] Anya's choices defined her development as a human once she was stripped of her supernaturally lethal capacities, which led her back to being a demon for a while, before her ultimate death, as a human, fighting the minions of the First.

The Buffybot—unlike Call, the aforementioned machine in the shape of a girl—never achieved self-awareness, or the capacity for choice. She was created by murdering prick misogynist bastard Warren as a lovebot for Spike—a particularly noxious Patriarchal development of a woman as an exploitable commodity. Though not created as a weapon, she was re-appropriated as a weapon by the Scoobies (via Willow's re-programming) during and after Buffy's conflict with Glorificus. While there is no real intelligence or sentience to the Buffybot, and "her" existence as a woman is debatable, the fact that Buffy re-appropriated her image, her ersatz lovebot body, for her own purposes as a weapon is pretty significant.

If the Buffybot is a weapon to be used against Glory, the question follows: Was Dawn also a weapon? Yes, in that she was a strategically created commodity that was used to thwart an enemy. The mysterious Brethren of monks created Dawn, the person, as a camouflage for the Key that they wished to keep out of the hands of Glorificus, the Beast. She was human, full of "Summers blood," as Buffy herself pointed out, and capable of human choice. But the fact is, as a human, manufactured

[4] It's sort of interesting that, given the vengeful legacies of female demons like the Furies, the male D'Hoffryn is head of this particular branch of infernal affairs.

out of memories and mystic energies, she was, at least in her inception, the tool of a Patriarchal organization.

Darla was not created as a weapon, but re-made as one. Before she died the first time, Darla was born a human being, then sired as a vampire. But when she was resurrected by the nasty suits at the law firm of Wolfram and Hart, it was specifically so that she could function as an implement of psychological warfare, to drive Angel mad and make him become Angelus once again. When that didn't work, she was weaponized again by Wolfram and Hart, retrofitted as a vampire when Drusilla sired her resurrected human form.

And Buffy herself has been known to re-write or recreate women as weapons, though not in the objectifying way that Wolfram and Hart rewrote Darla (or how she and the Scoobies reprogrammed the Buffybot). Buffy's rewriting of women as weapons can be seen as liberating, not appropriating. The Potentials, like Buffy and the First Slayer, carry their capacity for lethality by way of the Shadow-Men's Patriarchal appropriation of the female form in the distant past. During the escalation of her conflict with the First, Buffy appropriated that capacity in order to actualize all the Potentials as Slayers, subverting that Patriarchal authority and allowing the Potentials to shake off the limits imposed upon them.

River Tam

So, we have a distinct woman-as-weapon template here, in the Whedonverse. How, specifically, does it apply to River and her personal journey throughout the course of *Firefly/Serenity*?

First, River was a remarkable child, a prodigy. Her brother Simon in the pilot "Serenity" said that River makes him, who graduated in the top percentile of his medical school class, look like an "idiot child." We got a glimpse of her intellect and imagination in "Safe," when we saw little River playing with Simon, concocting a fantasy scenario in which they were surrounded by enemy forces who are attacking using . . . shudder! . . . *dinosaurs*! "Our platoon, Simon. We got outflanked by the Independent squad, and we're never gonna make it back to our platoon. We need to resort to cannibalism!" Looking at Simon's homework, River said it was wrong. When Simon said his homework answers were from the textbook, little River said, "No. The book is wrong. The whole conclusion is fallacious!" This was, of course, before River was sent away to the mysterious Academy. Though later, in "Jaynestown," we saw that River never lost the tendency to challenge authoritative texts when she "fixed" Shepherd Book's Bible.

Later, in another flashback in "Safe," we saw how River's capacity as a prodigy was being warped by the Academy through the letters she sent to her family, which only Simon could recognize as being written in code; they were full of misspellings, when River had been correcting Simon's spelling when she was three. River's capacity for imaginative play, which could invoke a military use for dinosaurs and which is a facet of her incredible intellect, was by necessity re-directed to a cry for help. Later, in the same episode, we saw a little bit of the old, playful, brilliant River come out when she was swept up by the need to dance at the town social on a backward planet.

River's talent, her remarkableness, her spirit, is a necessary component of her weaponization. In the Whedonverse, weaponization is partly the Patriarchal appropriation of something that belongs essentially to the woman being weaponized. This can be some inner capacity, a latent inborn talent, as is the case with Buffy and the Potentials. It can be a developed talent, as is the case with Anya/Aud and the knack for vengeance she demonstrated when she turned her philandering bunny-raising boyfriend Olaf into a troll. It can be a biological potential, as is the case with Ripley, and the traces of Alien DNA mixed with her own that the Government "kept on ice" until she, and the Queen chestburster, could be cloned. It can be an abstract or even poetic potential, as is the case with Dawn and what she meant to the Summers family as a being needing shelter and protection. Or it can be a psychologically symbolic meaning, such as the one that made Darla a mind-SCUD capable of frying Angel's brain. Even the Buffybot, not created as weapon, had an innate quality of "Buffy-ness" that made her tactically useful the first time she was used as a weapon to help rescue Spike from Glory and when she was used again by Buffy and the Scoobies for their final battle with Glory, during which Buffy was killed. The Buffybot continued being used as a weapon by the Scoobies after Buffy's death in that final battle with Glory, filling in for the dead Slayer until she could be resurrected on UPN.

It's this inner capacity that makes River and the other weaponized women *useful* as weapons. This capacity is subverted and rewritten by Patriarchal authority into something useful to that authority and that is lethal. While it seems at first like a fair deal that D'Hoffryn saw Anya's talent and offered her a job as a vengeance demon, an offer he also made to Willow after Ms. Rosenberg cast a particularly wicked spell, it was an offer that cost Anya her humanity. In the *Buffy*verse, full of non-human beings, this might not seem like so big a deal. But given the fate of Halfrek/Cecily, a close friend of Anya and fellow vengeance demon whom D'Hoffryn vaporized as punishment for Anya's defection from D'Hoffryn's stable of employees, working for D'Hoffryn probably wasn't all fun and dismembering games.

The taking, developing, cultivation, and perversion of these inner capacities by Patriarchal authorities is a dehumanizing act. The First Slayer became an exile because of her Patriarchally granted "gift" of "death." Dawn had an identity crisis as to whether she was human at all, cutting herself and asking, "Is this blood?"

River's capacity as a weapon, her psychic abilities and her physical prowess (as in "War Stories," when she saved Kaylee by shooting three of Niska's men with her eyes closed) made her an object to the Alliance. Stolen goods walking on two feet. As Dobson, the Alliance mole, told Jayne in the pilot "Serenity," "That girl is a precious commodity. They'll come after her. Long after you bury me they'll be coming." Referring to the aforementioned incident in "War Stories," Kaylee said of River in the episode "Objects in Space," "Not nobody can shoot like that that's a person." Whereupon Simon asked, "So . . . River's not a person?" Again, in "Safe," we got a sense of the objectification of River by the Academy scientists when Simon referred to River's mental disorders by saying, "This is paranoid schizophrenia, Captain. Hand-crafted by government scientists who thought my sister's brain was a rutting playground."

River herself articulates a conflation between the intrusions of Patriarchal authority (in this case specifically, the Alliance) and personal self-determination at the outset of the film *Serenity*, in the opening flashback/dream sequence that depicts her early days at the Academy: "People don't like to be meddled with. We tell them what to do, what to think: 'Don't run, don't walk.' We're in their homes and in their heads and we haven't the right. We're meddlesome."

With her inner capacity weaponized and commandeered, River became a danger to the very Patriarchal authority that made her a weapon. As the scary Operative in the film *Serenity* says to Doctor Mathias regarding River's telepathy, "The minds behind every military, diplomatic, and covert operation in the galaxy . . . and you put them in a room with a psychic!"

River's psychic abilities, prior to the events in the film *Serenity*, were also a threat to established Patriarchal authority in "Safe." She had the following exchange with the Patron of the isolated community of hill people who had kidnapped Simon so that he would be their town doctor: after the local teacher has accused River of being a witch, the Patron asked the girl warmly, "You're not a witch, are you? I'm the Patron here. Do you know what that means?" To which River replied, "Yes, you're in charge. Ever since the old Patron died. He was sick and you were alone in the room with him," with less than pleasant results.

The need for the Patriarchal authorities to control the female weapons they have created is another recurring theme in the Whedonverse. As mentioned above, Buffy butted heads with the Watchers Council to determine how the threat of Glorificus was to be handled, and to get Giles re-hired. It was a conflict that was a sequel to, and a final resolution of, her first conflict with the Council, in which she was forced on her eighteenth birthday to fight a vampire without her powers in a rite called the "Cruciamentum." The Cruciamentum was a particularly humiliating and violating rite by the Patriarchal Council, because it was designed to be a direct appropriation of a Slayer's body (in that the Council felt it could claim, limit, and remove the traits and strengths that made the Slayer unique) through the roofie-like administration of drugs that made her lose her powers. During Buffy's Cruciamentum, when things went haywire, the rite of passage also became an invasion of a safe Matriarchal home space when Kralik, the psychotic vampire Buffy was assigned to kill, kidnapped Buffy's mom. The resurrected and very tormented human Darla had to be brought under control by Wolfram and Hart, so she was re-sired as a vampire. The cloned Ripley is kept in a bunker-like prison. D'Hoffryn punished Anya for being a weapon with a conscience and stripped her of her powers before later sending demons to kill her. Though not made as a weapon, even April, the robot love slave that Warren built in "I Was Made to Love You" and the antecedent to the Buffybot, became a danger to the community at large when, as a device, she was left to her own destructive devices.

River was a danger not only to the Patriarchal authority that made her a weapon, she was a danger to the ersatz family she had onboard *Serenity*, as in "Ariel," when she sliced Jayne across the chest with a butcher knife, saying, "He looks better in red!" She was again a threat in "Objects in Space" when, in her own little fugue state, River found what she thought was a stick, but was in fact a weapon, which she pointed at Simon and Kaylee. In the film *Serenity*, Mal confronts Simon, saying, "You had a gorramn time bomb living with us! Who we gonna find in there when she wakes up? The girl, or the weapon?"

I mentioned earlier that it was human choice that determined the ultimate fates of the women of the Whedonvese who had been made weapons, and thus to varying degrees been made objects, by these Patriarchal forces. A weapon is a tool. Tools are made to be used. But in the case of these women and their ultimate fates, it's a specific series of choices made in specific contexts that lead them to what is often their self-determination to subvert their status as weapons/objects, to refuse to be used. In that this self-determination is other-directed, focused on the protection of immediate and domestic groups of real and substitute families, it can be thought of as the antithesis of the Patriarchal authority that has made objects/weapons of these woman. We can think of it as "Matriarchal" in that it is female-centered power—the empowerment of females independent of any external, "meddling" authority.

As said earlier, Buffy achieved a measure of self-determination by standing up to the Watchers Council, motivated by a desire not only to save the world, but to empower her close friends and family. Dawn reclaimed her life from the monks who created her as a device to deceive Glorificus, specifically by reclaiming her blood, which she had earlier been unconvinced was blood at all, as "Summers blood." The cloned Ripley, other-directed to save an Earth she has never seen and the remaining crew of the *Betty*, uses her weaponized blood to kill the Newborn Alien/Human hybrid to which she has a modicum of kinship. As mentioned before, the android Call has an other-directed need to save humanity from itself. The Potentials were actualized as weapons by Buffy, but it was an actualization that was a hijacking of the Patriarchal authority in the distant past that made the girls potential Slayers to begin with.

River, of all the weaponized women in the Whedonverse, began as the most un-actualized, aside from the Buffybot. Throughout *Firefly* and most of *Serenity*, she didn't have full control of her body, her speech, her mind. As we learned in "Ariel," her brain had been repeatedly opened and operated on. Simon explained to Jayne about River's stripped amygdala, "You know how you get scared. Or worried, or nervous. And you don't want to be scared or worried or nervous, so you push it to the back of your mind. You try not to think about it. The amygdala is what lets you do that—it's like a filter in your brain that keeps your feelings in check. They took that filter out of River. She feels everything. She can't not."

Because of River's near incapacity—in "War Stories," she felt incapacitated to the point of asking Simon, "What am I?"—her actualization as a person occurs as she becomes actualized as weapon. Her true journey to humanity free of the influence of the Alliance begins with her "use" as weapon. At the start of the film *Serenity*, even Mal sees tactical applications for River, bringing her along on a job for the first time as an early warning detection device because of her precognition. While this is on one level an objectification of River, it's also an act of inclusion, showing a level of acceptance of River on Mal's part. When River is activated by the Operative later in the film via the infamous Fruity Oaty Bars commercial, it triggers not only her capacity to kill, but her capacity to remember, to have a sense of a past that will help her reclaim her humanity . . . the memory of the mysterious "Miranda."

River's actualization, or her activation, as a weapon is at least partly an actualization of her self. Prior to her trigger through the Fruity Oaty Bar commercial, she had described her mental state in "War Stories" as a jumble of impressions, intimating that the jumble was keeping herself from being herself, from understanding her memories and controlling the functions of her mind: "I hate the bits. The bits that stay down. And I work. I function like I'm a girl. I hate it because I know it'll go away. The sun goes dark and chaos is come again. Bits. Fluids."

Other-directed, family focused (or, more properly, "crew focused") domestic issues override River's Patriarchal, "meddling" weaponization so that she can be her own person, and reclaim those unique attributes that had been hijacked. This family focus is at least partly defined by notions of "home," as was hinted at by way of the Council's intrusion on Buffy's home during the aforementioned Cruciamentum. The notion of *Serenity* as a domestic space, rather than your standard spaceship setting of most SF, is illustrated in the moment in the film *Serenity* when Zoe asks, after Mal has ordered the camouflaging of *Serenity* as a Reaver ship, "Do you really mean to turn our home into an abomination so that we can make a suicidal attempt at passing through Reaver space?" And the idea of "home" as a personal, mental, bodily, and domestic space is hinted at in River's comment above: "We're in their homes and in their heads and we haven't the right."

Yes, the confrontation on the planet Miranda and the revelation of the terrible secret of the Reavers' origins helps River reclaim her fractured intellect. But it's the threat of the Reavers to her domestic reality, much like the threats the Council/Kryec and later Glorificus posed to Buffy and Dawn's domestic reality, that fully realize River's potential as a human being and weapon. Faced with the deaths of Book and Wash, seeing Zoe and Kaylee and Simon horribly wounded, she overrides her function as a creation of Patriarchal authority and defends her family, telling Simon before she confronts the attacking band of Reavers: "You take care of me, Simon. You've always taken care of me. My turn."

Fully actualized as weapon, to the point that she can kill scores of blood-raged Reavers, she is from that point on again fully realized as a person, functional enough to pilot *Serenity* along with Mal.

The question arises: What is the overarching function of these "women as weapons" in the Whedonverse? I think the template is to be found in the story of the very first woman who was a weapon: Pandora.

Pandora was the first woman on Earth according to mythology, created by our friend Hephaestus, the armorer of the gods and the creator of women as tools, at the order of Zeus. Pandora was manufactured out of earth and water by the same hands that made Achilles's armor and Athena's shield as a kind of time bomb to punish the world for Prometheus's theft of fire from Olympus. Like River, Pandora was crafted with artificially enhanced abilities and gifts: beauty from Aphrodite, music from Apollo, cunning from Hermes, and so forth. Her name means "all-gifted." We all know the story of the famous box of troubles she opened (in the original myth, it's a jar or urn, not a box). But what doesn't get discussed much is the gift she also released—hope.

Buffy, Dawn, the cloned Ripley, and especially River—as re-directions of the punishing, meddling, Patriarchal authority that, Zeus-like, seeks to control us through force and fear—represent the hope of overcoming or subverting that authority. These women use that hope and actualize that hope by actualizing themselves, by taking control of their destinies in an other-directed way that is a boon to those of their immediate home and family spaces, and also to all of society. The freeing self-actualizations of all these women-weapons, impossible without their own capacity to feel hope, provide a means by which we all might be made just a little freer. They reclaim their use as weapons, saving us all from Glorificus and other apocalypses, alien genocide, and neo-fascist control. In so doing, they reclaim the strengths they have that Patriarchy has subverted and used for its own ends, and so make hope for us all a bit more viable.

Though he shares some things in common with Hephaestus as the creator of women who are weapons, Whedon's goal is ultimately the opposite, envisioning a recurring path of self-actualization that frees women, and us, from their limiting use as objects of force.

Since 1990, MICHAEL MARANO's work has appeared on the Public Radio Satellite System program *Movie Magazine International*, syndicated in more than 111 markets in the U.S. and Canada (www.shoestring.org). His commentary on pop culture has appeared in venues such as the *Boston Phoenix*, *Independent Weekly*, *The Weekly Dig*, *Science Fiction Universe*, and *Paste Magazine*. Marano's short fiction has been published in several high-profile anthologies, including the Lambda-winning Queer Fear series, *The Mammoth Book of Best New Horror 11*, and *Outsiders: 22 All-New Stories from the Edge*; his first novel *Dawn Song* won the Bram Stoker and International Horror Guild Awards. He is currently Fiction Editor of the horror publication *Chiaroscuro* (www.ChiZine.com). He can be reached via www.myspace.com/michaelmarano.

Sometimes it's hard to separate an actor from the character he plays, if for no other reason than the fact that they have a tendency to look so much alike. Sometimes actors come to resent this association with a character, and they struggle to carve out a space for themselves separate from the character, but sometimes they feel about it exactly as we all hope they would. Listen here to Nathan's voice . . . the humor, the authority. Isn't it a little . . . I mean . . . isn't it a little Mal? And isn't that fantastic?

I, Malcolm

NATHAN FILLION

Somebody once asked me what it was like to be Malcolm Reynolds. Usually I get, "Why was *Firefly* canceled?" and "Is there going to be another season/sequel?" But what was it like? Specifically, to be Mal? I wasn't quite ready for it. I mean, sure, it was great. Boots. Coat. Gun. Ride horses. Shoot guns. Shoot guns at horses. Stinks like awesome. But what was it like? It was so long ago it pieces together like childhood memories, complete with those moments of clarity that suddenly strike you with, "Oh, yeah! I remember that!" and a lot more moments of, "Really? We did that? Was I drunk?" But like those childhood memories there are images and feelings that are indelible.

Getting the job was stressful. I'm convinced the process of auditioning is designed to weed out the weak. Yet somehow, I still got it. There was the other actor up for the role, of whom I'm a huge fan. There was the fact I had to do the audition four or five times. There was the huge stack of contracts in triplicate to sign, potentially spelling out how I was going to spend the next seven years—or eight months, whatever the case may be. The stakes continue to rise throughout the process. Actors get knocked out of the mix, narrowing the choices. More and more faces show up to watch you pretend to be a spaceman. The offices get bigger and there's a special room for the audition. Meetings are held afterward while you wait outside. Trying to keep your cool during this traumatic affair is down to the individual, because there isn't anything that anybody can say to make it any easier. You are on your own. But I wanted this part badly. All the things we love about Mal were staring me in the face. The humour (spelled that way on purpose for Canadians), the questionable morality, the darkness, the anger, the almost imperceptible softness. It was all just out of reach like some toy in a window at Christmas, with Tiny Tim on the cold side, fogging up the glass. Or a brand new crutch or something. A gold crutch. No, a cure. Anyhow, it's safe to say the part was *all* I wanted.

So, there I was. Going to get a tour from Joss of the not-yet-finished ship. I met him at the *Firefly* production office (which weren't the offices we eventually wound up in) with the show logo on the door (which wasn't the logo we eventually used). The sound stages were huge, and we had three. The ship was enormous and incomplete. Strange, how it first struck me as so bizarre and unreal, and then later became a home. Know this: I had never been on an hour-long, single-camera show. The entire process, the scope alone was new to me and very impressive. They had built an entirely new world, made up of scraps from the past and future. There were a lot of people who put a lot of work into making the quality of that show what it was. As the show went on, I quickly understood how much I depended on those motivated, creative, hard-working ladies and bastards (typed with love, you bastards). Certainly, I was a small cog in a smooth-running (almost all the time) machine that produced product. Bottled sunshine? White lightning? Liquid gold? Red Kryptonite? Call it what you will, it was great, it had kick, and would probably take ten years off Superman's life.

The first scene we shot was up on the catwalks in the cargo bay. It was me and Sean. This was it. The ship was ready. The lights were moody and the camera was running. Nobody really knew anybody yet. I knew my lines, but I didn't have the handle on Mal that I have now. I was about to work with Joss. All the questions I had asked myself—"Will everyone get along? What will they be like to work with? Will I get along with Joss? Will people like it?"—were about to be answered. Then there are the questions you never think to ask that get answered. You learn these things as you go. It wasn't till "Our Mrs. Reynolds" that I knew Mal was a rancher. Yet it wasn't two days before I knew I could go to the little lunch camper out back and build a sandwich that would embarrass Dagwood. These things come with time. Until you experience them, the best you can do is smooth the gaps between the transitions, or bring lunch from home.

Certainly, there are a lot of technical considerations when acting on camera versus on stage. Three years of working with talented, seasoned professionals on daytime taught me how to ignore, or work with, the distraction of the technical. (Thanks, all of you at *OLTL*.) Past that, I got to live a self-centered kind of fantasy. As the captain, I got to be the center of my own universe. I got to be closed off, angry, bitter, and enraged. I fought my demons in bars, punished myself in fights I couldn't win, trying to feel *something*. In my daily life, I don't get the opportunity to swing myself onto a horse and feed my murderous energy into the animal for a primal burst of speeding revenge. Yet how many countless hours of my life did I spend daydreaming of heroic exploits? I needed that in my real life. I think maybe we all do, and sadly, few get the chance. When I played Mal, I wasn't playing me, I was playing me if I had been through what Mal had been through. I don't think of myself as a hard man, or closed-off, but I know this: Mal and I have a very similar sense of justice. I think comic books gave that to me, along with an over-developed sense of vengeance. I felt Malcolm was crusty, yes, but on the right track. More important than believing Mal was right, was knowing that Mal believes he is right.

I remember feeling like I owned the ship. When I was in costume and could find a moment on one of her two sets (lunch was the best time), I'd walk *Serenity* and just be Mal. I'd take in all her details. Nothing would escape my attention. It was just like the feeling I had for my 1975 Cadillac Eldorado, if the Caddy had somehow saved my life. I remember *Serenity*'s switches, lights, cables, and wires. I would try to fix things that were broken (*try*). I had a place at the head of the table. Either end, too. Other people could sit there, but it was understood that it was my place. 'Least in my mind. I had a rocker. I'd sit in it and space out in Mal's head. Very cathartic. The ship had a smell. Dusty garage and bitter metal, like a penny. As for what she tasted like, you'd have to ask Richard Brooks.

The cast . . . I can't say enough. The rest of the cast played a huge role in how I played Mal. By virtue of my role, I got to work with everyone. Sometimes all together, but mostly just one or a few at a time. What satisfied, and impressed, me most was the process of discovery. Putting a scene together with actors who could find the real life, the moments that define characters and the relationships that live between the lines. I didn't just watch; I was living it. Right there. Though for only moments at a time, I could be Mal. I couldn't help it. You've got everyone dressed up, in the cargo bay, looking at, talking to, and treating me like I'm the captain. There were strange moments, weird suspended seconds when I bought it all. If you have ever watched an episode and felt a connection with a character, felt he was speaking to you, or for a moment were somehow transported and felt you were on the ship listening to the conversation beside you—that's the feeling. Those instants that take you away, pull you in. I WAS THERE. I lived those moments. I got my ass saved by Zoe so many times. I mooned over Inara. I hit Jayne with a wrench. There were moments I could believe it. You'd have believed it, too, thanks to Joss. Looking at Kaylee, I could tell what kind of man Mal was. Speaking to Zoe, I could tell what kind of leader Mal was. Arguing with Wash and Jayne, I knew the limits of Mal's patience. They made me Mal. Looking back, I know now that everyone in the cast was, in essence, his or her character. What makes Jayne so Jayne, is that Adam is a Jayne. Jewel is a free spirit who was cast as a free spirit. Alan is a clever smart ass who questions authority. Ron once gave me the shirt off his back (true story—still a favorite of mine), Gina is alluring and powerful, Morena is elegant, Summer is grace, Sean owes me money. Off camera, I was able to spend my days with these people, and on camera, with their characters. I got to have them as friends twice. And I have been accused of being the leader when we were just hanging around. I've thought long and hard about this, because I feel it makes me sound pretty cool, but I want to be accurate. It is true that occasions arose when we wanted to spend some time together as a family—both cast and crew—be it a lunch date or a more serious shindig over the weekend. Sometimes I would watch as folks tried to agree on a time and a place, maybe an activity. As it can sometimes be when trying to organize ten or more people, it would get a little complicated, or no decision would be made at all. I remember taking the helm a little bit as far as saying, "We're going to this restaurant at this time." Or, "My house, Saturday." But that was the extent of it, really. So, it wasn't so much that the captain-y thing rolled over into my real life. More so, I simply had the desire to be with these people outside of work. I just wanted to continue connecting. I just wanted to be with my friends. I wanted them around me. I wanted to be around them. You've seen them. Can you blame me?

So, we've established it was great for me. The whole thing, heartbreak included. Super duper, really. (Realizing now I haven't the words to adequately describe the experience in a sentence, so: super duper.) I've also seen how the show has affected others. At unexpected times and strange places people reach out to me. They speak of *Firefly* with reverence, as a dear departed friend we had in common who did so much for them and died far too young. More than any other work I've done, I've seen that people are touched by *Firefly*. There is something in those characters that people identify with. I see it in people's faces when they try to convey to me why or how it hit home for them. A specific episode, a moment, or a line that was particularly truthsome to them. Others have trouble putting their finger on it, but I see in their eyes a little *Firefly* burning. I understand, my friend. You ask me? It's family. A group of people who, though flawed, would cross through hell for each other. For you. You're feeling what I was feeling. I understand. I was the captain.

It was only a short time, but *Firefly* changed me. It changed my whole life. Rotten it's over? Sure. Regrets? No. No way. What happened, happened. Anything bitter made everything else all the sweeter. I fought the good fight. I was a part of something that resonated with people, and still does. I made lifelong friends who have improved the quality of my life. So, what was it like to be Mal? I don't know. . . . I guess, imagine wanting, all your life, to be able to fly. Daydreaming about it, fantasizing about it. Imagine that flying was all you ever wanted. Then, for a few months, somebody gave you wings.

. . . Ooo. That's good. I'm going to write that down.

Nathan Fillion has permission to participate in your book, and is allowed to go on any field trips that may be included with promoting it. We are so happy that his university education was not for naught. He has had so much fun with that show and we can't believe how it just keeps popping up again and again! Let us know if there is anything else you need, and please make sure Nathan eats the apple we put in his lunch and don't let him lose his mittens.

—Cookie Fillion

Of all genres currently represented in television, science fiction is probably the one best suited to presenting genuine ideas. (Certainly America's Next Top Model *doesn't do it nearly as well.) By putting us at a distance in time and space, writers feel freer to explore ideas without feeling as if they're lecturing or preaching. I hesitate to attribute any specific political beliefs to Joss based on his writing, but it is certainly clear that* Firefly, *from theme song on down, held the notion of freedom very dear. Goldsmith dives into interesting waters here, taking seriously some of the more politically explicit implications of the series.*

Freedom in an Unfree World

P. Gardner Goldsmith

Yeah, I'm a stow-away. Proud of it, too. I wouldn't have been so happy if I'd gotten aboard a different ship, but I was tipped off to the one captained by Malcolm Reynolds, and it's led to amazing things. I boarded in New Hampshire, and got to travel the 'verse with the wildest, and in some cases the most principled, crew in existence.

My passage would not have been arranged if it hadn't been for people who had already recognized Mal's great heart, and seen in him something they cherished themselves: the unquenchable thirst for freedom.

I am a libertarian, and due to my work, I come into contact with many members of the expanding "Free State Project." The members of the FSP have been relocating to New Hampshire, and in addition to their devotion to things like first editions of Ayn Rand novels and the collected works of Lysander Spooner, they all seem to have one characteristic in common: they cherish the television series *Firefly* and its main character, Malcolm Reynolds, as much as they adore John Locke's "Second Treatise on Government."

The compelling question is *why*, and in order to provide an answer, one must understand the principles that drive libertarians in their political and social associations.

Most libertarians believe in, and adhere to, the Lockean Natural Rights tenet of "negative reciprocity," the idea that you have a right to be left alone by me, and I have a right to be left alone by you. I make my own decisions about my own life, and you do the same. Neither of us has a *positive* right to anything the other has or could peacefully acquire, and as long as we don't mess with each other, we'll be fine. According to Locke, we establish "the state" to stop such predation, and when a government does that which we formed it to *stop*, it becomes illegitimate. All consensual activities are supposed to be free from state interference, and if we are to form a government, it should be small, limited, and addressable to the people who gave it power.

The ideal libertarian hoping to live in such a system not only embraces those principles intellectually, but also *practices* them on a consistent basis, regardless of the hardship he or she endures. In his social and political activities, he endeavors to leave others alone, and merely asks for the same in return.

Malcolm Reynolds is one such man. He embodies those values, and practices them every day. And because he never waivers, he, like only a handful of fictional characters before him, can be appropriately identified as a libertarian archetype, fighting in a system that is inimical to freedom.

Our first encounter with Mal served as an introduction to this tyrannical universe, or "'verse," in which he would soon live. It was a world begat by violence, where the political structure would, in most respects, soon mirror that of the United States after the Civil War.[1]

In 1787, the United States of America represented the best hope for freedom in the world, and the Founders knew it. But the Constitution they wrote to replace the Articles of Confederation had within it the seeds of its own demise: the seeds of an all-powerful (and inefficient)

[1] True, one can see in *Firefly* subtle references to other time periods and historical events. The Alliance can occasionally be interpreted as a cipher for the United Kingdom prior to the American War for Independence, or the Soviet Union after 1917, their arbitrary rules and ham-fisted actions leading to more disasters, resentment, and resistance with each passing year. Whedon also made the Alliance banner an amalgamation of the Chinese and U.S. flags, a clear warning about the unification of large governments. But the core of the Alliance/Independent conflict in which Mal is thrust is a metaphorical derivative of the Federalist/Anti-Federalist battle that began in the late eighteenth century, and yielded as its most violent legacy the War Between the States.

bureaucracy under one centralized authority. As the Anti-Federalists argued, the U.S. Constitution gave too much power to the central government. Year after year, politicians like Alexander Hamilton and Henry Clay worked to build the strength of the federal government and shower favors onto their politically connected friends, and, as a result, States, businesses, and individuals are now at the mercy of arbitrary federal whim. There is little one can do today, no commercial transaction in which one can engage, that is not overseen or regulated by government agents and politicians with agendas quite different from one's own.

In *Firefly*, this is precisely the system in which Malcolm Reynolds tries to survive. The Alliance, like the U.S. government during and after the Civil War, is trying to enforce control over the planets of the 'verse, and it is not lost on the viewer that the planets are much like the States are today—the victims of majority sanctioned regulation and theft.

The opening scene of the first episode, "Serenity," introduced us to the violent birth of this world, and as Mal might say, "it ain't pretty." Serenity Valley was the place where liberty made its last stand, amidst explosions and gunfire, lasers and death. It was a fight for freedom, a fight Mal and Zoe would lose. The oppressive Alliance forces were working toward "Unification," an ironic term when one considers the questionable justification for any union that is created or sustained (as it was by Abraham Lincoln, the Soviets, and the Chinese) by force of arms.

Six years passed, and the Alliance had become hegemonic. But this power had not created a better galaxy. The centralized authority that controlled the outer planets of the 'verse had brought about death, sorrow, theft, torture, favoritism, corruption, biological experimentation, and stifling inefficiency in its operations. Indentured servitude was encouraged on Canton, and government schooling invited torture and brain surgery for "gifted" children like River Tam. The government health care system neglected the unconnected in "The Train Job" and showered favors on the elite in "Ariel." Unionized prostitutes wielded incredible influence while nonmembers struggled to survive. In most regards, the 'verse was a cesspool of moral ambiguity and perverted ideals. It was not, as the Operative claims in *Serenity*, a "better world" by any stretch of the imagination.

Shepherd Book understood the nature of the Alliance, and warned Simon Tam about the true danger of vesting any trust in those who would seize the reigns of politics. "A government," he said, "is a body of *people*, usually, notably, ungoverned."

Like Lord Acton, who observed that "power corrupts, and absolute power corrupts absolutely," Book knew that the psychology and base desires of men did not change when they were given positions in the Alliance. These men were simply granted more numerous and more dangerous opportunities to do ill unto others. The most recognizable philosopher aboard *Serenity*, Book knew that there is a difference between "government" and "society." Society is that which we create through our own volition, through private exchange and interaction, through free enterprise and commerce. The larger a government grows, the more society is put at risk, and the more the commercial interactions and moral decisions between consenting adults are threatened, thus diminishing prosperity for all.

It was out of this oppressive system that Malcolm Reynolds emerged as its most dangerous enemy—a seemingly powerless, sometimes cocky, typically soft-spoken and honest man whose broader dreams of fighting tyranny have been crushed, and whose sole goal is merely to survive. Mal may not be able to express as eloquently as Book the philosophy driving his actions, but in his heart, Mal holds the principles that fuel freedom, and even when he seeks only to "get by," his nature is such that he cannot help but skirt around the illegitimate Alliance law. Mal cannot help but do the right thing, and he ends up fighting the Alliance with the most simple and most powerful weapons tyranny can face: peaceful commercial exchange and unflinching personal integrity.

In the 'verse of Whedon's creation, commerce is monitored, manipulated, and tapped by the government, making it very difficult for peace-loving, honest people to survive. Of course, as Mal told Simon early in the pilot episode, "That's what governments are for, getting in your way."

Using flowery rhetoric, politicians often proclaim that employing force to "make a better world" is fine, is laudable—that it is, in fact, the very *raison d'etre* of government. But giving a legal patina to coercive acts and plunder merely allows those in charge to accrue more power and excuse their own coercive behavior.

Instead of siding with this pernicious and illegitimate authority to further his own ends, instead of collapsing under its oppressive weight, Malcolm Reynolds retains his principles. He goes "underground," engaging in black-market—i.e., free-market—exchange, in a supposedly lawless realm.

In this outlaw sphere, Mal is given choices, and presented with dilemmas brought about by the corruption of a society which itself has been perverted by an oppressive political system. Yet Mal always comes out in favor of individual liberty and personal integrity, and by doing so, he not only displays the attributes of a dramatic hero, he exhibits the personal inclinations and codes of honor that libertarians recognize are requisite for a market system to flourish.

This is an important point to stress. Many observers might glibly comment that under a corrupt legal system, those who break the law are the ones who are truly heroic. But, of course, that depends on how one breaks the law.

In the pilot episode, Badger, Mal's bowler-wearing, cockney acquaintance, described the captain of *Serenity* as a "man of honor in a den of thieves," to which Mal replied in a matter-of-fact tone, "I do business. We're here for business."

Though it might seem simple to Mal, his point of view regarding honor and integrity is profound. As libertarians know, even in a world devoid of government laws, in order to do business properly, one *does* have to be a man of honor, and this is how Mal distinguishes himself from people like the desultory Badger and even more unsavory characters.

Take the story "The Train Job," for example. At the outset, when the despicable underworld kingpin Niska offered Mal work robbing a train on a border world, he observed Mal's reputation as a man willing to steal from the Alliance. But this futuristic Robin Hood will not do so if it harms the innocent, especially those who might already have been hurt by the government.

When Mal discovered that he had stolen a shipment of the vitally important medicine Pascaline D, and learned that the Alliance troops were going to leave the citizens to fend for themselves, he wryly said to the Sheriff, "That sounds like the Alliance. Unite all the planets under one rule, so everyone can be interfered with or ignored equally." And in short notice, when he realized how much harm he was doing to the poor people living under Alliance tyranny who were dependent on the drug to survive, Mal actually chose to *give up* his booty in favor of what was right. Because of this, the Sheriff of Paradiso let Mal and Zoe go, revealing that he, too, was more concerned with honor and sustaining his local community than in upholding some form of abstract Alliance law. Here, both Mal and the Sheriff displayed in fictional form an understanding of what libertarian political philosophers call the principle of "spheres of control." The Sheriff knew better than the distant Alliance authorities how to deal with local problems; he was closer to the issues, knew the people, and truly cared about them. It was a powerful moment, when two neglected and forgotten men acknowledged their respect for one another, their devotion to their friends and principles, and their rancor for the central government that had placed them in this position.

In this tale of train heists and desperately needed medicine, Whedon perfectly illustrates what Nobel Prize winning economist F. A. Hayek and thinkers like the nineteenth-century writer Claude Frédéric Bastiat understood: large governments are bureaucratic, unresponsive, slow, and, often, threats to individual liberty. They alienate the people being affected by their laws, and generally retard the pace of progress for everyone. On the other hand, small spheres of control are more efficient and allow for greater freedom, responsiveness, and experimentation. They require people to deal with one another face to face, and with integrity, as Mal and the Sheriff did in the cold, tense darkness of Paradiso.

To bring the story full circle, and to stress Mal's strong moral stand, he then handed his payment for the job back to Niska's agents, saying: "We're not thieves. . . . Well, we are thieves, but. . . . The point is, we're not takin' what's his."

Though this comment was lost on the despicable Niska, whose dangerous, aggressive attitude would dampen the potential growth of any free-market system, it is one that has resonance with lovers of freedom. It indicates that Mal is a different kind of outlaw. By employing his morals, and keeping them in mind, he distinguishes himself from those who break the government ordinances *and* the Lockean law of negative reciprocity.

This is wonderful to see, because it is a form of morality that is at the heart of libertarian philosophy. Contrary to popular belief, libertarians are not *libertines*. We really do *care* about virtue and "the good." Yes, we believe that it should be legal to do anything one wants as long as it does not bring direct harm to the life or property of another. Yes, we believe that people should even have the ability to employ their right to do something harmful to themselves. But in our personal lives we recognize the difference between *license* and *licentiousness*. Just because libertarians extol the freedom to do whatever is consensual, it does not mean that we all engage in the panoply of activities that entails. We recognize the havoc that licentiousness and pleasure-seeking can play in our own personal lives and with our own emotions.

Mal's relationship with Inara is a perfect example of this. While the *legality* of prostitution may not be in question, the *morality*, or at least the emotional purity, of it is, at least for Mal. Even if the government grants legal status to Inara's line of work, it does not mean that Mal approves of *Inara* doing it. His own heart gets in the way. One sensed early on that Mal was in love with Inara, and Inara with Mal, but that their positions, and their natures, made expressing that love difficult. Inara's work made this doubly problematic for Mal, who had to see her meeting clients with whom she would engage in sexual activity but for whom she felt no true love. The problem built and built, becoming so intense that in one heated scene Mal told her, "What I do may be illegal, but at least it's honest!"

This was an interesting twist in the series, and contributed to the romantic tension between these two fascinating characters. Given the libertarian themes in *Firefly*, one might think its creator and writers would imply that the legality of prostitution meant it was also universally morally acceptable. But sex is a much more complicated interpersonal relationship than a mere transaction, for it involves one of the most intimate activities in which two people can engage. While it may be acceptable to some, all the training and respectability Inara can garner through her Guild schools do not help her with Mal. He may be fine with other prostitutes plying their craft, but he cannot help but feel upset by Inara's retail intimacy. He may search for any way in which he can be free from Alliance oppression, but he is still bound by his heart.

It is this heart that truly distinguishes Mal from others who operate outside the bounds of Alliance law. Like Rance Burgess, the local leader who tyrannized prostitutes in "Heart of Gold," Mal recognizes a distinction between that which is legal and that which is moral. But unlike the religious hypocrite Burgess, he would never go so far as to make his own law, or to claim a property right to the child he fathered with a prostitute at a brothel.

The outlaw Malcolm Reynolds adheres to the principles of peaceful exchange and respect for Natural Rights, while the outlaw Rance Burgess adhered to whatever furthered his own ends.

In the struggle between Burgess and the girls in the brothel over possession of a baby Burgess called his "property," Nandi pointed a shotgun at him and warned, "You don't get gone, we'll be well within our rights to drop you."

Burgess's reply was revealing: "Only rights you got," he said, "are the ones I give you!"

It's an attitude that stands in remarkably stark contrast with Mal's. Mal—a man who only steals from those who have not rightfully earned their possessions, a man who avoids killing people unless they are threats to his life or the life of another innocent, a man who avoids shooting unarmed men until he finally decides to take on the Alliance once and for all—was faced with an individual who flouted the unjust government law, but was actually lawless in his heart.

At first glance, one could believe that they were kindred spirits. When they met, Burgess's wife told Mal, "My husband makes a distinction between legality and morality, Mr. Reynolds."

Mal agreed, and replied, "I've said that myself."

But his mood was clear. He could see how Burgess operated, and he didn't like it.

When Burgess observed, "Bending one unjust law is a small thing when it comes to protecting one's family," Mal nodded. "I think I understand you," he said, with sarcasm lacing every word.

The distinction was clear. Burgess was, in fact, Mal's dark alter-ego. Mal favors peaceful relationships, even in societies with no written laws, while Burgess favored force, intimidation, and oppression. Mal will bend the rules to be left alone. Burgess would bend the rules, and make up his own, to get what he wanted or thought belonged to him.

Mal recognizes that no one has a property right to another person, even if he makes a law that says so. Each individual is unique—including a child with DNA distinct from his father and mother—and it is implied that because Burgess was already married, and had engaged in the commercial act of soliciting a prostitute, the living fruit of that sexual encounter was not his to raise, it was the mother's. Avoiding the tricky issue of abortion in this tale of feminist power and rights, something remarkable emerged as Mal fought to protect the ladies of the brothel and the mother of the baby Burgess had fathered: we saw an implicit acknowledgement of the sanctity of contract. It was understood that this religious maniac, this man of low moral character who imposed *his* law where Alliance law was pushed aside, had already paid for sex, and had given up his right to be a partner in the upbringing of the child. It was also clear that Burgess did not acknowledge that fact, and Mal was right to oppose him.

Burgess showed us the path Mal could have followed. Both men are individualists of a sort. Mal simply allows others to be individualists as well. It is because of Mal's strong moral character, and the effort he expends to keep it, that he walks this path.

In fact, it is this undeniable trait of the individualist-hero that leads to the weakening of Alliance authority at the triumphant conclusion of the film *Serenity*.

Though his decision to accept River and Simon Tam on his ship is often questioned by many in his crew, though the Alliance authorities hound them at every turn, Mal adheres to his principles—and his sense of obligation—and keeps them aboard. He grows to accept them, and to eventually realize in the film *Serenity* that River herself holds the key to the destruction of the Alliance rule.

We discover that River's great mental acuity was manipulated by the Alliance in terrible experiments, conducted at what was supposed to be a school for gifted students off her home world (a remarkable indictment of government education). But they did not count on River escaping with her brother, and carrying with her not only the scars of that state-sponsored torture, but the secret that no government official wants revealed.

With heroic strength of character, Mal and his company risk everything they have, including their own lives, to tear the façade off the government utopia and show what hides beneath: experimentation, mass murder, and the creation of horrific human monsters. The man-eating Reavers, infamous in every sector of the 'verse, are the product of Alliance attempts to create a better world on the planet Miranda, to placate subjects and make more efficient workers for the totalitarian utopia. Most of the subjects affected by the Alliance creation called the

Pax simply lay down, and died—a horrific metaphor for the diminution of man's ambition under the corrosive influence of socialism. But for a small cohort of the Mirandans, the drug had the opposite effect. Instead of losing the will to live, they acquired the desire to kill: they became the ultimate incarnation of the deadly side of government force, the final infringement of the Lockean rule. The madness, the horror, and the bloody slaughter of the Reavers is the responsibility of those who wished to force their will on others, just like Rance Burgess, and just like so many Alliance cronies from whom Mal and company fled throughout the series *Firefly*.

In a powerful speech, Mal tells his crew that they are done running. It is time to take a stand, and time to fight.

"A year from now," he begins, "maybe ten, they'll swing back to the belief that they can make . . . people . . . *better*. . . . And I do not hold to that."

For those who died at the hands of the government, for those who suffered due to their policies, for those who may be hurt in the future, the *Serenity* crew pit their wills and bodies against the forces of the Alliance in the "free-speech" broadcast facility of Mr. Universe. Following in the footsteps of Shepherd Book, Wash, the beloved pilot, dies; Kaylee, Simon, and Zoe are critically wounded as Reavers attack; Alliance troops invade; Mal nearly dies in one-on-one combat. But they succeed. They persevere in telling the horrible truth that lies behind the pristine mask the Alliance has worn for far too long.

After all the travails and adventures we've seen them endure, the remainder of the *Serenity* crew return to their ship to rebuild, fueled by new hope and optimistic resolution. River, the haunted girl who held the government's terrible secret, helps steer the ship up into the sky. She sits beside Malcolm Reynolds, the outlaw who adhered to a higher law from centuries past, and smiles at him as they dart into the black.

It is a remarkable conclusion to a story that began by chronicling the death throes of freedom at a place called Serenity Valley, and it is an amazing story of triumph for Mal.

We've taken a long and exciting journey with him, on a ship called *Serenity*, a ship that was its owner's only hope of finding a measure of freedom in this new, unkind world.

But really, the hope for freedom always existed within the heart of Malcolm Reynolds. He was a man willing to skirt the law to do what was right, willing to engage in private commerce even when it was verboten, and whose beliefs in loyalty, honor, and integrity will always represent the core human virtues that freedom requires to survive and prosper.

Take my love, take my land.
Take me where I cannot stand.
I don't care, I'm still free.
You can't take the sky from me.

At its heart, freedom is an intangible thing. It is a concept. It is an ideal. Malcolm Reynolds may have looked to the sky and seen his hopes for freedom embodied in his beloved ship, *Serenity*, but, in fact, the freedom was embodied in him, and his decision to live as freely as possible.

The same is true for each of us.

P. GARDNER GOLDSMITH worked in the script departments of *Outer Limits* and *Star Trek: Voyager*. He received the Writers' Guild Fellowship in 1998, and the Institute for Humane Studies Fellowship in 1996. His articles have appeared in *Investor's Business Daily*, *The Freeman*, *Human Events*, *SFX* (U.K.), *Naked* (U.K.), *Manchester Union Leader*, TechcentralStation.com, FEE.org, Mises.org, and LewRockwell.com. Gard was "2006 NH Libertarian of the Year," runs www.libertyconspiracy.com, and his first book, *Live Free or Die*, is due in July 2007. He would like to thank Leah and Jill. . . .

And to let you know that he owns a handsome brown coat.

There is something classic and powerful about two characters sharing the role of hero in a single world. I'm thinking of Butch and Sundance, Kirk and Spock, Stewart and Colbert. In the piece that follows, Swendson argues that Mal and Simon are co-heroes of the Firefly *saga, and she makes a good case. If the classic hero takes a familiar journey, Mal and Simon certainly travel roads that run through the fascinating tulgey woods nearby.*

A Tale of Two Heroes

SHANNA SWENDSON

Before you can tell a story, you have to know whose story you're telling, and when you're watching or reading a story, you want to know whose story it is. In other words, who's the hero? Not the hero in the sense of who wears the white hat and beats the bad guys, but more in the mythological sense—the man on a mission, the one who has to step out of his comfort zone and face potentially life-threatening situations and be forever transformed in order to achieve his goals.

Who's the hero of *Firefly*? In the television series, that changed from week to week, depending on the plot of the particular episode—Mal was usually the one taking the lead, but Simon was the criminal mastermind behind the caper in "Ariel," Wash refused to leave a man behind in "War Stories," River saved the day in "Objects in Space," and even Jayne got to be a hero in "Jaynestown." But whose story does the saga as a whole tell? At first it seemed pretty obvious that Mal Reynolds would be our hero. He was the first character we met, the captain of the ship, the one running the show. But after facing the battle of Serenity Valley in the opening sequence, he became a man very specifically without a mission. All he wanted was to make enough money to keep his ship and his crew going so that he never had to answer to anyone else ever again. As much as he hated the Alliance, he wasn't ready to start a rebellion, fight the Alliance (except in self-defense), or do much of anything other than stay out of the way. He was done with missions and grand fights, causes, and that sort of thing. He'd learned that great causes only get your heart broken.

Then along came Simon Tam, the young doctor who was very much on a mission: to rescue his sister, keep her safe from the Alliance, and figure out what they did to her and why—and then maybe, just maybe, fix it. He didn't know yet if that would involve something as small as finding the right dosage of the right drugs to make her sane again or something as large as changing the entire government so that it wouldn't try to get her back to finish whatever it was that it was doing to her, but he didn't much care. Whatever it was, whatever it took, he'd do it—and he'd do it willingly, without much thought for what it cost him. He'd already given up everything he had and everything else that mattered to him. Any further sacrifices—up to and including his life—would be relatively inconsequential to him.

Now, that's a hero of mythological proportions—the man on a mission greater than himself who is willing to take on all odds and overcome all obstacles to carry it out. And from a storytelling standpoint, that mission was also the element of change that kicked Mal's story into gear. Simon and River's plight was the catalyst that forced Mal into action and out of his comfortable world, into the unknown where he'd have to take a stand eventually. When he offered Simon a job instead of kicking Simon and River off *Serenity* at the end of the pilot, he forever changed life on board his ship. That put Mal on a path toward possible rebirth and transformation.

So, who is the hero of *Firefly*, the man on the mission, or the man who takes on that mission even though he's not quite ready to believe in it fully? Maybe it's both.

Superficial Differences, Volcano Similarities

At first glance, Mal and Simon couldn't appear to be more different. Mal is from a more rough-and-tumble part of the 'verse, a former ranch kid who grew up to be a soldier and then a mercenary/thief/smuggler/transport ship captain. He talks with a drawl and uses uncultured slang, dresses in Western/cavalry gear, and goes out of his way to subvert most rules of social propriety. He's comfortable with guns and violence as a way of life.

Meanwhile, Simon is from a cultured, wealthy background in the Core of the system. He's educated—a doctor—speaks properly, avoids swearing (unless it's appropriate), and dresses in perfectly tailored business attire. His concession to the more casual life in his first months on board *Serenity* was to stop wearing a necktie. He knows all the rules for proper social conduct and abides by them, even when nobody else around him follows those rules and even when that kind of behavior is seen as more insulting than polite. Before coming on board *Serenity*, he seemingly had little experience with violence. He'll pick up a gun if he has to in self-defense, or in defense of his sister or shipmates, but he's far better at patching up the results of violence (or being the victim of violence) than he is at committing violence himself.

Beneath the surface, however, these two men are very much alike, which could explain both why they clash so often and how they also manage to develop a certain respect for each other. Both of them use snark and sarcasm as weapons when they feel threatened or when they want to keep someone from getting too close to the truth. Both of them would do absolutely anything to protect the people for whom they have responsibility. Mal's protectiveness of his crew is very much like Simon's protectiveness toward River. They both also have an old-fashioned, courtly attitude toward women that occasionally gets them in trouble with their respective romantic interests. Inara wasn't particularly impressed when Mal got himself into a duel over her honor, and Kaylee was outright insulted at Simon's implication that she wasn't the kind of girl he'd get drunk and have sex with in a sleazy bar.

In spite of Mal's often gregarious nature, he has a talent for annoying others that's very much like a talent he himself noticed in Simon. Book remarked that Mal wasn't overly concerned with ingratiating himself with anyone, while Mal commented on Simon's remarkable talent for alienating folks. Neither of them is good at forming close, intimate relationships. Zoe is really the only person on *Serenity* who is what one might call Mal's true friend, and even their relationship is more businesslike than emotionally intimate. Whenever Inara gets close to anything resembling emotional closeness with Mal, he resorts to sarcasm or outright obnoxiousness. Simon is too new to have true friends on the ship, but he's not trying too hard, either. His focus is on River, and when he gets too close to intimacy with Kaylee, he falters, as in "The Message" when he managed to compliment her without thinking, but when she asked for more compliments he panicked and ended up infuriating her instead after he weakly turned the compliment into a joke. Both are shown to have a knack for planning. Mal's plans are usually mocked because they tend to rely on improvisation, but they often end up working in the long run, while Simon's effort at playing mastermind in "Ariel" was later referenced as the best job the crew ever pulled.

Both men also play big brother roles—Mal with Kaylee and Simon with River. These interactions serve as a humanizing touch for both characters. In "Serenity," when Mal was generally being a jerk to everyone, he was nice to Kaylee—and since the audience couldn't help but like Kaylee, we figured this meant he was basically an okay guy. Almost every scene of Mal being mean, harsh, or cruel was balanced by a scene of him being a good "big brother" to Kaylee. In that same episode, Simon's devotion to his sister thawed his personality significantly. He was introduced as a potential villain, the one we were led to believe was the Alliance spy, and even after we knew he wasn't the spy he still could have been a bad guy—he was a wanted man desperate enough to essentially use Kaylee as a hostage to ensure his escape. Until his sister was revealed, he came across as cold, distant, calculating, and a touch arrogant, but once we saw him with River and learned what he'd done for her, all was forgiven.

Even those similarities are still somewhat superficial, though. If you want to really know a man, you have to see how he reacts in a crisis. Or, in the words of the *Firefly* universe's psychotic dictator/warrior poet Shan-Yu, you have to tie him up and hold him over the volcano's edge. When either Mal or Simon is held over that metaphorical volcano's edge, they both react the same way—with sarcasm, stubbornness, and a touch of recklessness. Both of them come into their own in a crisis, where even if they're not in control of the greater situation, they're totally in control of themselves and willing to stand up to or take on anyone. They don't back down, even when all looks lost.

We first saw this trait in Mal during the flashback at the beginning of the pilot "Serenity," when he was able to keep his troops together and get his job done under fire, even if that required improvising. Simon first demonstrated his ability to think under pressure when he coerced Mal to make a run for it by refusing to treat Kaylee until Mal agreed not to turn him over to the Feds. Later, we saw that he didn't let a death sentence hanging over his head slow him down at all. Instead of groveling and begging for his life, as many people would do, he kept arguing with Mal, up to the point where he got himself decked. He flung himself off a catwalk and fought with the federal marshal when River's safety was at stake—the kind of reckless move you could imagine Mal making. Mal never gave a straight answer as to why he hired Simon instead of stranding him on Whitefall, as he'd originally planned to do, beyond "You ain't weak, and that's not nothing," but it's not hard to guess that Simon's feistiness under pressure had a lot to do with it.

These core traits repeated themselves throughout the series: Mal thinking his way calmly through the life-threatening crisis when the ship died in the middle of nowhere in "Out of Gas"; Simon's icy dressings-down of both a hospital resident and the federal officer who captured him in "Ariel." They even have similar ways of dealing with Jayne. When Simon quietly lectured Jayne about his disloyalty during the Ariel caper in "Trash," he echoed some of the terms and arguments and even the hint of ruthless menace that Mal used when lecturing Jayne on the same event at the end of "Ariel." Both focused on the concept of crew unity and loyalty.

The similarity under pressure, however, was most obvious in the episodes "War Stories" and "Objects in Space." In "War Stories," Mal never lost his sarcastic edge while being tortured by Niska. He looked for and found his opening to strike back at his captors, and he didn't let himself stop fighting until the fight was over. In "Objects in Space," Simon reacted in much the same way when he was taken captive by bounty hunter Jubal Early. He kept his sass thoroughly intact, no matter how threatened he was, waited for his opportunity, and then tried to take on an armed, armored man nearly twice his size while he was unarmed, barefoot, and in his pajamas—and then kept trying to fight even after he was shot, because he thought he was all that stood between Early and his sister.

You could probably swap these characters in these situations and get almost identical results. Simon being tortured by Niska might have made different snarky wisecracks, but he would have kept up the sarcasm until the very end—and as a doctor he might have been even more creative about the way he turned the torture implements on his torturer. Likewise, Mal, put in Simon's situation with Early, would have been just as sarcastic, defiant, calculating, and reckless, though he probably wouldn't have used the word "incorporeally" in his taunts.

Although Simon and Mal had very different upbringings, there is one major element in their backgrounds that they have in common. They've each faced their own "Serenity Valley" of sorts, a time when they were disappointed and betrayed by something or someone they believed in, and when they found out that they really were all alone in the universe.

Mal had the literal Serenity Valley, the battle where he and his forces were left without support to face the enemy on their own. According to a deleted scene from the episode "Serenity," the soldiers were left in that hellhole without supplies or help while the leaders negotiated a settlement. It was in Serenity Valley that Mal lost his faith in God, when he learned that prayers aren't answered, and his faith in his cause, when he learned that his loyalty wasn't returned by the people to whom he gave it, those who left him and his people to die in the aftermath of battle. He was left believing in nothing but himself and Zoe, with no greater cause than just getting by.

We saw Simon's metaphoric Serenity Valley in flashbacks during the episode "Safe," when he learned that the parents who had seemed supportive of him wouldn't be there when he really needed them. They wouldn't believe him when he was worried about River, and they didn't support the actions he took to help her. His father's declaration that if he got in trouble again, he would be on his own, his father would not come for him again, was for Simon the equivalent of the moment when Mal learned that there would be no air support at Serenity Valley. Someone he believed in and counted on had let him down, bringing everything else he believed in into question. The fact that it was the government Simon had previously supported that had harmed River was yet another betrayal.

Both Mal and Simon even responded to their own Serenity Valley experiences in a similar way, by escaping society and heading for the blackness of space—the only place where they could have any semblance of freedom. We don't know the whole story of how Mal went from the immediate aftermath of Serenity Valley to purchasing *Serenity*, but he makes it clear that he wants no part of the government's control over his life, and he took the person who mattered most to him at the time—Zoe—with him. Simon's escape was somewhat less than voluntary, as he had government agents chasing him, but he, too, wanted to get away from government control and took the most important person in his life—River—with him. And of course, both of them ultimately ended up in the same place, on board *Serenity*, and they both found a new kind of home and family there.

FROM "SERENITY" TO *SERENITY*

So, is Mal the hero, or is Simon—or is there even a distinction? In a sense, these aren't two separate characters but rather different reflections on the same character, which allows us to see the hero in different phases of his life and on different parts of his journey. The two of them represent the range of possibilities for each other's futures. Depending on what happens to them, how they react to events, and the choices they make, each could end up very much like the other.

The comparison between the two characters and their journey as the two heroes of the saga is most obvious between the episode "Serenity," which begins the story, and the movie *Serenity*, which completes the story arc (for now, we can only hope). These two "episodes" taken together present a complete mythic hero's journey for these two characters.

The two characters were constantly depicted as reflections of each other throughout the episode "Serenity." When Simon was first introduced, there was a long shot of him and Mal, facing each other across the cargo bay ramp. They stood on either end of the screen, framed as though they were looking into a mirror at each other, establishing the sense of comparison and contrast. At that point, Mal was a man without any mission greater than finding a customer for the cargo they were carrying, and he believed in nothing other than his ship and his crew. Simon was the one with a capital-M Mission, the one that would affect the rest of the story and change everyone's lives. He was still idealistic enough to believe that good and right would ultimately win—enough so that when he was later caught by the federal marshal he felt that if he could just explain what had really happened, if the marshal could only understand why he'd taken River, everything would be okay. Even though he'd lost absolutely everything, he was still able to believe strongly enough in his love for his sister to get them both through the crisis and to hope that love would influence others.

In a structural sense, the moment when Simon boarded *Serenity* with River in the cryosleep chamber was when the story really began for the crew of *Serenity*, because it was the moment of change—yet another reason why FOX should have shown this episode first during the series's original run. Simon's story had already begun off-screen, when he learned River was in danger and accepted the responsibility of saving her.

Plot-wise, Mal and Simon have similar story arcs in the episode. Mal brought a box on board the ship and kept the secret of what was really in it (the marked goods) from his crew. He tried a dangerous plan (dealing with Patience) because he was desperate to keep flying. He ended up in a gunpoint standoff that was resolved in part by someone outside the standoff (Jayne) intervening. Likewise, Simon brought a box on board the ship and kept the secret of what was really in it from the crew. He tried a dangerous plan (essentially holding Kaylee hostage) because he was desperate to keep running. He ended up in a gunpoint standoff that was resolved by someone outside the standoff (Mal) intervening.

When Mal became aware of the change Simon had brought to his ship, he wasn't welcoming of it. He decked Simon in the cargo bay as a suspected spy; planned to space him or, if things went well, strand him on an inhospitable planet, even after learning Simon's true story; and decked him again when Simon remained defiant. As much as he hated the government, Mal wanted no part of Simon's mission, and he didn't want it associated with his ship. But then Mal had a change of heart after seeing Simon holding the federal agent at gunpoint, and instead of putting him and his sister off the ship, Mal offered Simon a job.

Mal knew what he was getting into at that point. He knew he was taking on fugitives, that by doing so he was in effect taking on Simon's mission of keeping his sister safe, which also meant that he was putting himself in more active opposition of the Alliance government. He knew that he was forever changing life for his crew. As the two men discussed the specifics of the job offer and what it meant for them, again they were framed as though they were looking into a mirror, on either side of the screen in nearly identical poses. The story question that seemed to be raised in this moment was how the decision would change them both, since they both had similar potential. Would Simon change to be more like Mal as he faced life on the fringes of society, becoming hard and bitter from having his ideals shattered? Or would Simon's influence revive Mal's long-lost idealism, his ability to believe in something greater than his immediate surroundings, to the point where he would be willing to take action to right a wrong instead of just keeping his head down and staying out of trouble?

The other story question raised in this moment is a central, unspoken conflict that would go on to drive much of the series and provide the core emotional conflict in the movie. We knew that the things these two believed in the most strongly were bound to be mutually exclusive at some point. Mal wanted to protect his ship and crew and stay out of major trouble, as much as possible (minor trouble is just a bit of fun). Simon wanted to protect River at all costs. As long as protecting the crew was the same as protecting River, they would be fine. But we knew that if there was ever a situation in which protecting River meant putting the crew at risk, or protecting the crew meant putting River at risk, well, there were two very strong-willed, determined, and occasionally reckless men who would be at odds. Mal's promise to Simon in "Serenity" that if he ever shot Simon, "you'll be awake, you'll be facing me, and you'll be armed," had the ring of foreshadowing to it (though the premature cancellation of the series that required the shortening of the major arcs meant we never got to see that foreshadowed moment—or we haven't yet). A couple of times during the run of the series situations arose that skirted such an opposition between River's safety and the crew's, but it never came to all-out war between Simon and Mal.

Which brings us to *Serenity* the movie. As we pick up with the crew after a gap of several months, the questions raised at the end of the pilot episode seem to be answered. Simon has become like the Mal of the series—harder, angrier, more confident, more defiant. He's also become emotionally closed off to everyone but River, barely even looking at

Kaylee, with whom things had been looking up in the final episode of the series. We don't have much indication of what happened to Simon in the timeframe between the series and the movie, but whatever it was stripped away most of Simon's softness, youth, and vulnerability. As the ultimate sign of his transformation, this time he's the one to hit Mal with a sucker punch in the cargo bay. Because they seem to have reached an impasse in which, in Simon's opinion, Mal's view of what's good for the ship and crew isn't in line with what's good for River, Simon plans to leave the ship. He's ready to stand on his own.

But it also seems that some of Simon has rubbed off on Mal. He may act colder and harder-edged, but when River collapses after the fight in the Maidenhead, Mal's instinct is to bring her and Simon back on board, and he can't even explain why. She's proved that she isn't helpless at all, but Mal seems to sense that this actually puts her and her brother in even more danger, not least because Simon is ill-equipped to handle a semi-psychotic fighting machine armed only with a safety word. In making the decision to bring River back on board and keep her on board even though he knows that the Alliance is actively seeking her, Mal takes on Simon's original mission to a degree he never had before, and this time willingly instead of by chance. And in doing so, he picks up again with the same battle he was fighting in the first scene of the pilot, openly rebelling against the Alliance.

By the midpoint of the movie, Mal has totally taken over what once was Simon's mission. Mal is the one meeting with the Operative, coming up with the plans, and making the decisions. In doing this, he frees Simon to lay down his burdens and focus on just being a big brother. Keeping River out of Alliance hands isn't solely his responsibility anymore. Even though the whole situation is about his sister and himself, Simon is just along for the ride. The Operative wants River and Simon; they are his quarry, and he has no quarrel with Mal or *Serenity*. But Mal puts himself in the position of intermediary. Simon and River never meet the Operative face-to-face during the entire film. In fact, at the film's climax, Mal goes on alone to complete the mission that will ultimately make River safe from the Alliance.

Although Mal is unquestionably the hero of the movie, Simon is still a co-hero of the saga, and he gets the proper ending to his hero's journey. One of the final stages of a mythic hero's journey is a symbolic death and resurrection, a moment when all seems lost and the hero is as good as dead, before he comes back, reborn, a new man. Both Mal and Simon go through this phase in the movie.

Mal is nearly defeated by the Operative during the final battle. He's run through with a sword, and only an old war wound saves him from paralysis that would have ended the fight. He comes back from what appears to be certain death, and he returns from completing the mission a changed man. After what he's gone through, he's learned to believe again in something greater than himself. He's taken on the kind of cause he'd given up on and, as his final scene with Inara demonstrates, he's begun allowing himself to open up more emotionally.

Simon also faces death in the climactic battle, when he is shot and gravely wounded. As he lies dying, he and River change roles. He lets go of his personal mission to protect her, as she comes into her own and becomes the protector. His letting go during this symbolic death means that he returns from his injury a changed man. He's reborn as someone who is open to love, who allows himself to live his own life, to do something for himself—something he'd forgotten how to do in his preoccupation with River's safety. His mission is complete and he has the chance to enjoy his reward: being able to start a relationship with Kaylee.

In the end, Mal and Simon have each learned, changed, and grown from the experiences they've had because of the other. If Simon had never boarded *Serenity*, Mal might never have learned to believe again. He might never have opened himself to a cause greater than himself. If Simon had never boarded *Serenity*, he might never have learned to be part of a family again, to trust in those around him and know that they trusted him, too.

The story, such as it is, is mythically complete. Our heroes have taken on their mission, faced death, and returned as new men. But we can always hope that there's another mission out there, some other wrong that needs to be set right, some other learning experience. The way these two characters reflect, contradict, complement, and reinforce each other opens the door to a variety of future storylines. Their different backgrounds mean that they're bound to clash, while their similarities could mean that they don't provide much in the way of checks or balances. If they ever agreed fully on something and went after it together, their combined stubbornness, persistence, and recklessness could be a force to be reckoned with—or a disaster in the making. And wouldn't that be fun to watch?

SHANNA SWENDSON became a devoted Browncoat a few minutes into the first airing of "The Train Job" and still hasn't given up. Although her comic fantasy novel *Enchanted, Inc.*, was published by Ballantine Books in 2005, the highlight of her year was attending the Hollywood premiere of *Serenity* (although she was too shy to actually talk to anyone involved in the movie). In between watching *Firefly* DVDs, discussing the series with anyone who'll listen, and meeting up with other Browncoats, she's written two more novels, *Once Upon Stilettos* and *Damsel Under Stress*, as well as contributing to the Smart Pop books *Flirting with Pride and Prejudice*, *Welcome to Wisteria Lane*, *So Say We All*, and *Perfectly Plum*. Visit her Web site at www.shannaswendson.com.

Of all the characters of the Firefly *universe, Book was almost certainly the one we got to know least well. Greene suggests, aptly, that "Book reflected Mal that was, but is no more: Mal as believer." The analysis goes beyond that, into a look at what belief—at what faith—typically means in a Jossian world. It also presents a very compelling political reading of the* Firefly *world. Whether or not you feel, as Greene does, that something important was neglected when Book died, we can all agree that if the show had been allowed a longer run, there was much more we would all have liked to have known about the good shepherd.*

The Good Book

ERIC GREENE

"I wish they hadn't killed you in *Serenity*," I earnestly protested to Ron Glass at a recent screening of Otto Preminger's celebrated yet lamentable *Porgy and Bess*. He smiled a smile that could best be described as, well, serene, and told me how nice everyone on the production had been, what good people they were. And I don't doubt it. I didn't think it was malice that led to Shepherd Book's demise. But I wish he had lived.

Book was an endless font of paradox that drew me in, made me want to know more. We all have our share of complexity, of course, but sometimes you encounter people whose inner worlds seem so rich that you could spend a lifetime delving into them and never get bored. That was Book. Perhaps it was the juxtaposition of a man of faith running with a gang of criminals, Friar Tuck in outer space. Maybe it was his discomforting familiarity with secret military operations and the tantalizing suggestions of a shameful hidden past as an Alliance agent/interrogator/torturer ("I don't give a hump if you're innocent or not so where does that put you?"—how chilling is *that* in these Abu Ghraib/Guantanamo days?). Or the fact that, as Joss Whedon says on the DVD commentary for *Firefly*'s pilot, Book was "a man of peace, not at peace." It could simply have been the elegance and beauty Ron Glass brought to the character. But definitely part of the fascination was Book's relationship to Mal.

All of *Serenity*'s denizens were defined in large measure by their relation to Malcolm Reynolds. One of the remarkable things about *Firefly*'s very large ensemble is how vividly the characters were drawn, both by the writers and by the actors. There is an impressive consistency to how they behave, react, and speak which might not seem very difficult with only a few characters, but poses a challenge with a large cast sharing limited screen time. Often TV characters exist to convey information or advance a plot and are therefore largely interchangeable. On *Star Trek*, for instance, Kirk, Spock, McCoy, and to a degree Scotty, were distinct individuals but, outside of job-specific lines like "hailing frequencies open," much of what was said by Sulu or Chekhov or Uhura could have been said by any of them. Reading a line of dialogue from *Star Trek: The Next Generation*, one would be hard pressed to guess if it had been written for La Forge or Riker, O'Brien or Crusher.

But *Firefly*'s crew members were more like the people we meet in real life: who they were was more than just the functions they performed. The characters had a personality, a recognizable—and distinct—way of inhabiting and responding to their world. It's hard to imagine the things that came out of Jayne's mouth being said by, for instance, Inara. A Wash joke is very different from a Zoe joke. The characters' internal continuity made them come alive as individuals—but they all had a link to Mal that made them come together as an ensemble.

Mal's crew was an extension and reflection of Mal. Echoing attributes of the central character in the supporting characters is of course a time-honored technique. *Star Trek* again offers an instructive example in the way Spock reflected Kirk's intellect and McCoy embodied Kirk's emotions. Watching McCoy and Spock argue was like seeing Kirk's internal dialogue externalized. This dynamic made both Spock and McCoy vital to Kirk's success as a captain and integral to his wholeness as a person. It also helps account for why the trio was so compelling as a unit.

Firefly achieved a similar effect but with three times as many characters. This was perhaps most easily observable with Mal and Simon. Simon's absolute dedication to his sister, his unbreakable loyalty, his foolhardy willingness to risk everything for the one he loves, echoes Mal's commitment to his ship and his crew. Thus, Simon earned Mal's respect. (In the *Firefly* DVD commentary Nathan Fillion mentions that the Simon-River relationship was his favorite in the series and that he loved Simon's devotion to his sister. For all the conflicts between Mal and Simon—Simon's background and adherence to formal conventions of propriety mark him as a creation of the Alliance, after all—something of that love, however unspoken, is expressed through Fillion's performance.) Mal kept River and Simon on board not just because Simon was useful as a medic but also because the captain saw something of himself in the doctor.

Standing in direct contrast to Simon's impractical dedication, Jayne reflects Mal's elemental pragmatism. Jayne could easily be mistaken for, and could have thoughtlessly been played as, stupid. But he is not. Rather, like a space-faring Stanley Kowalski, Jayne's is an inate, physical—as opposed to intellectual—intelligence (nicely manifested by Adam Baldwin's acting choice to have Jayne relate to the world largely through senses like touch and taste). Whedon points out on the *Serenity* DVD commentary that it is Jayne who is always apt to ask the practical questions. He is also the one most apt to grasp the practical, physical implications of a situation. In "Out of Gas," for example, Jayne stopped Mal and Wash from fighting, not out of a principled objection, but simply because they were using up precious air. Yet his particular intelligence has no way of accommodating displays of altruism which exceed the confines of practical self interest. Acts such as Mal sheltering River and Simon or the mudder sacrificing himself to save Jayne in "Jaynestown" are likely to puzzle him. Jayne's strictly rational common sense and Simon's Quixotic and chivalric devotion established the two men as opposites and repeatedly led them to butt heads.

And so on with the rest of the crew. Zoe shares Mal's experience as a soldier, the primal bonds developed by comrades in arms, and understands his special relationship to Serenity Valley. Kaylee shares Mal's love of the ship, Inara his emotional guardedness and fear of intimacy; River, like Mal, has been interfered with and wounded by the Alliance. And Wash? Well, I was a bit stumped about Wash, figuring he was something of a fish out of water, like the wisecracking Jewish guy who married into the mid-western family, until my friend Jeremy pointed out that Wash represents Mal's spirit of resistance to authority and is the one most likely to challenge Mal's orders. That sounds right to me.

Just as children often pick up different traits from their parents, the members of *Serenity*'s crew had different parts of their captain. Dispersing parts of Mal amongst the other characters helped forge a cohesive ensemble, and gave the audience a sense that these individuals were part of an organic whole, distinct but related. It also partially explains why so many fans reacted to the travelers on the Firefly as if they were a family. Not all the residents of *Serenity* had much of a relationship to each other, but they all had a relationship to Mal.

But while the rest of the crew tended to reflect Mal that is, Book reflected Mal that was, but is no more: Mal as believer. Mal's religious estrangement was foregrounded early in *Firefly*'s pilot episode. Joss Whedon has Mal invoke God and angels and kissing his cross in the opening sequence, then sharply juxtaposed that behavior with Mal's forbidding Book to say grace at the table a few scenes later. This is a textbook example of showing, rather than telling, the audience what they need to know. In a few concise gestures an entire arc was implied and understood. Mal believed once, but no longer. While Book, a former sinner we may assume, now believed. It would seem that just as the defeat at Serenity Valley stripped Mal of his belief, something pushed the shadowy Book into the light. While belief in something larger disappointed Mal, that very belief may have saved Book. Thus, like the rest of the crew, Book reflected an aspect of Mal, but it was more of a reflection in the literal sense: a reverse image.

More than any other episode, "Jaynestown," with its "broken" Bibles and fallen idols, addressed the role of faith and the divergent views of the captain and the shepherd. Book maintained that "faith fixes you," whereas when Mal acknowledged that the mudders' belief in Jayne was not about Jayne but "about what they need," his use of the word "they" marked faith as something strictly for those that need it, not for himself.

In the pilot episode Book worried about his suitability for life on *Serenity*, but by "Bushwacked" he had come to understand that the way of things on the frontier was "not so plain as on the central planets, rules can get a might foggier." Though Book inhabited a religious world he balanced that commitment with the need to adjust to the nature of life in "the black." While Mal had left Book's spiritual world and showed no interest in it, at times ("War Stories," "Our Mrs Reynolds," "The Message," and, especially, the *Serenity* feature) Book understood Mal's world better than Mal. A clergyman schooling a former soldier on military tactics certainly posed an interesting challenge to the captain.

The affinity and the tension, the pull and the push, between Mal the non-believer and Book the believer held much promise, not only as an exploration of the Western genre conventions of disillusioned rebel and preacher with a past, but as a reflection of and engagement with our own complicated contemporary relationships between faith and hope, disappointment and doubt, belief and proof. Sadly *Firefly*'s premature death and Book's death in *Serenity* left that promise largely unfulfilled

But while Mal no longer believed in Book's book, it is not right to say that Mal believed in nothing at all. It is more accurate to say he believed in nothing that was abstract, only in what was immediate. Like many a pragmatic hero in the American Western, Mal is compelled almost exclusively by practical considerations, immediate survival needs, and personal loyalties. Mal is primarily instinctual rather than ideological. Having lost the great cause, Mal was left uninterested in causes or ideals or abstract principles. On the *Firefly* DVD's making of *Firefly* documentary, Fillion recalls being drawn to Mal precisely because he "didn't have any grand dreams, he didn't have any great causes or goals, all he wanted to do . . . was continue living his life." No longer driven to rebellion by Alliance injustice, Mal's interest was more in avoidance than defiance. He travelled the frontier planets where Alliance influence was weakest and tried to stay away from the core as best he could. As Mal says in *Serenity*, "The war's long done, we're all just folks now."

Being an outlaw, a "petty criminal" as Inara calls him in "The Train Job," allowed him to remain a rebel, but only in petty ways.[1] Having lost the war, Mal became neither a guerilla warrior fighting entrenched power (like the heroes of so many Westerns who, after losing the American Civil War, migrate to Mexico and join theirs), nor an errant knight carrying on the noble cause of a shattered Round Table, nor a Robin Hood avenging the downtrodden—"stealing from the rich, selling to the poor" (note: *selling*), as Wash puts it in "Ariel," is the closest he comes.

[1] It's a little like prominent 1960's activist-firebrand-turned-businessman Jerry Rubin, who was killed in 1994 while brazenly violating the law . . . against jaywalking.

This is not to say that Mal was a villain: he was not a sociopathic gun for hire like Jubal Early in "Objects in Space," a cynical opportunist intent on getting others before they get him like the pirate captain in "Out of Gas," nor a heartless predator like Niska in "The Train Job" and "War Stories." It is not that Mal was without morals or honor but that he did not abstract those personal morals into an overarching ideology. As Simon said in *Serenity*, "what's of use" was Mal's "guiding star." For Mal practicality trumped principle, what he did was determined by what he needed and what he saw rather than by conceptual constructs (perhaps a reflection of Mal's creator, who acknowledged on the "Objects in Space" commentary that he is "very literal about everything I do").

Repeatedly Mal rejected overarching principles and constructs in favor of the specific demands of the moment. In the pilot episode, for instance, Mal, unmoved by the injustice of what he dismissed as Simon's "tale of woe," was concerned strictly with the peril Simon and River had brought to "me and mine." In "The Message" Mal was willing to shoot Tracey because protection of his current crew was more important than devotion to a former comrade.

"Out of Gas" was particularly rich with examples. When Mal saw that Kaylee could do the job and Bester could not, he fired Bester on the spot and gave the job to the better woman. It was a straightforward, simple calculation: competence outweighs contract. The same pragmatism which counsels Mal to take a better option when it comes along allowed him to intuit that Jayne would betray his employers if Mal offered a better deal (and also alerted Mal that Jayne had betrayed him in "Ariel"). And while principles of loyalty and familial devotion might dictate that a man should stay with his wounded wife, for Mal the need for survival demanded that Wash get to the bridge to help save the ship rather than tend to Zoe.

In "Ariel" Mal insisted that River and Simon were "on my crew. No one is getting left." But in "Safe," faced with choosing the principle of leaving no one behind and the immediate need to get help for Book, Mal left Simon and River so he could seek a medical facility. For Mal even the imperatives of self-preservation and survival are contingent, not absolute, principles—they too are subject to practical considerations. Mal was willing to go to the Alliance to get medical help for Book and there was no reason for Mal to think he would get out of that a free man.

Furthermore, a strict pragmatist might have opted to save Simon before Book, calculating that the doctor's skills were more essential than the shepherd's. Thus, Mal's pragmatism notwithstanding, he is capable of self-sacrifice

Putting himself at risk of Niska's wrath by returning the medicine in "The Train Job" might seem like an act motivated by an abstract principle, but there again Mal was responding to the immediacy of what was before him. Perhaps Mal would have chosen to return the medicine to Paradiso if he had simply heard about, rather than seen, the suffering of those in need of the medication. But having seen the reality of that suffering with his own eyes, Mal felt that he had *no* choice other than to return the medicine.[2]

But, while not insensitive to the needs of others, Mal's main loyalty is to the well-being of the small community he has built around him, an egalitarian community that allows equal membership to preachers and prostitutes, doctors and mercenaries, the young and the old, the healthy and the sick, browncoats and unification supporters, Black people and White (though, disturbingly, not Chinese people, whose presence, culture, and language are reduced to mere adornments[3]), all bound together not by allegiance to any code, cause, or principle, but by the bonds formed by common peril, mutual reliance, and the fact that, as Mal said in "Our Mrs. Reynolds," they "trust each other, do for each other, and aren't always looking for the advantage." Again recalling classic Western themes, the *Serenity* is a space where meritocracy, as a microcosm of an idealized America free of race, class, and ideological divisions, can flourish; where social status gives way to merit; where the talent you bring means more than the title you bear; where, in the most stunning image in the series, a priest can receive the benediction of a prostitute.

Like *Firefly*'s other characters, Mal is remarkably consistent in his core characteristics, and that opened up an intriguing space between

---

[2] "Heart of Gold" may be the exception to this pattern: Mal's first instinct after seeing what he was up against was the practical desire to run. By changing his mind, however, he seemed to put himself and his crew in danger unnecessarily. But, like Simon's determination to defy the Alliance and protect his sister, the women of the Heart of Gold appealed to his respect for those fighting for self-determination. Maybe it was a way of re-fighting the War for Independence on a more manageable scale.

[3] See Leigh Adams Wright's thoughtful "Asian Objects in Space" in BenBella's *Finding Serenity*.

him and Book who, as a clergyman, by definition was guided by overarching principles and ideological constructs. Again, had the series had a longer run it would have been nice to have seen that space and those tensions explored more deeply. But with Book dispatched after two short scenes in *Serenity*, Book's role as the believing counterweight to the non-believing Mal is taken up by the Alliance operative.

Having so clearly defined Mal in *Firefly*, in *Serenity* Whedon gives him an adversary who is his diametric opposite. Mal, the pragmatist who reacts only to what he sees, is opposed by an agent known only as the Operative,[4] a fanatic who blinds himself to the reality before his eyes and who, as Whedon says on the commentary "believes so strongly that he would do anything." The Alliance and its Operative, unlike Mal, act almost exclusively in the name of abstractions like order, law, and morality. Yet these ideals have been severed from the true values that arise from lived human experience: the need for self-determination, the importance of dissent, the simple moral imperative that children should not be kidnapped, killed, or turned into killers.

When killing his targets the Operative is fond of telling them what their sin is, but his sin is the big one in the eyes of the film: unlike Mal, the Operative ignores what is in front of him, the true morality of slaughtering civilians or murdering a child, in favor of serving an *idea*, an abstraction. "We're making a better world," he says, destroying Haven in order to "save" it, clinging to the idea of the world to come while ignoring the reality of the world that is. Perversely, obedience to an abstracted morality means that normal moral impulses to empathy and compassion must be subsumed to *concepts* of righteousness. Therefore even his own recognition that he is "a monster," doing "evil," leaves him unmoved.

With no name, no history, no rank, the Operative is less a person than a function, so committed to abstraction he becomes one himself. Continually watching holograms, surveillance recordings, and video monitors—but never looking in a mirror—the Operative sees all, but understands little. The Operative stands not only in opposition to Mal but in opposition to Book as well. Book and the Operative embody two very different kinds of

---

[4] Perhaps a call back to Dashiell Hammett's fictional Pinkerton Agent "The Continental Op"?

faith. Book's faith leads him to engage the world. The Operative's faith leads him to dominate it. Where Book might try to convince, the Operative, like the Alliance, seeks to control. That characteristic of the Alliance, the urge to control, is at the heart of its crime on Miranda. It is also a crime that Book likely would have objected to on theological grounds.

A standard trope in cautionary science fiction is that human beings should not "play God." But the Alliance goes way beyond that. In the Hebrew Bible the God of Genesis, Chapters 6–9, deems that the inclination of the human heart is toward evil continually, decides to wipe out the human race with a flood, but then relents and allows a remnant led by Noah to survive and rebuild humanity. But in so doing God does not "reprogram" the essential nature of human beings, which, presumably, God had the power to do. God does not extinguish human free will. God does not eliminate the capacity to do evil, even as God hopes that humans will do right. God will send commandments and prophets, promise punishment and reward, in order to cajole, exhort, and inspire humans toward virtue. God may weep and mourn when we sin, but unlike the Alliance, God does not try to instill docility in order to control people. God knows better than to "play God." So the Alliance does more than try to "play God," it tries to play a part that even God, wisely, turned down.

Conventional wisdom is that Book's dying wish that Mal "believe in something" helps initiate a change in his character. But I am not convinced. Mal never embraces anything like faith, or even belief in any abstraction. He does not come to believe in the way that Book believes and certainly not in the way the Operative does. On the commentary track Whedon says that Mal's arc in *Serenity* is from not admitting that he cares in the beginning to being self-sacrificing at the end. Perhaps that is the case when looking strictly at the film, but looking at the whole of Mal's arc throughout the series, I don't think that's quite it. Yes, by the end of the film Mal is willing to risk his life and the life of his crew for something beyond self-preservation, but he had been already willing to do that in *Firefly* episodes like "The Train Job," "Safe," and "Heart of Gold." Mal always cared, but who he cared about tended to be narrowly circumscribed to those in his immediate circle (a circle which included Simon and River in the series but which, probably to serve the needs of the arc Whedon intended for the movie, did not include them when the film began).

But there *is* a transformation. When over the course of the movie Mal sees with his own eyes the damage that the Alliance has done—to River, to Haven, to Miranda—he widens the circle of his concern from those in his immediate community to the rest of the Alliance's current and potential victims. He responds to both the fact of what the Alliance has done and to his fears of what the Alliance will do in the future, and is willing to risk his life and the life of his crew for something beyond the immediate needs of survival.

Key to that transformation is Mal's conversation with the Operative following the destruction of Haven. At the moment the Operative expresses his belief in "a better world" his image is on a video monitor, at the right of the frame, while at the left of the frame are Haven's smoldering remains. The image juxtaposes the Operative's dream—removed, clean, theoretical—with the reality of his actions—immediate, bloody, real. When the Operative admits, "I'm a monster," we see his head on several monitors simultaneously. The multiplied image of his disembodied head literalizes his confession, making him indeed look less like a human being than like a technologically enhanced, many-headed monster. Appearing on multiple screens at that moment his face is in front, beside, and behind Mal, literally surrounding him. Mal had eluded the Alliance for much of the series but now here it is boxing him in, choking him, leaving "no ground to go to." Like young Jesse seeing his mother killed by the railroad in *Jesse James*, or Luke Skywalker seeing the burning skeleton of Uncle Owen and Aunt Beru in *Star Wars*, Mal's seeing the remains of Haven, the deaths of those he cared about, shows him that he cannot remain just an observer, that he cannot forever run. Rather than forcing him to surrender, by squeezing tighter, the Alliance awakened the rebel in Mal just as they triggered the warrior in River.

The Operative follows his superiors' orders, even though he neither sees, understands, nor even wishes to understand their grand plan. He does so because he trusts that, despite the undeniable ugliness of his actions, there is purpose and order and rightness to them. The word we use for trust in what you can't see is "faith." And faith, in the eyes of *Serenity*'s atheist writer/director is a problem. Faith that ignores what is in favor of abstractions of what *should be*, the faith eschewed by the hero, is what enables the Operative's crimes. Faith here leads not to compassion and comity but domination and murder.

"Was blind but now I see" is a classic statement of rebirth through faith, but here believing suggests blindness while seeing signifies being freed from the bondage of faith. And rescue from the horrors of faith comes at the hands of Mal, a man who has renounced his own. Shown the truth of his desired "world without sin" the Operative is stripped of the abstract beliefs that blinded him to his actual reality. He sees he is about to murder people for no reason and orders his soldiers to stand down. His faith shattered, the Operative loses his reason to be, ceases to exist, becomes merely a shadow. Having disabused the Operative of his faith, Mal, like Richard Dawkins with a six shooter, aims to disabuse everyone else's.

Firefly and *Serenity*'s theme of anti-establishment skepticism toward hierarchy, piety, and hypocrisy is consistent with the deep veins of individualist sentiment that run through the Westerns which were Whedon's templates. But *Serenity*'s theme strikes a cord that resonates beyond the confines of *Serenity*'s story and seems like more than genre nostalgia. I know nothing about Whedon's politics, but I wonder if the characterization of faith in *Serenity* might at some level be a reaction to our own time when Jihadists, Theocrats, Neo-Cons, and others who have cast themselves as the protectors of virtue have perverse notions of how to pursue it. Might *Serenity* be in part a reaction to an era when the certainties of faith have become the enabling ideologies of terrorism, when codes of honor drive deeds of horror?

Perhaps these are unintended associations rather than deliberate parallels, but is it possible that the portrayal of the Alliance is a response to a religious right which has mobilized against gay marriage but has been silent on the issue of American torture? Or Catholic Church officials who shield pedophile priests while arguing that politicians who support reproductive choice should be denied communion, elevating that one issue above a politician's views on poverty, war, the death penalty, caring for the widow and the orphan, or any number of Catholic religious imperatives? Is a shrill rectitude that insists on Christian superiority and the damnation of non-believers, that would police private morality while ignoring the morality of shredding the safety net, the real target of Whedon's indignation? Might the Alliance's intolerance of dissent be a reaction to Islamic supremacists and their Jihadist terror campaigns against "infidels"?

Is *Serenity* a critique, veiled perhaps even to its creator, of a President who says that Jesus—the teacher of "how you treat the least of these is how you treat me"—is his favorite political philosopher, but then defunds programs for the poor in order to give tax breaks to the wealthy, who professes allegiance to the "Prince of peace" but wages a war of choice, who swears an oath to uphold the Constitution but then eviscerates due process? (In fact, how different is the Alliance Operative, killing innocents in order to serve a government in which he has blind faith and to fulfill a vision of a better world to come, from those at Abu Girhab, Haditha, and Guantanamo who, through torture and murder, violate American legal and ethical values in the name of serving their country?)

Going further, is "terraforming" in *Serenity* just fancy science fiction lingo for "nation-building"? Is transforming a planet's atmosphere to make it hospitable for colonization and trying to pacify a planet's population with experimental drugs akin to the hubristic act of trying to remake the Middle East in our image? When the film takes us to Miranda and we learn of the pacification plot gone horribly wrong, of the unwitting creation of the brutal Reavers, the specter of Iraq seems to lurk in the background. As the holographic image of the Alliance scientist on Miranda insists, "We meant it for the best, to make people safer," and the Reavers attack her, I cannot help thinking about the sectarian militias tearing apart Baghdad. When I hear the Operative earnestly proclaim, "We're making a better world," as the smoke rises from the ashes of Haven, I hear echoes of Donald Rumsfeld's facile defense in the midst of post-invasion chaos that "freedom is not tidy" and George W. Bush's boast of "mission accomplished."

Were these intentional allusions? I can't say. But it's tempting to think at least some of them might have been when Whedon says on the *Serenity* commentary that "the film is about the right to be wrong. You can't impose your way of thinking even if your way of thinking is more enlightened and better than theirs. It's just simply not how human beings are." When Whedon says that the outer planets' message to the Alliance was, "You don't belong here, you don't belong on our soil . . . we have a right to be ourselves," it's hard not to think of the overreaching of our own exceptionalist super power, convinced it has a divine, perhaps messianic, role to play in the world. And young River's statement at the beginning of *Serenity* that the Alliance is objectionable because it "meddle[s]. People don't like to be meddled with. We tell them what to do, what to think," clarifies the problem of the Alliance, specifies it in a way it had not been specified in the pre-Iraq war TV series and in a way that seems consistent with a post-war critique. The galactic superpower now seems more explicitly like our global superpower.

Whedon maintains on the *Serenity* commentary track that "a leader is by nature something of a monster." That distrust of authority, so very characteristic of American Westerns, helps explain why for Whedon true virtue—responding to the human need in front of you rather than to abstract principles, forming community based on mutual respect and aid rather than conventional titles or status—had to be vindicated by unlikely candidates: fugitives, prostitutes, mercenaries, and outlaws.

After September 11, the neo-con fiasco in Iraq, and a host of tragedies past and present, at home and abroad, we might all be rightfully skeptical of grandiose theories and messianic agendas. After all, for the September 11 hijackers "God" was their co-pilot. Point taken. At the same time dreaming big should not easily be abandoned. Cautious as we may be of arrogant presumption and over-ambitious agendas, we should not recoil so far as to eschew big ideas entirely. The Four Freedoms, liberty and justice for all, the Universal Declaration of Human Rights—abstractions all, but abstractions that could be truly liberating.

On the *Serenity* commentary Whedon sensibly argues that we can't control others, but adds the claim that "sin is just how people are . . . all of those things we take as faults are also the source of pleasure and decency." But while those convinced of their own ideological purity, be they named Stalin or Bin Laden, are indeed a threat to all, is Whedon's summation regarding sin really satisfactory, or does it just *sound* enlightened and sophisticated? I'm sure Whedon would never look someone in the eye who had just been raped, someone trapped in a sweatshop or subsisting in slum housing, and blithely say that "sin is just how people are." These people could probably all testify to something true about sin. Not sin as an abstraction, but sin as real. Sin as experienced, sin as lived, sin as cruelty. Other people's sin as the source of their suffering. Might seeking to overcome sin, to secure justice and promote mercy also, maybe even *more* so, make us human? We celebrate people like Harriet

Tubman, Frederick Douglass, Martin Luther King, Jr., and Nelson Mandela, certainly not sinless people, for their efforts to end at least *particular* sins. Is the problem really seeking to end sin, or is the problem trying to do so through control and domination rather than through reason and persuasion? Is the problem those who strive to be righteous or those content to be self-righteous?

Whedon states on the *Serenity* commentary that "the person who believes . . . is capable of terrible things," and indeed, that conviction runs throughout both the series and the film. Repeatedly in *Firefly*, Mal faced adversaries whose professed belief in principle licensed brutality and repression. The Alliance captain in "Bushwacked" believed he was serving civilization, Atherton Wing clung to aristocratic pretensions and rules of honor in "Shindig," and the superstitious villagers in "Safe" used scripture to justify killing River. Referring to Burgess in "Heart of Gold," Mal says there is "nothing worse than a monster who thinks he's right with God." And even Jubal Early in "Objects in Space" claimed to live by "a code." The Operative is the latest villain in the *Firefly* 'verse who is used to switch the traditional moral valuation of believer and non-believer. It is precisely the Operative's status as a "believer" that makes him so dangerous in the film's terms. Book tells Mal that the "sort of man they're like to send believes hard. Kills and never asks why," and Inara maintains that "we have every reason to be afraid *because* he is a believer." In the Whedonverse those who believe are typically pathological, reliably dangerous.

But might there be something a bit too sweeping in Whedon's condemnation? Should we not distinguish between the absolute faith of the Operative and the more humble devotion of the Shepherd? Throughout *Firefly*, *Serenity*, and his *Serenity* commentary Whedon seems to suggest that the very act of faith is inherently dangerous. Given the intimations of Book's Alliance past, he and the Operative seem linked, as if the capacity to murder is dependant on the capacity for faith, as if the Operative is merely a sociopathic version of Book, as if the Operative is where Book was inevitably headed had he not left the Alliance and become a Shepherd. The suggestion that Book did leave the Alliance holds out the possibility that faith need not become fanaticism but nevertheless, by the end of the film Whedon denies both Book *and* the Operative a place in *Serenity*'s community.

Did eliminating Book, and the more benign, compassionate type of faith he represented, reflect an under-appreciation of what he brought to that community, an under-appreciation of the good that can come from those committed to abstractions: Evangelicals in comfortable suburbs who nevertheless advocate aid to Darfur, Rabbis who organize to raise the minimum wage, white-collar religious activists who believe serving God means fighting for the rights of blue-collar garment and hotel workers, clergy committed to the separation of faith and state and to the dignity of other religious groups? Book would have made common cause with all of them. But eliminating Book seems to deny a place in the Whedonverse to the type of faith Book practiced, the kind of commitment to principle he represented. Doing so was Whedon's prerogative, of course, but since, in so doing, something worthy was lost, I say of Book, again, I wish they hadn't killed you in *Serenity*.

ERIC GREENE is a graduate of the Religious Studies department at Wesleyan University and of Stanford Law School. Hailed as "groundbreaking," his first book was the critically acclaimed *Planet of the Apes as American Myth: Race, Politics and Popular Culture*. Eric recently examined *Star Trek* and Cold War politics in BenBella's *Boarding the Enterprise* and wrote about *Battlestar Galactica*'s treatment of September 11/Iraq War anxieties in BenBella's *So Say We All*. Greene works as a civil rights activist in Los Angeles where his professional hats have also included actor and commentator on politics and the arts.

When something is wrong with, say, our lunch, we probably like it less. But characters are not like our lunch. Often, the things that make us like a character, that make us identify with a character, are his flaws. This is especially true about a hero, because without flaws a hero can be truly insufferable. Bledsoe gives us a good look here at some of Mal's more charming/violent moments of human weakness, and points toward the progress the character eventually makes toward a purer flavor of heroism.

Mal Contents
Captain Reynolds Grows Up

Alex Bledsoe

See how I'm not punching him? I think I've grown.
—Mal, "Shindig"

In the first scene of "Serenity," the pilot episode of the series *Firefly*, Malcolm Reynolds was introduced as a loser. His cause had been lost, the specific battle he was fighting had been lost, and his personal command was lost. He stared up in despair and wonder at the victors as they descended in all their might and glory, an overpowering visual image of just how *badly* he'd lost.

Flash forward to the climactic moments of the film *Serenity*. By exposing the treachery behind the Alliance government's benevolent front, Mal finally wins the battle he'd lost so long before. As with all worthy victories the cost has been high, and there is no sense of righteous triumph, only the hope that this victory will be the first of many. But it is a true victory.

The path from one "Serenity" to the other is marked by Mal's gradual maturing from the inherently adolescent impulse that led to his rebellion to the adult sense of responsibility that causes him to fight to send the transmission from Miranda. He has finally learned (and fully accepted) that he owes as much to the people who don't follow him as to those that do, and that their lack of appreciation for him does not absolve him of this obligation. Mal has, at last, grown up.

May have been the losing side. Still not convinced it was the wrong one.
—Mal, "Bushwhacked"

To start with the obvious, Malcolm Reynolds is a rebel. Not, and this is an important distinction, a revolutionary. Revolution seeks change; rebellion seeks separation.

Rebellion is a standard aspect of adolescence, whether within a family or a community. Defining yourself by what you're against, rather than by what you approve, is the first step toward differentiating yourself from your parents. In Malcolm's case, this phase never fully ended, although since little of his childhood is ever explored we have no idea why. Like many men his age (mid-thirties), the transition to adulthood in a world that still admires childish traits is harder and slower than it might be otherwise. The men who survive the transition in this environment tend to be men of singular courage, able to face the darkness in both the outer world and their own hearts. Mal becomes such a man by the final scene of *Serenity*.

Mal volunteered to fight against the Alliance when it tried to incorporate all the system's planets whether they wanted it or not. We are never told how widespread the resistance was, how many planets fought the Alliance, or how long the war lasted. The parallels with the romantic version of the American Civil War are clear, and Mal is a noble loser in that grand tradition (trust me on this, I'm from Tennessee). He even wears a brown coat, the symbol of revolution, much as the Confederate battle flag remains a visible presence in my home town. He picks fights with Alliance supporters, just as good ole boys do with Yankee tourists. And most importantly, he remains convinced of the rightness of his cause. This faith in his ideals, and by extension himself, drives him to the only place where those ideals can still function, the outer planets. Each brush with the Alliance reinforces his certainty about the revolution, and fuels the rebellion that keeps him isolated.

Mal grew up on a ranch, pop culture shorthand for the kind of free-spirited anarchist who bristles at the notion of being told what to do. This implies that Mal fought the Alliance not only because he disagreed with its principles, but also because he could not bear the idea of living under anyone's authority. The war against the Alliance can be seen as a true revolution, wherein one system of ideas fights for supremacy over another, and intellectually Mal probably agrees with the principles involved. But for Mal emotionally, it is a rebellion. As any parent of a teenager will recognize, he was saying (with guns and death instead of whines and slammed doors), "You're not the boss of me!" He hides this immature defiance behind bluster, stubbornness, and a pretty malleable (no pun intended) code of behavior, but it informs his every major decision. And if the Alliance had lost, eventually he would have run afoul of whatever organization took its place in the outer worlds (see Inara's comments below on his relationship with other criminals). Revolutions end; rebellion tends to be a lifestyle choice.

After the loss, Mal heads to the farthest edge of the system to ply an iffy trade with his nondescript spaceship, fixed up and tweaked like a teenager's first car. And *Serenity* the ship may very well be Mal's first car, with all the emotions and male attachment that come with that. He speaks often of how he loves his ship, apparently the only form of that emotion with which he feels comfortable. How many young men are the same way, able to say they "love" their car, boat, or favorite team, yet unable to express it to wives, children, or friends? This has its root in an immature ego's fear of rejection and loss, something to which Mal is clearly sensitive. Friends and lovers may prove inconstant, but *Serenity* the ship will never say she doesn't love him, or that she's met another captain but still wants to be friends.

He is careful to assemble a crew he both trusts and can dominate. His second in command, Zoe, is so devoted to him that she seldom seriously questions him; if any of the others have the temerity to suggest that he might be wrong, Mal quickly reminds them that it's *his* ship, and they are never to dispute his orders. The fact that his history as a commander is checkered at best does not matter to him. What matters is never letting anyone be "the boss of me" again.

This is the Malcolm Reynolds we met at the beginning of the series.[1] His wit and humor made him entertaining, but his hard edge kept us, and the other characters, at a distance. The series and subsequent film gradually close that gap, until Mal can at last drop his guard completely, as he does with River in the film's final moments.

Can I make a suggestion that doesn't involve violence,
or is this the wrong crowd for that?
—WASH, *Serenity*

Mal is comfortable to an unhealthy degree with violence. Although he does not appear to be physically intimidating (he's neither overly muscular nor towering), he can take a punch like no one this side of Bruce Campbell in his prime, and his military training allows him to compensate for any lack of size or brute force with tenacity and smarts. In his line of work these qualities are assets, and he's not above killing people for no more than the sake of expediency, as when he kicked Crow into the engine at the end of "The Train Job," or shoots the Alliance survivor trying to surrender at Haven in *Serenity*. Although these moments are played in entirely different ways (the first comedic and the second to illustrate Mal's wrath), they both spring from childish impulses not controlled by maturity. Death is never casual, and should never be used by an ostensible hero simply to illustrate a point. Allowing Mal to initiate death in this way shows him to be severely, if not fatally, flawed.

But on occasion, Mal successfully fights his violent impulses. In "Trash" he didn't kill Saffron even though he knew she would likely cause him more trouble in the future. He fails to kill Niska in "War Stories," even after the gangster literally tortured him to death. In "Heart of Gold," he did not kill Burgess even though he had a personal, and justifiable, reason to do so.

[1] This is also the Malcolm Reynolds we meet at the beginning of the film *Serenity*, which—when taken as part of the canon—implies quite a bit of personal backsliding by Mal. The dramatic necessity of giving the character an "arc" in the film is most likely the real explanation, but it does make Mal more interesting when taken in context of the *Firefly* universe as a whole. What caused his nascent maturity to fail to take? Inara's departure? Hm. . . .

This contradiction implies that Mal only sees people with whom he's interacted *as* people. Those to whom he has no emotional connection, whether love *or* hate, are fair game, but if Mal gets to know them, even as enemies, he cannot arbitrarily kill them. Although this still results in a high body count, it *is* a step toward maturity, and leads to the final commitment to strangers Mal makes in *Serenity*.

Mal may not kill an acquaintance casually, but he's not above physically brutalizing them to keep them in their place. He often punches and threatens his ostensible friends, especially if they have the temerity to disagree with him. Caught between adulthood and adolescence, he is grown-up enough to admit he's not always right, yet still childish enough to insist everyone play by his rules in *his* backyard. The struggle leads to repeated instances of physical confrontations with his friends, with only Zoe immune from his wrath. He punched Simon in the first episode,[2] surely one of the most childish things he's been shown doing, asserting his schoolyard authority over the new rich kid. The bookend of this is found in *Serenity*, when Simon decks Mal for putting River in danger. By this point *everyone* is standing up to Mal, disputing his much-vaunted authority and showing him the limits of his adolescent people skills, but Simon has made the greatest journey, from quivering fear of Mal to utter disregard: when Mal warns him about giving ultimatums on "my ship," Simon continues as if Mal had not even spoken.

Mal lives a violent existence in a violent world, but must learn to separate his professional self from his role as head of *Serenity*'s family. Since violence is always expedient and sometimes speed is essential, the challenge for a ship's captain is even harder. But Mal discovers that respect is a far greater motivator than fear.

[2] The idea that a real punch to the jaw can just be shrugged off is such a fallacy, it must be created by people who've never really been punched in the jaw. In "Objects in Space," Early slammed a *metal handgun* into Inara's face, and she got nothing more than a delicately split lip. To borrow Early's rationale from that episode, a writer should only be allowed to put moments like that in a script after finding out what it's like to be hit in the face with a three-pound piece of jagged metal wielded by a strong, pissed-off criminal.

[Sings] *My love for me ain't hard to explain. The hero of Canton, the man they call . . . me.*
—JAYNE, "Jaynestown"

To see where Mal could end up if he remained locked in this adolescent mode, you only have to look at Jayne Cobb. Jayne is Mal writ large and crude, with all his sociopath tendencies given free reign. Mal will kill strangers with no regrets; Jayne will kill *anybody* with no regrets. Mal puts the arbitrary conceits of "ship" and "crew" ahead of personal consideration, often not seeming to realize these terms represent actual human beings; Jayne puts himself first, not caring that anyone else might *be* a human being. He was bribed to join Mal's crew, and was not above selling out crewmates in "Ariel." His loyalty is entirely based on money and fear.

What separates Mal from Jayne is the very self-awareness that forces Mal toward emotional adulthood. Jayne, so self-absorbed he often only knows he's the butt of a joke when everyone else starts laughing, will never have this quality. Perhaps that's the real reason Mal keeps Jayne aboard; surely armed muscle isn't that hard to acquire among the outer settlements they frequent. Jayne may serve as his personal moral barometer, alerting Mal to his own excesses before they can get out of hand. If Jayne believes something is a good idea, Mal knows to stop and think about it some more.

In the film *Serenity*, Jayne is the one who, at last, brings up the one undeniable fact about Mal's past. When Mal insists on a dangerous, profit-less mission and demands the crew's loyalty because, as always, it's his backyard, Jayne challenges him with the question, "How many men in your platoon came out of [Serenity Valley] alive?" Significantly it's not Mal but the loyal Zoe who stands up to Jayne, while Mal does and says nothing. Jayne's point, that blindly following Mal could very easily get them all killed, is undeniably true; and to accept it, and move past it, is Mal's greatest challenge.

In the episode "The Message," we met another "alternate" Mal: Tracey, a former soldier who served with Mal and Zoe in the rebellion. Like Mal, he hid his serious side behind a flip exterior and after the war drifted into crime and smuggling, only without the benefit of a ship (he smuggled experimental internal organs in his own body). Yet *unlike* Mal, he didn't catch the same breaks that have clearly favored Reynolds from the first moments we saw him. Mal possesses two qualities Tracey lacked: intuition and luck.

Mal is a far better intuitive judge of people than Tracey, although (as "Our Mrs. Reynolds" ably demonstrated) he's certainly not infallible. Still, it's hard to imagine him making the blatant mistakes that led to Tracey's death. Tracey failed to accurately anticipate the reactions of both his enemies and allies, something Mal excels in doing. By the end Tracey recognized this as his fatal flaw.

And "lucky" might not be the first adjective that springs to mind to describe Mal. But from the first scene of the first episode, he was clearly protected from an arbitrary and pointless fate. As he gazed up at the descending Alliance warships, the soldier beside him was shot down; Mal, oblivious to the danger or the death, continued to stare, just as exposed to enemy fire as the dead man, yet he emerged unscathed. In flashbacks to their time in battle, both Tracey and Mal behaved carelessly, even recklessly; Zoe saved Tracey, but only luck, or fate, saved Mal.

Tracey had no such luck (or savior) when they met again. Each decision he made turned out to be wrong, based on misunderstanding (and the fact that he didn't blindly trust Mal). Mal was clearly affected by his death: there, but for the grace of the God not welcome on his ship, goes him. But one wonders if Mal really understood how similar he and Tracey were; when Tracey said, "Wasn't never no good at life, anyhow. Couldn't seem to make sense of it. Always running scared . . ." he could just as easily have been speaking about Mal as himself.

Mercy is the mark of a great man. [He stabs Atherton in the side.] *Guess I'm just a good man.* [Stabs him again.] *Well, I'm all right.*
—MAL, "Shindig"

Throughout the series there were glimmers of Mal's growing discontent with his own approach to life, most notably in his relationship with Inara. Although he referred to her as a "whore," disparaged her lifestyle, and generally hid his obvious attraction to her from himself (if no one else), there were many instances when he took painful steps based on her guidance and example. She was, of course, completely familiar with the territory: after she helped a young man lose his virginity, he asked, "Aren't I supposed to be a man now?" She replied, "A man is just a boy who's old enough to ask that question."

To keep that question at the fore of Mal's thoughts, she continually punched holes in his juvenile "manly man" self-image. In "Shindig," Mal insisted that he never backs down from a fight, to which she responded, "Yes, you do! You do it all the time!" In "Heart of Gold," when Mal asked if Inara would "stoop to being on my arm," she replied, "Will you wash it first?" When Mal found himself dueling for Inara's honor and tried to blame it on her "society," also in "Shindig," she fired back, "You never follow the rules, no matter what society you're in! You don't even get along with ordinary criminals either, which is why you are constantly getting in trouble!"

Oddly, the man who *should* have been providing Mal with both guidance and an example, Shepherd Book, had few significant encounters with him. Book, a Brother Cadfael-like man of God with a dark secular past, is very under-developed in the series and film, no doubt a casualty of the series's brief run. His few exchanges with Mal consisted of set-up moments for Mal to demonstrate his disillusionment. Most pithily, Mal told Book, "You're welcome on my boat. God ain't" ("The Train Job"). In fact, Book really discussed his beliefs only with River, in a scene from the episode "Jaynestown" notable for its sheer awkwardness.[3]

MAL: *You know . . . they walk just as fast if you lead 'em.*
JAYNE: *I like* smackin' *'em.*
—"Safe"

So what events mark Mal's moments of change? When does the overgrown boy become the sadder, wiser man?

[3] I suspect that the character of Book pays homage to the presence of religion in the great Westerns of John Ford (i.e., *My Darling Clementine* and *The Searchers*), but since creator Joss Whedon is an avowed atheist (see his October 9, 2002, comments in *The Onion*), it seems no one understood exactly what to do with him. Luckily Ron Glass had charisma to spare in fleshing out the part.

Obviously the Battle of Serenity Valley marked the end of his childhood, if not childish, idea of independence. The larger "adult" world simply will not allow him to make his own rules and behave however he wants. However, his reaction to this universal truth indicated his refusal to outgrow his failed ideals; instead, he created a microcosm—his ship—where these ideals could still function.[4]

Mal insisted the stolen drugs be returned to the miners in "The Train Job," a standard-issue noble gesture used early in the series to indicate Mal's basically decent nature. It showed an aspect of his personality not seen again until the film *Serenity*: the idea that he owes something to people he doesn't really know. By refusing to profit from their misery, he clued the audience in to the maturity at his core struggling to express itself.

In "Our Mrs. Reynolds" he refused to bed the eager Saffron. The moment that really said something about Mal was that he steadfastly, if shakily, resisted her charms until she switched from offering herself to him, to asking for *his* attention to *her*. Only when he believed he was granting her a kindness she sought, rather than taking a gift she offered, did he give in to her entreaties.

In "Heart of Gold," Mal had a sincere romantic liaison with a friend of Inara's, who was then killed by the episode's villain, Rance Burgess. Mal chased Burgess down, beat him up, but didn't kill him, despite having both emotional and rational motives to do so. He did *allow* him to be killed in cold blood, but he did not pull the trigger himself. The implied rationale within the episode is that a) the other killer had a prior claim on Burgess, and b) Mal might have enjoyed it too much. But taken as part of his progression toward maturity, it shows that Mal understands at least a little that enjoying killing is wrong.

In the final moments of "Objects in Space," River asked for permission to return to the ship. Mal granted it with a smile by saying, "You know, you ain't quite right." After fourteen episodes where River's presence was often questioned, and the option of turning her in for the reward given serious thought, this represented Mal's first acceptance of her as a real member of his crew, and broke the ice for his later acceptances in the film *Serenity*.

It wasn't all forward progress, though. Like all of us, Mal won't give

[4] Of course, without this microcosm we'd have no show to discuss.

up old behavior patterns without a fight and falls back on them in moments of stress. After the massacre at Haven, Mal commits a massacre of his own by shooting an Alliance pilot who tries to surrender. He does this to make a point, the same reason he kicked Crow into the engine. He wants his crew to know he's serious, and to emphasize that he also threatens to shoot *them*. In his state of mind at the time he certainly seems capable of it, much as John Wayne seems genuinely determined to kill Montgomery Clift in *Red River*. This is the final last gasp of the old immaturity, before the revelations at Miranda force a different action.

During the trip to Miranda, there is a short, wordless scene where Mal, alone in the depths of *Serenity*, shows how affected he is by the recent tragedy. He can drop his façade to this degree only with his ship, the one thing he fully, totally trusts. The audience knows what he's thinking *about*, but not what he's actually *thinking*. I believe that, in these few silent moments, he's realizing that all his old ways of acting and behaving, of all the arbitrary lines he's drawn for himself and others, simply don't function without a staggering cost he's no longer prepared to pay. He must find something new within himself, and fast.[5]

When they reach Miranda and Mal comprehends the true horror of what's happened, he knows something must be done. In part it's his standard revenge impulse, since only by striking back can he supposedly give meaning to all the deaths surrounding the secret. But there's a larger altruistic impulse, not really seen since the climax of "The Train Job," that leads him to undertake a mission for which there is no profit, either monetary or personal. In an extraordinary speech he tells the crew (whom he'd threatened to kill to get them to even go to Miranda), "I'm *asking* more of you than I have before" (emphasis mine). For the first time in fourteen episodes and a two-hour feature, he does not order his crew to undertake a dangerous mission based solely on his own judgment, or threaten them with violence or abandonment if they disagree. He treats them with the respect of equals, and as a result, they stand with

[5] A similar change comes over that other great space rogue, Han Solo, in *Return of the Jedi*. After spending two films resolutely refusing to officially join the Rebellion, Solo changes his mind after his friends rescue him from Jabba the Hut. Typically, Lucas relegates this major shift in the character to a brief voice-over, but in Solo's next scene he's "General Solo" and is preparing to lead a team of Rebels to knock out the shield generator on Endor.

him of their own free will. For a man terrified of losing again as he did at Serenity Valley, this is a moment of real change, when he understands that the things he fears losing most (the people who mean something to him) are beyond his control. He can only be honest with them now, and hope they understand the importance of what he wants to do.

The fact that they do (symbolized quite wonderfully by the passing of a bottle from which they all take a drink) rewards his trust in a way that must touch him deeply. In fact, when he next speaks to them in a non-crisis situation, he is kind, concerned, and unafraid to show his softer side, as he does in the final scenes with Zoe, Inara, and River. He has grown, and grown up. Mal becomes a true hero not just for slaying the dragon before him, but the one within him as well.

You want to meet the real me now?
—MAL, "War Stories"

No discussion of Malcolm Reynolds is complete without mentioning the actor who embodied him, Nathan Fillion. Without the inherent intelligence and decency he brought to the part, Mal would have been an insufferable bastard and no one would have cared what happened to him. Fillion's edgy, meaningful portrayal gave Captain Reynolds a surprising level of subtlety, and the depths of pain and fear beneath the bluster made it unfortunate we never got to know him better.

ALEX BLEDSOE entered the *Firefly* 'verse through the film *Serenity* and then blasted through the series in four days. The author of many short stories published in magazines you've never heard of, and a novel from Night Shade Books, *The Sword-Edged Blonde*, you hopefully will hear about soon, Alex now lives between two big lakes in Wisconsin with his patient wife and son, the Original Squirrel Boy.

Did anyone watch Firefly *alone? It, like* Buffy *before it, seems to have been a show that people watched in groups, some small, some large. Viewers formed communities and they held debates and they formed personal attachments and they formed personal opinions. Opinions that make collections like this one possible, by the way. Rich provides us with a funny view of one small viewing community with very strong opinions.*

Curse Your Sudden but Inevitable Betrayal

Things My Husband and I Have Argued About While Watching *Firefly*

LANI DIANE RICH

Before we get started, there's something you need to know about my husband and me: We're geeks.

And I'm not talking the kind of casual geek that's popular nowadays, the person who enjoys the Lord of the Rings trilogy and plays the occasional hand of online spades. My husband and me?

We're *geeks*.

My area of geekspertise is television. I did my undergrad in television, radio, and film back when ¾" tapes the size of your typical VW were the height of the new technology, and I started taping shows religiously about a week after the VCR was invented. Somewhere in my mother's basement are piles of VHS tapes containing most of the episodes of *Moonlighting*, *Northern Exposure*, and *The X-Files*. When *The X-Files* launched a trend by releasing entire seasons on DVD, the skies of my world broke open with a thousand angels singing the hallelujah chorus.

My husband, he's a fantasy game geek. He was on the Internet role-playing a text-based dwarf in 1991. He had first-person experience with Rogue. For Christmas one year, all he wanted was a copy of *Deities and Demigods*. He's lost countless hours of his life to *Ultima Online*, and indeed only stopped playing when I told him I would take the baby and go far away if he didn't. To this day, I think he's okay with the choice he made, but we're engaging a don't-ask-don't-tell policy. Just seems safer for all concerned that way.

Now when two people such as us get married, the geekitude increases exponentially. You combine my love of television with his love of fantasy, and it's completely unfathomable that we didn't discover Joss Whedon until 2004—and then only because so many of my romance writer friends were talking about the incredible love stories. We started with *Buffy*, which had us completely sucked in by the time Xander's buddies ate Principle Flutie. Then, after Netflixing *Buffy* all the way to the end, we started on *Angel*. When that was over, there was only one thing left:

Firefly.

The thing about *Firefly* is that, at the time, I was only beginning to realize that engaging storytelling is not genre-dependent. I am a fan of neither Westerns nor science fiction, so for me, believing that I would be remotely interested in a combination of the two was way beyond my limited vision. I had loved all things Whedon up to this point, and was fairly certain I'd be only meh about *Firefly*, so I was understandably resistant. Fast-forward twelve months, and you and Irony would find me fastidiously knitting my husband a cunning hat in anticipation of the opening of the feature film extension of the story, but at the time, I was less than enthusiastic.

But my husband—we'll call him Fish because that's what I call him—was insistent.

It was time for *Firefly*.

I dug my heels in. Even if I *did* like it, which was doubtful, I knew the history. There were only thirteen episodes before the short-sighted bastards at FOX canceled it. If it was bad, I'd be disappointed, and if it was wonderful, I'd be heartbroken. There was no possible good to come from getting involved with this show.

But Fish merely shook his head like a Buddhist Zen master and said, "*Firefly*. It's time."

It was our first argument about *Firefly*. As it turned out, it would not be our last.

Winters are long and brutal in central New York, and in the tiny apartment we lived in at the time, the TV was right next to the fireplace. One night, Fish got me drunk on cheap wine and took advantage, slipping the first *Firefly* DVD into the player. The rest, as they say, is history.

I fell in love with Wash immediately. The second I saw the loud print shirt and the dinosaurs on the ship console, I was all about Wash. He was the ultimate beta hero, the funny, smart guy who could fly a ship like a master and was secure with himself even in the face of his wife's ability to kill a man at thirty paces without so much as a shaky trigger finger. Add to that the fact that Wash and Fish are so similar in personal style and temperament as to be brothers, it was the perfect fictional crush, one that reflected amiably upon my real-life chosen loved one and set the tone for marital harmony.

Fish, on the other hand, fell instantly for Kaylee. For the record, while it's admirable and romantic that I would lust after the character most like my husband, he fell for the girl least like me. Kaylee is tiny and delicate, a whiz with mechanical things, and sweet and naïve, always seeing the best in people. Me, I'm of stocky Anglo-German stock; I haven't had a delicate moment since somewhere in the fetal stage. I laugh heartily, I speak crudely, all things mechanical mystify and frequently zap me, and I'm always surprised when I meet someone who is genuinely sweet to the core, not just pretending in order to put other people off their game. Fish readily admits that I remind him more of Zoe than Kaylee, and yet, Kaylee is the one he loves.

I try not to take it personally. Sometimes, I fail. What can I say? I'm human. And, as you can tell by the description I gave you, kind of a tough one to live with at that. Still, every now and again, Fish winds up the courage to ask me if I'd dress up like Kaylee, to which I respond by suggesting he bite one particularly unsavory part of my anatomy. He finds this amusing.

Between you and me, sometimes, so do I.

In the pilot, "Serenity," there is a moment when Inara was entertaining a client, and he made a crack about her speeding up the clock to cheat him out of some of his time with her. A look of surprise and offense flashed across her face, and Fish said to me, "She doesn't like her job."

This was on a recent viewing, at least our third joint viewing of the total series, so I was understandably shocked that he could even say this. I grabbed the remote, hit pause, and stared at him like he was crazy. Which, he was, but I'd known that going in.

"What the hell are you talking about?" I countered, with my typical verbal dexterity.

He motioned toward the TV. "Look at her face there. She's obviously ashamed."

"She doesn't like being *insulted*," I said, still stunned that we were even having this conversation. "No one likes being insulted. But that doesn't mean she doesn't like her job."

"She's a *whore*."

"She's a *companion*," I said through gritted teeth. "What she does is about the soul as well as the body, and she lives a completely respectable life. There might be elements of her job that she doesn't like, and yeah, being in love with Mal complicates things, but she's not ashamed."

Fish turned his head toward me with a facial expression that said, "Lani, you ignorant slut," but he didn't actually say this because he'd lose an eye and he likes his eyes. Instead, he repeated, "She's a *whore*," as though that made his entire argument, which it did *not*. It did, however, buy him a full hour of stony silence from me, which he probably saw at the time as a win-win. Later that night, however, as the wonky spring in the couch gouged permanent marks into his backside, he came around to my side of it.

I am nothing if not persuasive.

FF03. "Shindig." This episode was written by Jane Espenson, a writer who won over both me and Fish with her hilarious and insightful work on *Buffy*. It had gotten to the point where Fish and I would play The Jane Game: without looking at the credits on our second run through the full series of *Buffy* (I always have to watch the full series, in order, because I am mentally unbalanced) we'd guess whether it was written by

Jane or not. More often than not, we were right; there was something about Jane's quirky voice that put a stamp of individuality on her episodes. So when we saw Jane Espenson's name on this episode, our little geek hearts leapt for joy.

As an example of Jane's stamp, there's a scene in "Shindig" in which Kaylee was admiring the poofy dress in the store window, and Mal made a comment along the lines of, "What are you gonna do in that rig? Flounce around the engine room? Be like a sheep walking on its hind legs."

"Oh, man," I said, cringing as Kaylee and Zoe got their frost on. Then Jayne leaned in with, "Is she mad or something?" and both Fish and I cracked up. Then Fish turned to me thoughtfully and asked, "Who do you think writes the opposite sex better? Jane writing men or Joss writing women?"

Wow. I had to pause the DVD for that one so I could take a moment and think about it. I decided that I couldn't really judge Jane, because I wasn't a man, although I felt like she got them down pretty damn well—especially their total cluelessness when it comes to the complexity of female psychology. Joss, for his part, is brilliant at writing women, never cheapening their strength by sacrificing their femininity. Zoe, Inara, Kaylee, even Saffron/Bridget/Whatever—they are all allowed to be both strong and girls, which is a simple but amazing thing to have done.

I stammered for a while, expressing some of these thoughts while others hung amorphous in the air around me, and eventually came up with, "I dunno."

Fish shrugged, hit the play button on the remote, and said, "So, what are you making me for dinner, woman?"

I stared at him, my red-lasered gaze boring smoking holes into his skull. Eventually, he turned to me, his eyes widening to match the depth of his cluelessness, and said, "What?"

"Jane's better," I said flatly.

"Our Mrs. Reynolds" is easily our favorite episode of the entire season, and the most quoted. On any given day in our household, you will hear odes to this episode flying around the house. It is not unusual for one of our daughters (who have earned the ironic nicknames Sweetness and Light) to say something to each other like, "If you don't give me that doll, I swear by my pretty floral bonnet, *I will end you*!"

They may be too young to watch *Firefly*, but they're not too young to quote us quoting it.

However, despite our abiding love for this episode, there is always a point when the friction hits between me and Fish. It's usually when Wash says, "Good myth."

For those of you playing along at home, this episode revolved around a conwoman who pretended to be a wide-eyed virgin but was really out to deliver *Serenity* into the hands of scavengers; the fact that this would require the deaths of the crew was not a big concern for her. So, like any clever girl with a prodigious rack, she drugged her lip gloss and planned to get various crew members to kiss her, thus knocking them out long enough to take over the ship and deliver it to the scavengers. Mal, of course, fell for this after Saffron quoted a lengthy, and very sexy, Bible passage, to which Mal responded with a husky, "Good Bible." For Wash, Saffron chose a myth about Earth-That-Was, and while Wash was affected, he would not succumb, citing his love for a woman who could "kill me with her pinky." At which point Saffron failed in her attempt at seduction and was forced to knock him out with a well-placed kick to the back of his head.

At this point, for some reason, Fish said, "Yeah, right."

"Excuse me?"

"Look, Zoe's hot and everything, and yes, she probably can kill Wash with her pinky, but this gorgeous woman who gives good myth just offered him sex on a platter." He met my eyes. I could tell by his expression that he knew he was in dangerous territory, but there was really no going back, so he continued with false bravado. "To which I say, 'Yeah. Right.'"

I crossed my arms over my chest. "So you're saying that if Saffon offered you sex, you'd take it."

Right about this point in the conversation, smart got a lead on bravado. "I don't fly a spaceship. That would never happen to me."

"But if it did—"

"But it wouldn't—"

"But *if it did*, you would have sex with her."

He swallowed, and as the smile curved over his mouth, I could see he was going to try to hop on the back of a joke, hoping it would lead him out of very scary waters. "Of course. You can't kill me with your pinky."

"But I can make you miserable for the rest of your life."

He patted me lovingly on the knee. "You're gonna do that, anyway. Might as well get good myth." Then he laughed the weak, scared laugh of a man who knows he's not getting out of this alive.

Twenty minutes later, I was enjoying a nice bubble bath with a glass of wine while he made dinner for Sweetness and Light.

That one had been almost too easy.

"The Message" started out with the crew of the *Serenity* on a planet collecting their mail, and Jayne received a cunning knit hat—complete with goofy earflaps—from Ma Cobb. As we were watching this, the Big Day—September 30, 2005, the day the movie *Serenity* would finally be released and give us another much-craved *Firefly* fix—was just a few months away.

With no attempt at subtlety, Fish echoed Wash's comment: "Man walks down the street in that hat, people know he's not afraid of anything."

Fish waggled his eyebrows at me, as though I've been waiting my whole life for the opportunity to knit him a cunning hat, and who'd have guessed I'd ever have such luck?

The fact was, the idea of knitting him the cunning hat made me all warm and gooey inside. We'd already lined up a sitter. *Serenity* would be our first date night in months. As I planned out the trip to the yarn store in my head, I smiled at him and said, "Yeah, right."

He took my hand as we watched the rest of the episode, and I knew he knew he was getting the hat.

But I didn't argue about it.

September 30 finally arrived, and I had never been so excited for a date in my life. We left Sweetness and Light learning how to draw horses with the sitter and headed off for dinner and a movie. Over dinner, Fish wore his cunning hat in the restaurant, and we got the occasional odd look, but we were in upstate New York; most everyone here had seen odder. When we got to the theater, we were giddy. The cunning hat was recognized by others waiting to hit the movie on opening night, and we all stood around chatting about episodes, and each of the boys (in our little group, including Fish, there were three) jumped on any opportunity to quote Jayne's famous, "I'll be in my bunk," line.

I exchanged a friendly eye-roll with the only other woman there, but we were both smiling.

Fish and I took our seats in the theater, holding hands as the lights faded, ready for the movie experience we'd been waiting for all this time. It was both exciting and overwhelming. Everything moved at lightning speed and I could hardly catch my breath, but it was so wonderful because it was Joss, and someone else was minding the children.

Then we got to the climax.

Wash was killed.

Wash was *killed.*

I felt as though I'd been speared through the heart myself. The rest of the movie happened, the survivors of *Serenity* fought the good fight, and the Big Story ended Big, just as it should have.

But I was still in *Serenity*'s cockpit, with Wash, a mantra repeating in my head. *He is not dead. I do not accept that. Something will happen. Something will bring him back.*

He. Is. Not. Dead.

The movie ended and the lights came up and Wash was still dead and I felt horribly betrayed. I looked at Fish and, despite Jayne's cunning hat, I knew why I was so attached to Wash, and why Wash meant so much to me, and even as Fish joked me through the lobby and out to the car, I couldn't shake the feeling like part of him was dead in the cockpit of *Serenity*.

On the way home, we discussed the film, and I got angry.

"Joss made a mistake," I argued. "Zoe was already a bad-ass. So, Wash dies, and she just becomes more of a bad-ass? There's no arc in that. It should have been Zoe. Can you imagine how much more powerful it would have been if Zoe was killed, and Wash turned into a badass? Plus, for the future movies, there's so much story there, so much to do with that. With this, it's just Zoe being more of a badass."

"I don't know. I think—" Fish started, but I didn't let him finish.

"I love Joss, and he's a genius and everything, but this was wrong. It was a weak choice. A bad call."

"But, look at it this way—"

"*No*," I said, and at that point, Fish got the hint and changed the subject.

In the fifteen months since that day, we've had variations on this argument probably about half a dozen times. Fish thinks I'm being silly, which is a point I'm often forced to concede, and he even offers to sit with me and hold my hand through the whole thing so I can feel him live and ticking by my side. Still, I haven't been able to bring myself to do it. I've watched the opening sequence a few times, but I always end up picking a fight about something stupid, and then I find an excuse to leave the room.

It's nuts. I know it. And someday soon, but probably not today, I will sit down and watch *Serenity* again, because it is Joss, and it is brilliant, and it's not Fish in that cockpit. Hell, the guy can barely maneuver the mini-van without knocking the sideview mirror off on a tree branch. In a lot of ways, he's not Wash. But he's devoted, and funny in a quirky way that not everyone gets, and he has questionable fashion sense, and if Saffron tried to seduce him with the lip gloss of death, I think that he *would* say no, and only partially would it be because deep down he believes I *can* kill him with my pinky. Mostly, it would be because he's faithful and loving and despite my faults, he wants only me.

Don't tell him I said so, though. I can still squeeze at least two more bubble baths out of that argument. Three, if he brings up Nathan Fillion's naked butt in "Trash."

And if I know my guy, he absolutely will.

Lani Diane Rich lives in upstate New York with her husband and two daughters. Most of her time is split between writing women's fiction novels, singing songs from the *Buffy* musical episode with her kids, and fighting with her husband. You can find out more about Lani at www.lanidianerich.com and www.literarychicks.com.

Visual effects were clearly an important part of the Firefly *series as well as the movie. But we rarely hear from the people in this part of the process. Peristere points out here that, at least when Joss is involved, visual effects aren't just the tasty sauce on the story. They're made of story, all the way through.*

Mutant Enemy U

LONI PERISTERE

Living is learning and in living a good life we teach what we learn to others. At a very young age my family exposed me to all kinds of creative arts, from painting and sculpture to opera and Broadway; the good ones had a lasting message. Some person somewhere had something important to teach, something so compelling they produced a work of art, which concisely or otherwise served up a big idea for others to enjoy, interpret, love, or hate. With great art, it is impossible not to feel *something*, and whatever that feeling might be, it means that—for a moment, at least, as you watched or read or admired—you felt a part of an experience you had no part in. The phenomenon is an awesome one. To experience it is to live, however temporarily, a "false life," one that charges and inspires you to do things in your real one.

Of all the teaching arts, I found motion pictures to be the most exciting. They tell the biggest stories, in the most exotic places, with the most extraordinary people. And they use full size toys to make them. How cool is that? And millions of people of all kinds, shapes, and creeds see it and hopefully feel it.

Growing up in a small town in Massachusetts, I imagined I might become a writer and a director for motion pictures. The journey to becoming is long and different than we expect; today, I am a visual effects supervisor, and I have been Joss Whedon's "mildly insane" visual effects guy for ten years. I discovered Joss Whedon while working for Digital Magic, a post-production and visual effects company in Santa Monica. There, while making labels for videocassettes, I watched the first season of *Buffy the Vampire Slayer*. I was an instant fan.

After a good deal of fan nudging I convinced David Solomon, an executive producer on the show (who would later be the director of "Out of Gas"), to give Digital Magic the opportunity to pitch a new "dusting" effect. The original "dusting" was a quick transition from an actor to a series of computer-generated dust explosions. The effect wasn't bad, but in my opinion it lacked a story and therefore felt flat in its execution. So somewhere after midnight one evening, in a half sleep, I gave it one. When a vampire turns to dust, I theorized, it begins with a chemical reaction in the heart. The wood and the organ react violently, causing all of the moisture in the body to evaporate from the soft tissue out, leaving only dust behind.

For the pitch, we drew some pictures and did some tests. They were okay, not great. But Joss was much more interested in the story behind the effect. To be a part of Joss Whedon's team, story comes first. Digital Magic was hired to do season two because our approach was founded in storytelling.

Thus my enrollment in Whedon University began. My major was storytelling; *Buffy* and *Angel* were my undergraduate focus, *Firefly* would become my master's thesis, and *Serenity* my doctorate project. All through, Joss emphasized clarity in narrative. We were writing visually: turning vampires to dust, transforming humans into vampires, creating big bad guys, casting spells. All of which played a part in a bigger picture, a bigger story.

Like most series, the development of the final show begins with the script. Once written, the department heads get together with the writer and the director and decide what part they will play in realizing it. Joss constantly called the script the instructions and reminded everyone how important it was to follow them. He didn't mind change in the script, but if there was change, he wanted there to be a reason for it.

In visual effects, Joss was interested in enhancing the drama. The demons we were building often represented an idea central in the theme of the script. For example, the Gentlemen in "Hush" (*BtVS* 4-10) stole the voice of the town and by design they needed to be quiet; therefore the Gentlemen floated through space. Their motion was fluid and quiet. Our job in visual effects was to make sure the gentlemen came across as visually quiet.

When we found out the mayor was a snake, it felt as if we had known it all along. Joss wrote him as a slippery character, a liar. He wasn't a dragon or an ogre, he was a snake. Eventually the snake in him got so big he had to shed the human skin and become the monster he really was. His true purpose revealed itself, finally out in the open. Once the snake was revealed, Buffy stepped up and took care of it, blowing up the high school because inside it was the biggest snake you have ever seen, one that had corrupted the whole infrastructure. The only thing to do was to blow the school up with him in it and start over. It's a metaphor that was repeated in the series finale when the Hellmouth fell in and literally took all of Sunnydale with it, leaving a gaping hole. Once again writing visually, Joss had Buffy's (and *Buffy*'s) whole world collapse beneath her. When we were storyboarding this sequence, Joss meticulously placed Buffy on the edge throughout. She saved the day, but her world had collapsed on an epic scale, a direct reflection of the epic end of her world on the inside, and also, in a way, the world of those of us making the show.

Angel's ending was slightly different. It was left unfinished: Angel stood before an army with his sword drawn, ready to fight. Joss called me into his office late in the afternoon during production and showed me the end of the last episode. The army wasn't big enough. Joss needed to be sure the audience understood that Angel was left in the fight against insurmountable odds, and that he was going to keep on fighting even after the show was canceled. As homage to both *Buffy* and *Angel*, we threw in every major creature from both shows; they were what we left Angel to defeat. Joss wanted to be sure the viewer knew Angel was going to continue to fight on past the credits, and that had to be represented by the army we saw in that final rainy shot.

I had learned from Joss that good visual effects were about story, but working on *Firefly* was our first real opportunity to apply this not just to demons and monsters, but to entire scenes. From the beginning, everyone involved knew we were doing something special, and we were excited and determined to do something that had never been done in science fiction: not simply use a spaceship as our primary set, but have space travel play a significant role in what the cast was doing and how they were doing it. Visual Effects played a significant role in this. We generated scenes in the computer, from scenes in Joss's script, which were important to understanding the whole narrative. In our own small way we were a part of the story generation, and we had to be close with those people, Joss and Tim specifically, who were telling the tale. Our department debated the origins of everything we designed; we scrutinized, fought about, and relished our part in the story. And we argued over every choice we made as if it might throw the viewers out of the story if we didn't. We did this to the point of driving Joss and Tim nuts.

Our first job was to develop the ship, *Serenity*. Who was she? Where did she come from? Where was she going? What did she like? What didn't she like? What made her special?

Serenity is a home to the characters that live inside her, a character in the story herself. *Serenity* is a place of quiet, a center where one can focus, where one might find peace or love. *Serenity* is a Firefly-class spaceship, a transport ship with room for crew and passengers. She has a large modular cargo bay, which was used, prior to Mal's purchase of the ship, for carrying things. As Carey Meyer planned the ship's interior layout, we worked on a logic for the external one. We wanted people to believe the ship worked in every way.

Many of the crew on the visual effects team are Star Wars fans, myself included. I personally own a few books, technical guides created for fans that explain how things work. I loved the fact that there was a logic, realistic or otherwise; it made the universe feel authentic. We wanted our audience to have the same feeling. We wanted them to be able to "kick the tires" of *Serenity* and feel what Mal feels about her, to love her. We invented a false logic for the ship's functions and made sure everything worked according to its rules—everything. (I will explain some of these below.) As we did this we debated the purpose of every detail. Those debates made the design even richer.

One of my favorite debates about the ship had to do with the functionality of the cargo bay. We pitched to Joss and Carey Meyer that the cargo bay should detach and be changeable, just as shipping containers can be swapped out between trains and cargo ships and eighteen-wheelers. Joss felt the concept was too akin to the detaching disk in Star Trek; we just wanted this class of ship to be able to pick up and detach large shipments with ease. In the end, Joss didn't feel it was necessary, and the ship's cargo bay remained a permanent part of *Serenity*. However, if you look closely, you can see that some of the engineering for this changeability still remains. Tucked under the side engines on either side of the ship, you'll find a large locking device, which wraps snuggly around the cargo bay and snaps into place to hold it. If the ship were to drop the cargo bay, these metal holders would be left behind. We were hoping there would be a place for this in the future.

Serenity has three main engines, two for atmospheric and guided space flight and one for unidirectional space flight (the Firefly). She also has thirty RCS (Reaction Control System) thrusters, to help set her course in space.

The two atmospheric engines can rotate a full 360 degrees. They carry *Serenity* as modern day VTOL (Vertical Take-Off and Landing) engines do the Harrier jet or the even more modern Joint Strike Fighters. These engines are fueled jet turbines; they function like today's engines, only with a bit more power and on a larger scale. Their rotation in flight is what allows *Serenity* to fly like a plane at high speeds and like a helicopter when she needs to slip into a tight spot in the woods. These engines also tuck in. We set them up to do so to allow better access for maintenance and maneuverability while parked (it also allows free access for the shuttles), but I don't know if we ever showed this function on screen. If we did, it was just something happening while we were looking at something else. The design of these engines often affected the way the writers scripted stories. The "Crazy Ivan" (the term comes from a submarine move where a sub turns 180 degrees underwater instantly) Wash did during the pilot was a good example; the engines' ability to rotate is what made it possible for Wash to turn on the Reavers and then go to full burn, leaving them in the nuclear blast left behind and propelling our crew to safety.

The "Firefly" engine on the back is a bit of a contained bomb. In development, we talked about a military project called "Icarus," where NASA looked at the detonation of a nuclear weapon as a potential form of thrust in space. The "Firefly" effect is something like this. The engine lets out a big radioactive blast, which propels the ship at high speed in a direct course. During this propulsion she has limited maneuverability.

In the pilot, when they set off the engine so close to the planet's surface, they were essentially detonating a nuke in atmosphere. That is why the blast has such a significant visual effect; the big bright burst behind her is basically an oil slick. The Alliance commented on this class of ship being a dirty burner in the pilot, a reference to the color display left in her wake. It's beautiful, but it is waste. The glow on the panels is part of the cooling process for the engine. After full burn it takes some time for the coils to cool off, and the result is the firefly glow.

The "Firefly" effect, much like the dusting on *Buffy*, evolved every time we used it. We always wanted it to be prettier, more magical. It represented the journey the crew was on, the mission they had to fulfill, and we really wanted it to be a passionate effect, full of emotion. If we were still flying, we'd probably still be working on making it better. Joss was always asking why it kept changing; we just kind of avoided giving him a direct answer. Why did we avoid it? Because he liked it as it was, and we wanted it to be better. It was the most spectacular thing *Serenity* could do, and for us it was just never good enough. In a way, it became a constant pitch, a way of proving ourselves over and over again.

In addition to the big engines, *Serenity* has her RCS thrusters. These work the same way as they do on our real world space shuttles: they emit small amounts of compressed gas, which meticulously alter the ship's direction. Originally we wanted these guys to play a big part in the rules that defined for the animators how *Serenity* could move. In space, a ship does not bank or sweep. It drifts until its motion is corrected. RCS thrusters correct their ship's directional drift. But these rules didn't stand the test of time. *Serenity* needed to move well, and moving with RCS doesn't look that cool—it often looks angular and frankly unimpressive. We always had them running, even in the big battle with the Reavers and the Alliance at the end of the film *Serenity*; we just stretched their capability to allow for some sexier motion.

Serenity has two shuttles, which are used to get around when there isn't anywhere to park a Firefly. These are utility vehicles. Like *Serenity*, they are VTOL craft, but unlike *Serenity*, they have fold-up wings for more nimble flight. They also tuck neatly halfway inside the ship when docked. During take-off they are pushed out by two small arms, allowing them to press straight up off of *Serenity*'s wings.

Serenity doesn't have any guns. Her best offense is defense and those who live inside her. When she's in a pickle, she always has Jayne and Vera. That's what really makes her special: her crew will put on space suits and open the cargo bay doors to take the bad guys head on.

She is a bit odd looking. When Joss originally described what we wanted *Serenity* to look like, it was a cross between a bird and an insect, with her head perched high in the air. He drew a picture, which I wish I still had. Joss draws more often than you'd think and he is good at it. He sketched her out and this sketch was the beginning.

When Mal picked *Serenity* out of the sand, he raised her up and put her back together piece by piece. Patched and welded the steel into a solid machine to travel in. Joss wanted to feel that she had been kept together through hard work and maintenance. When Carey Meyer drew her up and we built her, we built this care into the design. There are many varieties of steel that make up the body of the ship. They stopped making Firefly-class ships years ago and every repair is custom, built and scrapped together with parts from other ships. She is never quite sound; ships as old as *Serenity* are always in need of repair.

When we put her together for the first time she looked abstract and unfit for flight. Carey Meyer pieced her together out of cardboard and painted her blue. She was a Lebbeus Woods sculpture. When we put her together in the computer we dragged her more toward a Klingon "Bird of Prey." We wanted her to be space-worthy and cool. Joss wanted her somewhere in-between. Joss wanted her to be unique, singular, and beautiful, a ship created just for her crew, a ship for Mal to find and feel safe in, a ship that could take him and his family where they needed to go. In the end the pushing and pulling we all did made her what she is. Which is what she is, a sculpture of voices all heading in the same direction with a whole lot of heart. She evolved a bit too over the years, just like the effect that drove her. She didn't evolve because she needed to, but rather because we wanted her to be real, to work in every way. So we kept adding pipes and pistons, heating coils and fly panels, all in the hope that her fans would see them, see her, and love her as much as we did.

For the film, Joss was asked if he wanted to change the ship. He said,

"I didn't change the cast, why would I change the ship?" The only changes we made to her were in the details. We took our fine paintbrushes out and made sure she didn't have any bald spots or stray hairs for that wonderful opening shot where we got to show her off, from the painted name on her side to the flapping panels that slow her down enough that she won't burn when she skips into atmosphere.

Let's digress a bit here, because this shot by design tells you much of what you need to know about the ship. The shot opens with a smash cut to the logo, which also happens to be the name of the ship, and the name of the movie; it's quiet at first, which adds to the mystery. Slowly we change the light a bit and bump the camera, which is now pulling back. As it pulls back even further we begin to see the silhouette of the ship. We see her long neck, her body against the clear deep black of space. The panels begin to close on her *Firefly* cooling coils as she prepares to enter the atmosphere. We look at her against the big black and know she is a spaceship. As we come around her rear the camera bumps some more and we reveal her from the top. She is heading down to a planet below. Now she is backlit by the planet. She is a planetary traveler. She starts to buck and bump and the camera plummets to her side as the twin jet engines fire, breaking her fall into the heat of the Terran atmosphere. It's rocky but she's got it together. We pull all the way back around to her neck and approach the cockpit where we see her captain and the pilot. She doesn't fly by herself. She is guided on her journeys. A piece of her nose breaks off as we approach the cockpit. She is fragile. Now on the inside we meet the family that lives inside her, the family that brings her to life. This is probably my favorite shot we ever made in either the series or the movie. It's gorgeous and singular. One shot to tell us all about this piece of metal which does so much for the people who call her home. It was the last shot we delivered to the movie, as it included titles. It may be the last shot we ever work on with *Serenity*. If there has to be one, I am glad this was it. She sure is pretty.

Home is a relative term, used to describe a place where we live, where we eat, where we return, where we invite our friends, where we feel safe. When we began to work on *Firefly* Joss gave us a number of books and films to look toward for tone. *The Killer Angels* in particular meant a great deal to me, as it deals with great loss and the search for hope and a home when you are cast away by a moral society. It calls into question what morality means in the face of war and what you do with yourself when what you have been taught as moral is turned against you, when faith fails and you are cast out of your house. Malcolm Reynolds was cast out on the battlefield in Serenity Valley. On his ship *Serenity* Mal finds home again, he finds his family, and he finds hope. We knew *Serenity* was all of these things when we made her, when we lit her, when we flew her, and when we photographed her. We cared for her, as if we were caring for someone's home.

Beyond creating the ship herself, our role was to create pictures in support of the stories. When we read "EXT. SPACE" in a script, it meant we had a part of the story to tell. Whether we were flying through a ring of death made out of spare parts or bringing Jayne in for a surprise rescue during a witch-hunt, our scenes moved the story forward and often toward climax. How did we do this without real cameras or physical sets, and with limited actor involvement? We pretended we did have them. We pretended in the same way you pretend when you use your imagination, only we pretended with computers that created pretty recordings of our play sessions. We pretended with the stakes of the words in the script driving us, knowing that, dramatically, we were responsible for story beats.

Being the good geeks we are, we pretended with toys first. Carey Meyer made Joss a miniature of *Serenity* to use in our meetings. It was small enough to fly around and we used it. At the office we used stand-ins, matchbox cars and such; these objects became our ships. We used the toys to show the animators how we wanted the ships to fly and where we wanted the camera to photograph them.

From the start Joss insisted that this play be different and singular: he always wanted the viewer to be in the room, to be present in the way he told the story visually. This *verite* approach persisted whether we were creating close-ups or wide matte paintings. The camera was looking for the story, following the emotion. In CG this meant setting up rules which were new to the field—camera rules that seem to be everywhere now. We put documentary photographic language into the animation we created. We used zoom lenses, soft focus, lens flares, and faulty cameramen. We wanted human imperfection to be a part of our work in finding the story, the way it was on the set. Our animators were told to set up the action, and then find what was interesting within it without discovering it right away; and upon discovery, they were told, they were to only "look" at it until the viewer understood what they needed to.

In the pilot we used this technique as punctuation. The crew knew the Reavers were on their tail. We put a camera there, on *Serenity*'s tail, and the Reavers were nowhere to be found. In deep background, there was a tiny line of black against the blue sky. The camera focused on this line, zoomed in, and refocused, revealing the very formidable ship gaining on them. As the camera adjusted focus, so did we, the viewers. We were focusing on this very dangerous and very ugly thing chasing after us.

In "Objects in Space," Jubal Early snuck up on *Serenity* from behind. He put his ship in pace with ours. He got out and snuck onboard. He wreaked havoc on the ship. Mal and River confronted him in space. Jubal was left floating in space for all time. There was a lot more to the story on the inside, but these scenes were significant and important. Jubal was an invader and River is an empath. How did we introduce Jubal to the ship? He crept in through her pipes and air ducts like a thief in the night, startling the vulnerable young River from her sound sleep. The shot design told the story of invasion and danger. As we found River, the camera shifted focus from the vents we had been slinking our way through to the sleeping girl. She opened her eyes. She felt our intrusion. We knew, by design, that Jubal had penetrated the ship.

Every computer-generated shot in the series had meaning, like these did. As we worked with the computer—and working with a computer takes time—we took the time to be meticulous. Perhaps the greatest proof of the influence of shots like these in the field is that other folks took on their aesthetic as a new standard. *Battlestar Galactica* uses these rules, the Star Wars prequels picked them up, and now John Favereau promises the motion picture *Iron Man* will as well. It's a storytelling aesthetic that focuses on story over spectacle.

The movie *Serenity* again would provide another pinnacle: the space battle. We have all dreamed of fighting heroically in an epic war for good, using laser beams and photons. We have all dreamed of saving the day and destroying the Death Star in order to defeat an evil empire, but Joss took this dream and rewrote it for value and point. In less capable hands the battle scene in *Serenity* would have been an effects extravaganza without meaning, but instead it was handled with the uttermost care and design. And again Joss used his singular invented documentary camera aesthetic to do it. He used his camera and action to build his Shakespearean tragic finale.

It plays out in an operatic ballet, as Wash flies *Serenity* for a final time "like a leaf on the wind" through the giant space battle. The camera fights the mayhem around it just to stay with our heroic ship and her pilot. As it all unfolds, we never leave *Serenity*. Keeping up with her and Wash is harrowing, as all hell unfolds around us. The crew, and their message, is at the center. The battle itself is almost an afterthought. In design we had many more epic scenes laid out, but they were dropped on the cutting room floor in exchange for a focus on Wash and his mission to get us through. Joss designed each shot to build an atonal drama. The scene plays against our instincts, spending very little time in the pinch of pursuit by the Reavers and assault by the Alliance, and by doing so he makes Wash a bigger hero than ever before. Wash almost floats through this Trojan encounter. Joss builds his hero up as the very best pilot our *Serenity* family could ever have, knowing full well that all of us would be patting him on the back agreeing with him as he congratulated himself on being "a leaf on the wind" . . . and then takes him from us. He builds our emotion and our courage, flying through the battle above, and then rips it away. And here again we must rise up.

Making *Firefly* in partnership was thrilling and revolutionary. The passion to be unique and yet absolutely familiar is paramount. We wanted characters, places, and things we all knew, in extraordinary places doing extraordinary things. We did this week after week and we did it well. Perhaps it was the ever-looming threat of network cancellation that pushed us, but I'd like to think that it was just one of those singular situations where all of the right people are doing all of the rights things, creating a perfect space to be creative. We all fought hard all the time to be the best.

The movie was much different. The movie was Joss's entirely. Making a movie is a personal battle. When it is over you are wounded and tired. Joss was exacting and focused, and he led us tirelessly. Great movies are great battles won by heroes in art. That thing you feel when you leave great art, that thing that stays with you, that makes you think, that inspires and thrills, is what happens when you win a battle in art. We won the battle of Serenity because we went into the battle with a solid plan. Our script, our story, our plan is what you see in the finished film. It was our directions. It was our plan and Joss fought tirelessly to make sure we followed through.

In the beginning of this essay I called making the movie *Serenity* earning my doctorate at Whedon University. This is why. When Joss managed to bring *Serenity* back from the dead and to the big screen we were given a gift, an opportunity to continue with something that meant so much to so many, to give more, to say more, of what Joss wanted to say. I knew that every story beat I would be involved in needed to resolve to Malcolm Reynolds's final speech on the bridge to River. That was what I focused on throughout the process. The final shot became the summation of everything. It was meticulously fashioned to underline the word love: *Serenity*'s turn, her punch through the clouds, her breach against the sun, and her burst into space came from love. And what made the shot even better was Joss's end to it, the panel that breaks and falls right into camera. That broken panel sums up the final lesson: love is frail, and frailty makes us mighty because we must overcome it. Joss gave me a great deal over the last ten years but his most important gifts were the very same gifts we have all been given. His stories, populated with emotional hills and valleys, which never end. Sisyphus pushes the stone up the mountain and it rolls back down and he must push it up again. Joss helped me understand that there is greatness in every part of Sisyphus's task, and knowing this I will always look for greatness in all things. I can laugh and expect that the rock will always fall down when I reach the top of the hill, just as *Serenity* breaks after giving the world truth. And this makes us mighty.

LONI PERISTERE was born in Natick, Massachusetts. He graduated from UMASS Boston then went to work for Joss Whedon as Visual Effects Supervisor on *Buffy the Vampire Slayer*, *Angel*, *Firefly*, and *Serenity*. Loni co-founded the multi-award winning visual effects company Zoic Studios. He has won an Emmy, two VES awards, a Clio, a London International Advertising Award, and a Gold Pencil. Loni recently turned his focus back to writing and is currently developing several projects.

Television shows and movies tend to be written neither by muscle-bound hunks nor by high-bosomed hunkes. We may or may not be tech-savvy (I know of one high-level writer who has an assistant stay at hand during late-night writing sessions to perform the tricky "save as" operation at the end of the night), but we certainly execute our work in front of monitors, our fingers on keyboards. Most of us, I would venture, self-identify as nerds or geeks of some variety. So how do we depict our brother geeks? Giardina looks at the question of geeks in Serenity, *in sci-fi, and in the real world.*

(Note: My first real paying gig as a television staff writer was for a show called Monty. *The younger son on that show was played by a brilliantly talented teen actor named David Krumholtz, who has gone on to great things, including starring in the CBS series* Numb3ers, *and playing a certain geek called Mr. Universe.)*

Geeks of the World, Unite!

You Have Nothing to Lose but Your Lovebots!

NATASHA GIARDINA

Mr. Universe? Mr. Who?

I bet you didn't even notice him when you first watched *Serenity*. Admittedly, he only has a few lines and doesn't really get involved in the blood-and-guts action of the story, except, ultimately, in a rather *terminal* way. He isn't what you'd call a hero, and while you could say he is necessary to the plot, you'd have to think twice to remember what he personally did to make the world a better place.

And yet, on reflection, I think you probably can remember him. In fact, I can practically see your brain ticking over: "Mr. Universe, Mr. Universe. . . . Hey—wasn't he that geek with the lovebot?"

Sigh. Yep, that's right. Mr. Universe—not only a person of great knowledge, skill, and intelligence, but also a being of immense potential in terms of social and political power—is best remembered for the fact that he married the futuristic equivalent of a blow-up doll. He's a nerd, a geek, a dork, a dweeb even. He has all the social cachet of a fungal infection. But why is it so? Why, in our technology-dependent era, is the geek marginalized and effaced in our stories and our society, an object of amusement and derision when s/he appears at all, while the action hero is king?

Let's face it, in a film exploring the nature of right and wrong, the crimes perpetrated in the name of a "greater good," and the triggers that turn human beings into monsters, Mr. Universe provides some welcome comic relief. We first meet him in his fortress of solitude: a scrappy-looking young guy in a rumpled shirt and old trainers, with the complexion of something that lives under a rock. His repartee is nails-down-a-blackboard cringe-worthy, and the knowledge that he's so lacking in social skills and experience that he's sating his lusts upon his lovebot is . . . just ick. Just really, *really* ick. You get the feeling that if you cut him in half, the word "dork" would be written all the way through.

Of course these things are funny—all humor is based on someone else's misfortune—but I suspect that much of the laughter has that odd, nervous quality that comes from barbs striking slightly too close to home. Specifically, while *Serenity* may be set in an interstellar future age, Mr. Universe looks awfully early twenty-first century: he looks like someone who was the butt of jokes in your high school. In fact, if you're the kind of person who takes your science fiction seriously (which you probably are if you love *Firefly* and *Serenity*), it's just possible he may look a teensy bit like you. I'll be honest here: apart from, like, the stubble and the Adam's apple and associated stuff, he looks quite a lot like me. So I laughed at him, perhaps like you, because I remembered the feeling of being ostracized for geekiness, and I was laughing at myself, really (sure I was); I don't have a chip on my shoulder about it at all (yes, that's right, this three-pound chunk of hardwood I'm sporting here is for decorative purposes only, I swear!). In short, I laughed because it's nice to be the laugher and not the laughee and because, deep down, there was a small voice that said, "You know, geeks aren't cool."

Sometimes it seems like no one wants to be a geek. I mean, taking Mr. Universe as an example, if there's going to be a quest to spread truth and justice throughout human civilization, to right wrongs and cream the bad guys, who wants to be relegated to background scenery, with a lovebot, a few amusing lines, and a half-sad, half-creepy death scene? No, I suspect that the vast majority of us would rather be Zoe or Mal, because we all know that action heroes rock. It's as if we've got a little voice in our heads that says, "Action heroes! How cool are they?!"

It's not surprising; after all, action heroes have been around for at least 4,000 years. Gilgamesh was one of the earliest action heroes, and the stories of him and his manifold literary descendents—Hercules, Beowulf, Arthur, Robin Hood, Tarzan, and Aragorn, to name a few famous ones—have become part of the mythos of Western civilization, framing the ways we think about life. The hero story just seems *right* to us: a young man (and yes, most of them are still guys) leaves his home, goes out into the world, learns things, acquires power and strength, fulfils a quest, and returns home triumphant, usually making that home a better place in the process. It's arguably the reason why we idolize explorers and elite athletes over scientists and philosophers. (For proof on this point, consider how many philosophers have major sponsorship deals. Advertisers know where the money is.)

We are so attuned to action heroes that we rarely stop to think about them critically, but we know that they're cool in the same way we know that geeks aren't. Again, a lot of it comes down to image. For example, action heroes are usually buff like you *don't* get from sitting at a computer for fourteen hours a day. Nor can the blue glow from a screen (or in Mr. Universe's case, many screens) create the kind of muscle-defining tan the action hero often sports. Unlike geeks, action heroes look good in whatever they're wearing, be it animal skins, loincloths, chain mail, cowboy gear, or the blood of their vanquished foes. And they look far, far better in celluloid, backed by multimillion-dollar budgets and the very latest in stunts, costumes, and special effects. Even *Serenity*, which admittedly did not have the budget of, say, *Blade 3* or *Terminator 2*, featured a couple of pretty hot action heroes in Mal and Zoe. They had the look down pat: tall, young, fit, well-tailored clothes, bad-ass guns, and a keen sense of justice. They talk the talk too: like great action heroes they're laconic, but witty—they "aim to misbehave" but never cry "like a baby. A hungry, angry baby."

And yet geek heroes, too, have had moments in the pop culture sun, especially in science fiction: think of Captain Nemo in Jules Verne's *20,000 Leagues Under the Sea* (1869); the scientist in H. G. Wells's *The Time Machine* (1895); Isaac Asimov's *Foundation* series scientist-hero Hari Seldon (1942–1950); Robert Heinlein's young astrogators, spaceship captains, and explorers in *Starman Jones* (1953), *Citizen of the Galaxy* (1957), and *Space Family Stone* (1969); and the engineer Vannevar Morgan in Arthur C. Clarke's *The Fountains of Paradise* (1978). Scientists, engineers, and other tech-savvy heroes also made their presence felt in early television science fiction including *Doctor Who* (1963+) and *Lost in Space* (1965–1968).

But it was a later subgenre of science fiction—cyberpunk—that really put geeks like Mr. Universe on the map. This was the first kind of fiction to explore the potential effect of computers and cyberspace on interpersonal relations, politics, the economy, and society generally. Suddenly, we realized that the new frontier was not "out there" but all around us—it was electronic. Hackers emerged onto this stage as the new tech-savvy heroes; skilled at surfing the cyberseas, they were freedom fighters battling the corporate giants. Case, the hero of William Gibson's *Neuromancer* (1984), is widely considered the quintessential hacker hero, but an earlier example is Nick Haflinger, the talented hacker who breaks his government's control over information in John Brunner's 1975 classic *The Shockwave Rider*.

If the seventies and eighties were the era when hackers became heroes, then the nineties were when these geeks became cool. An early forerunner here is Hiro Protagonist from Neal Stephenson's *Snow Crash* (1992). Hiro is one of an elite cadre of hackers who created the Metaverse, a 3-D Internet analog. Yet this guy is far from a pocket-protector nerd: he wears a black leather kimono, drives a very mean street machine, and carries a matched set of samurai swords. He has all the accoutrements of cool, but he most definitely uses his brains and not his brawn to save the day.

It was in the late nineties, though, that the hacker hero reached its apogee. And significantly, the greatest hacker hero of science fiction film was also the most popular with the mainstream (that is, non-geek) audience: Thomas A. Anderson—office johnny by day, hacker extraordinaire by night, and eventual freedom fighter against the dominance of machines over the human race. The fact that most know him by his hacker handle rather than his real name is evidence of his street cred. And, like his ancestor Hiro before him, this hacker is cool. He may be an unappealing, hairless gray blob in real life, but plug him in, and his virtual self kicks butt in black leather and PVC, leaping from tall buildings, fighting hand-to-hand battles with evil computer agents, and brandishing some pretty hardcore weaponry.

The main problem with Neo is that we remember his black leather and martial arts and too readily forget his geek origins, because the action-hero meme is pervasive and resilient and out-guns the geek-hero meme every time.

The action hero responds to our deepest desires: we look at this hero with a thousand faces and we dream that one of those faces could be ours. It is the ultimate consolatory fantasy, evoking some mythical time when life was simpler, quests involved scaling mountains (not commuting to work), and problems could be solved at the point of a sword or a gun. The trouble with this consolatory fantasy is that it has no useful translation into the real, contemporary world. This problem occurs even in the fictional universe of *Serenity*: the really cool things about the crew of *Serenity* are their retro Wild West accents, outfits, manners, and sensibilities, but in the world of the film, the high-tech world of tomorrow, this only serves to mark them as creatures of the past, and in the bigger scheme of things, not all that successful. They may be the heroes of their own story, but they're eking out a rather precarious existence in the margins of human civilization in the future.

Beyond the silver screen, the consolatory fantasy of the action hero is both more seductive and more dangerous. It affects us on personal levels: got a dead-end desk job, a mortgage, and three kids to support? Well, that truly blows, but in another universe, you could have been a hero with a sword to wield and a dragon to slay. You could've been a contender. You could've gone up to all the people who made you feel small and said, "You looking at me?" before resorting to your fists or a gun and teaching them some respect. The same principle afflicts our politics and national identity—just take out the fists and guns and substitute missiles, armies, and coalitions of the willing. Because that's been such a *successful* conflict resolution strategy . . . hasn't it?

The ideologies underpinning the action hero emphasize individualism, isolation, and confrontation. They say that the hero is an island, alone—he may have friends and compatriots, but the ultimate responsibility for their well-being and his own rests solely with him. In the action hero's universe, right and wrong are clearly demarcated, an action hero knows the difference between the two instinctively, and because he is always right, he can make the world fit his views. But this world he inhabits is a difficult and dangerous place, populated by far more foes than friends, and so the hero *must* meet them head-on and aggressively.

It's a fantasy that is simply not useful for the ways we live our lives today and may very well be a recipe for disaster. It's time to stop buying into it. It's time to accept that we're never going to be action heroes, and think about what we *are* instead. Because when we look around at the world we actually live in, that world is digital. It's time for us to embrace our inner geek.

Let's re-evaluate what it means to be a geek by taking another look at Mr. Universe. Sure, the image is a little unspectacular, but the substance is awesome. He's able to access all digital information everywhere, so he's practically omniscient. He's extremely intelligent and knows how to get the most out of the technology available to him. Moreover, this must be a financially successful strategy, because he seems to own his very own planetoid, as well as the fortress, satellite dishes, and associated computer hardware, including the lovebot. (And may I just point out here that the *Serenity* crew, by contrast, own little more than the clothes on their backs and the junk-heap they fly around in. Action heroing may look good, but it doesn't seem to pay the bills too well.) So if you're starting to think that maybe geeks aren't that unappealing after all, I have some good news for you: if you have an Internet connection, can make your computer go, and have ever bought or sold anything on eBay, then there's really little difference between you and Mr. Universe, it's only a question of degree.

Looking around at the ways we're using technology and the kinds of activities we're engaging in, we can start to discern the emerging ideologies of geekdom, which sit in opposition to those of the action hero and are much more life-affirming. The first of these is what Mr. Universe would call the truth of the signal: everything is information and information is *everything*. This doesn't simply mean that knowledge is power or that the pen is mightier than the sword, although these clichés are indeed applicable. Saying that everything is information acknowledges that we're all the same in binary code. If the things that define us can be expressed in a series of ones and zeroes, then concepts like gender, race, age, religion, and politics are simply different patterns of on and off, rather than chasms to divide us.

More than that, information is communication. Unlike the action hero who stays strong and silent with no one to turn to, geek culture is predicated on the constant flow of information. Admittedly, this can occasionally seem like a bad thing, especially if the main way people communicate with you is to dump hundreds of e-mails in your inbox every day. But Generation Y will assure you that e-mail is, like, so *yesterday*. They're the first generation to grow up with computers, and they've turned constant communication into an art form, expressed creatively through a variety of media. Like a democratic hive without a queen, they communicate constantly to maintain the networks of their peers. SMS and IM are among their most commonly used communication tools (Lenhart et al.), but MySpace, Facebook, Habbohotel, blogs, YouTube, and MMORPGs are also important arenas for social interaction. And it's a very reassuring thing to know that you are never alone: your peers are all around you in cyberspace, only a click away.

This hive, or ambient peer network, provides excellent opportunities for fun and play. Unlike the ideology of the action hero, which sees life as a grim battle between right and wrong, geeks prefer their battles to come with magical items, ph4t l3wtz, cool graphics, and the prospect of resurrection. Online role-playing games like *Guild Wars* and *World of Warcraft* enable us to play a good guy or a bad guy as the mood takes us, with consequences restricted to the fictional universe. Alternatively, we can take advantage of the many opportunities for more . . . adult social "play" and make virtual love not virtual war; either way, it's still healthier than real war. The ideology of geekdom says that life should be fun, that play is part of life and should be undertaken with great enthusiasm.

The implications of the democratic hive are starting to make themselves felt far beyond the social arena. In Australia, for example, viral e-mail campaigns from key NGOs have educated the public about the implications of new workplace legislation, spread the word on public protest days, and provided efficient and effective ways of petitioning government ministers (*Your Rights at Work*). In the Philippines in 2001, anti-Estrada groups used text messaging to organize smart mob rallies, which were instrumental in overthrowing the government (Rheingold). As Mr. Universe says, you can't stop the signal. In the era of instant digital communication and the democratic hive, geeks are making sure the truth gets out.

Our digital connection—the signal that brings us together—is not only creating global communities, it's also disrupting traditional hierarchies of knowledge. Where once we accepted that corporations, universities, governments, and traditional news media were the authorities of public knowledge, now we're much more likely to create and vet that knowledge ourselves, and to take for granted our right to do so. It's no wonder then that blogs are gaining ground on traditional media as consumers' preferred source of news; they offer an immediacy and personality to news that old media just can't match (Loewenstein), and more fundamentally, they provide a multiplicity of perspectives, which come together to create a composite image of the truth. Similarly, the online encyclopedia that anyone can edit and contribute to, Wikipedia, has destroyed the canons of knowledge and famously spawned "wikiality"—truth or reality as established by consensus (a term first coined in 2006 by Stephen Colbert in *The Colbert Report*).

But perhaps one of the most pertinent examples of the power of the democratic hive is *Serenity* itself, or more specifically, the Internet-connected, international fan networks of Browncoats and others who kept interest in *Firefly* alive after the series was canceled. Meeting online through fan sites, spreading the word through blogs, e-mail, and in my personal case, earnestly thrusting the series DVDs into the hands of friends and saying, "Watch this. You will love it. Tell everyone!", the democratic hive created enough lasting popularity that Universal Pictures decided to take on the project of the *Serenity* film. Significantly, Universal took advantage of the fan networks in its marketing campaigns for the film, with a range of Internet-based promotional material including the "R. Tam Sessions." Even now, the Browncoats have remained active in many areas, using their connections to raise money for charities and *Firefly*-related events.

Welcome to geek culture: you're standing in it. It's democratized, decentralized, viral, and playful. There's no room for action heroes here: if anyone's going to save the world, it's going to be all of us, together, each doing our own thing but communicating with the others all the time. The future we make can be a consensual one, if we forget about being heroes alone against the world and accept that we're heroes-in-common. We only need to stop valuing image over substance, belittling our achievements, and ascribing to an ideal that will never make us happy. Instead we should take heed of the reminder contained in Mr. Universe's name—that smart, tech-savvy people are out there, everywhere, universal. Geeks of the world, unite!

I am indebted to Terry Pratchett for his philosophy on the eternal popularity of kings, which I have adapted for the case of action heroes.

NATASHA GIARDINA is a lecturer and senior research assistant at Queensland University of Technology in Brisbane, Australia. She is currently investigating the ways young people engage with new media technologies and the kinds of online and offline spaces they inhabit. She wears her "Geek Pride" badge with honor and encourages others to come out of the server room.

REFERENCES

The California Browncoats. 2007. 28 February 2007. <http://www.californiabrowncoats.org/CABC/index.htm>

Campbell, J. *The Hero with a Thousand Faces*. Princeton, NJ: Princeton UP, 1968.

Giardina, N. "'Paladins rule, okay?!' Young people constructing identities and forming communities through online and offline fantasy role-playing systems." Paper presented at *E-merging realities: youth/media/education*. Australian Teachers of Media Conference, QUT: Brisbane, 6-8 October, 2006.

Lenhart, A., M. Madden, and P. Hitlin. "Teens and Technology: Youth Are Leading the Transition to a Fully Wired and Mobile Nation." Washington, D.C.: Pew Internet & American Life Project, 2005.

Loewenstein, A. "Bloggers of the World, Unite." *The Sydney Morning Herald Online*. 20 January 2007. <http://www.smh.com.au>

Pratchett, T. *Feet of Clay*. London: Victor Gollancz, 1996.

Rheingold, H. *Smart Mobs: The Next Social Revolution*. Cambridge, MA: Basic

Books, 2002.

Wikiality: The Truthiness Encyclopedia. 2007. 4 February 2007. <http://www.wikiality.com/Wikiality>

Your Rights at Work. Australian Council of Trade Unions, 2005. 3 February 2007. <http://www.rightsatwork.com.au>

Sometimes reality reads like an excerpt from The Handmaid's Tale, Brave New World, 1984, *or pick your own favorite toe-tappin' dystopia. Government secrecy hides alarming agendas, freedoms are curtailed for our own "protection," and religious ideology grows stronger as it encroaches further into our daily lives. When religion and government begin to view science as an enemy, or even more sinisterly, as a tool to manipulate for their own purposes, we would do well to become concerned. Wharton reminds us that our now is Mal's yesterday, and—geez—that makes more and more sense.*

The Alliance's War on Science

KEN WHARTON

After watching the movie *Serenity* and the episodes of *Firefly*, one might come to the conclusion that the show's creators did not like science.

Or scientists, for that matter.

After all, the movie opens with white-coated "doctors" plunging needles into a young girl's brain, and builds up to the revelation that secret scientific experiments killed 10 million innocent people and created the Reavers. True, the scientists are not portrayed as the main "bad guys"—the soon-to-be-skewered whitecoat in the movie's opening scene seems particularly hapless—but without these scientists and their hideous secrets, the Alliance would probably seem like a pretty decent group of people.

You might also draw the same conclusion from the quite different scientific leanings of the "good guys." Malcolm Reynolds and his gang don't much care for fancy research. *Serenity*'s only technician has never had any formal training—machines just "talk to her." True, they have a well-trained doctor on board, but that's just a bit of happenstance. Indeed, we're continually reminded throughout the series that medicine can be used for evil as well as for good. In the *Firefly* pilot episode, even Simon threatened to withhold medical treatment for Kaylee unless Mal helped him escape the Alliance.

And Captain Reynolds himself hardly ever mentions anything technical. When he does, he demonstrates that he understands the basic principles well enough, but has no interest in anything he can't put to direct use. For example, in the *Firefly* episode "Shindig," Reynolds saw an impressive floating chandelier at a ball on Persephone. "What's the point of that, I wonder?" he said. "I see how they do it, I just don't get why." A telling remark: pure science is not of much interest to our heroes.

So, do these stories carry an anti-science message? I'm going to argue just the opposite. The *Firefly* universe is just showing us the consequences of the perversion of science, extrapolating some of today's anti-science trends to their logical conclusions. The open scientific method that human beings use to find truth and discard falsehoods—untrammeled by government or corporate interference—simply isn't evident in the *Firefly* universe. In its stead, we see a future in which the enemies of modern science have won. By showing us such a future, I argue that these shows are actually pro-science, right to their very core.

Like all good science fiction, the *Firefly* universe supposes that there is a plausible path that connects our current reality to the imagined future. If it weren't obvious enough from the languages and slang used in the show, Joss Whedon has come right out and said that the Alliance is supposed to be the fusion of two different cultures from Earth: American and Chinese. The "science" practiced by the Alliance presumably also has its roots in these two cultures. And sure enough, one can find a lot of parallels between what is portrayed onscreen and what has happened—and is happening—here on Earth. Of course, many technological advances have come out of both China and America, but these advances were accomplished in spite of certain anti-science trends—some of which seem to be getting worse every year.

Ancient China was arguably the most technologically advanced civilization of its time on Earth-That-Was, inventing gunpowder, printing, and the compass. Six centuries ago, China had a vast navy, with boats reaching lengths more than twice that of a typical Firefly-class vessel. But that navy was soon decimated by a sequence of top-down decisions from China's emperors; by the year 1500, it was illegal to sail in a ship with more than two masts, and by 1525 such ships were being actively destroyed. The net effect was irreversible for centuries; in a few decades,

China's leaders had thrown away an entire field of useful technology.

How was such an act possible? Many of us have become accustomed to viewing science as a steady march toward more knowledge—indeed, used properly, that is what the scientific process *does*. But here is an example of a few decisions by a few leaders negating centuries of technological advances. It is certain that such a large step backward was made possible by the fact that China was politically centralized, effectively giving complete power to a single person. The Alliance, as portrayed in the *Firefly* universe, is not *quite* so centralized, but they are still in the position of letting a few bad decisions do enormous damage to particular scientific fields. Indeed, if they could cover up the existence of Miranda for years, surely they also have the power to quash any area of scientific research they find politically unpalatable.

But China's anti-science sentiments did not reach their zenith for another 400 years, when Mao Zedong—deeply suspicious of intellectuals—effectively stopped all education for a decade. Ironically, this misguided effort immediately followed a period in which tens of millions of Chinese starved to death because Mao could not distinguish between science and ideology.

That story revolves around a Soviet politician named Trofim Lysenko, a pseudo-scientist in charge of the USSR's Academy of Agricultural Sciences. Lysenko claimed to be a biologist, but did not actually do any science—he merely claimed politically acceptable results from his falsified and uncontrolled "research." He claimed, for example, that seeds exposed to cold conditions actually changed the heritable genetic makeup of the plant. True, this flies in the face of genetics, but Lysenko encouraged the official proclamation of genetics as a "Bourgeois pseudoscience"—its teaching and practice were banned throughout the Soviet Union. When actual biologists pointed out Lysenko's errors and misrepresentations, they were persecuted, sent to prison camps, or simply killed.

As a result, in the mid-1900s, Soviet biology ceased to be a science and became an ideological game: inconvenient truths were simply denied, while any viewpoint that agreed with the ruling political philosophy was assumed to be correct. Over in China, Mao imported these ideas and put them into agricultural practice—clearly because he was unable to distinguish between scientific knowledge and his similar ideological beliefs.

Tens of millions of Chinese starved, simply because these ideologies were passed off as scientific fact.

The lesson here is that science—the pursuit of factual knowledge using the scientific method—can be perverted and destroyed by ideology. Consider the fictional scientists who added the "Pax" to Miranda's air processors. The movie *Serenity* argues that this was ideology-driven research; they *believed* that human nature could (and should) be changed, and they evidently made some horrible mistakes as a result. Given the existence of such ideological "scientists," the mistakes almost seem inevitable. There must have been negative side effects during the original test studies; *no one* reacted to the drugs as expected. But it's not too difficult to imagine an ideologue ignoring such reports, if the inconvenient facts didn't fit with their mindset. Maybe scientists who raised questions about the whole line of research were quickly discharged from the project and sent to the Alliance's version of Siberia. Subjecting science to political whims and fancies not only degrades the science, it can even stop science from working in the first place, as in the case of Lysenko.

After Mao's disastrous "Great Leap Forward," China slowly re-embraced scientific knowledge, and they are now making great efforts to "catch up" to America and Europe. They're spending big research money on particular fields—but most of the papers they manage to get published are not important or interesting enough to be cited by anyone else. Plagiarism, bribery, and data forgery appear to be widespread; peer-review of scientific papers is more about political schmoozing than the quality of the research. And the mandated research directions are not chosen by scientists, but rather by politicians. Consider their state-directed push toward a manned space program, geared more toward boosting national pride than any novel technological achievement. Still, the overall problem that continues to hobble Chinese science is the same as it was in the Soviet Union: a simple lack of scientific freedom.

The scientific method thrives off a free exchange of ideas and information. All of the various perversions of science are naturally self-correcting, given time. That's what science does—it roots out mistakes and wrong results in a never-ending quest to understand the way things really are. And it's been remarkably successful in this, using tools such as open peer-review and reproducibility. Still, these tools only work in an open environment; you can't root out a mistake that you don't even know exists. That's the danger of secret scientific programs.

Try to envision the backstory of the Miranda tragedy. How could such a thing have happened by purportedly well-meaning individuals? No matter how ideological they were, the storyline doesn't really hold together unless you also assume a vast cloak of secrecy over the whole project. It's hard to imagine that the Alliance doesn't have any ethical safeguards on their research—but maybe those safeguards didn't apply on Miranda. After all, how could safeguards have been enforced without at least an even general knowledge of the project?

It's important to imagine the type of scientists who might have agreed to work on the Pax. The movie *Serenity* asks us to believe that well-meaning people might act in this manner, even in the absence of ethical safeguards. Well, why do scientists work for secret government programs in the first place? What might these scientists have said, when asked? Probably the usual excuses: "I'm just developing technology, not deciding how it will be used." "If I refuse to do this, they'll just hire someone else." "This has to remain secret, because no one else can be trusted to use this wisely." Throw in money and power, and yes—it's imaginable. Scientists are just as human as everyone else, and everyone likes to know a secret, everyone likes the illusion of control. But it is just that—an illusion—and scientists have been far too slow to learn this lesson, even after the experience of the development and use of the first atomic bombs.

During World War II, America concentrated many brilliant scientists and engineers under tight security in a major effort to create these weapons. Dr. Robert Oppenheimer, the physicist running the effort, kept the exchange of information relatively open (within the large project), and the scientists were able to produce two different types of atomic bombs—from scratch—in just a few years. But despite their quick work, the war in Europe had already ended, leaving only the war with Japan. Japan was effectively already defeated; they were simply holding out for face-saving surrender terms. The Russians were about to declare war against Japan, clinching the victory. All of this was known to the U.S., and yet they deployed not one, but *two* atomic bombs on civilian populations before Russian involvement could end the war on less favorable terms. The death toll was hundreds of thousands.

Would the scientists in charge of the project still have completed the bombs if they knew that Russia was about to declare war on Japan and end the conflict? We will never know—because the government never told them. And after the war, when Oppenheimer and other scientists proposed strict controls over these weapons, they were persecuted by the very government that they had served so faithfully. Then as now, scientists "in charge" of secret projects have been manipulated into producing what is desired of them, but upon success, they inevitably lose their imagined control. The weapons becoming militarized, the knowledge becomes classified, and the scientists become obsolete nuisances.

But America's primary cultural contribution to the Alliance's anti-science attitudes—our present-day link to future Miranda-style atrocities—is not a culture of secrecy. With a few exceptions, we're less guilty on that front than most. No, our primary anti-science innovation has been the rise of the Corporation.

This is ironic, because most people naturally associate Corporations with research and development. Many Corporations *require* science to keep moving their products forward via technological innovations. But to a Corporation, science—and everything else—is subservient to their only reason for existing in the first place: to make money. And if any obstacle gets in the way of that goal, the full might of the Corporation is brought to bear against it. Because of this, scientific truth is a frequent casualty of capitalism.

In the *Firefly* universe, the Mega-Corporation "Blue Sun" pops up in logos everywhere. In the DVD commentary for the pilot episode, Joss Whedon tells us that Blue Sun is a powerful corporate conglomerate: "practically half the government was Blue Sun." Sounds like the direction today's trends are pointing, especially in our modern one-dollar/one-vote society. In a separate interview, Whedon tells us that the two "Hands of Blue" men work for Blue Sun. It's not much of a stretch to imagine that Blue Sun might also have been involved with the Miranda experiments.

But would a universe with an all-powerful Blue Sun Corporation really be more anti-science than, say, the U.S. today? After all, money's influence on science isn't unique to Corporations. The same can be said of any individual willing to bribe their way out of government regulation or into a fat government contract. But the difference between an individual and a Corporation is that one is human, and one is not.

Prior to the rise of multi-national Corporations, the main influence of big money on government was through ultra-rich individuals, who actually *controlled* the pre-corporations. While these rich individuals sometimes could convince/bribe governments to favor them, at least this was still a *human* influence. And we humans tend to have a respect for the truth, especially as revealed to us by science. Indeed, the scientific method is not merely the best method we have of learning facts about our physical universe—it is our *only* reliable method. No other method has ever come close.

But inhuman Corporations have no bias toward the truth. Even though every decision and action in a Corporation is made by individuals, these organizations are probably best viewed as higher-level organisms, subject to their own Darwinian selection pressures. It is becoming less and less possible for the CEO, or the Board of Directors, or the shareholders, or any human group to actually *control* such a corporation. By the time a Corporation evolved to Blue Sun-like status, such a notion of control would probably be as laughable as if a group of cells in our bodies claimed to have control over us. Corporations use humans the same way that humans use cells—and they are "naturally selected" to perfect a single trait: a higher rate of return.

Scientific knowledge can indeed be a path to making money, but it can also be an obstacle. People will not buy a product if they know it will not work, or is harmful to them, or is harmful to those that they care about. But if people do not know such facts, they will continue to infuse the Corporation with its lifeblood cash. Manufacturing processes that make dangerous chemicals or pollution are in similar danger from scientific facts; sometimes the science implies that the processes should be regulated. From a corporate-logic perspective, science is just another commodity that needs to be controlled to maximize profit.

Still, until this millennium, Corporate efforts to relax government regulations and health warnings had met with mixed results, precisely because the scientific facts won out. So Corporations converged on the concept of attacking the scientific method itself. Much is made of the supposed adversarial nature of science and religion, but *Firefly* and *Serenity* may be correct in predicting that science's most dangerous adversary will actually be the future Corporation.

Of all the corporate anti-science strategies, the most obvious has been to simply perform Lysenko-style "research" to yield the desired outcomes. The methods by which Corporations force certain conclusions vary widely, from simple funding threats to outright data fabrication. But the result is the same; careful science is being discarded in favor of Tobacco Institute-style falsehoods. The scientific method requires an objective assessment of *all* the evidence, and, most importantly, potentially falsifiable hypotheses. A typical corporate research "hypothesis" is just the opposite: a purported truth that must be supported by any means necessary—no matter how much evidence needs to be sifted through, processed, or flat-out ignored. America is fast becoming the leader in such "research"—often in the guise of Research Institutes set up to churn out pseudo-scientific results. The end result is public confusion as to what is scientific fact, and what is spin.

And that is precisely the Corporation's desired outcome: a confused public, and scientifically illiterate politicians dependent on large campaign donations. And manufacturing false research is only half of the battle-plan; they also need to cast doubt and aspersions on the actual science. These efforts also take many forms—magnifying and playing up scientific uncertainty, packing review panels with ideological supporters, misrepresenting scientific findings, and more often than you might think, intimidating and ruining the reputations of actual scientists.

It's not hard to fast-forward these trends to see where science might end up—and sadly, it's not too far off from how things are portrayed in the *Firefly* universe. The worst scientific offense in the series is not the Pax release on Miranda; that, at least, was performed by "well-meaning" ideologues. The worst portrayal of science is what was done to River Tam.

Imagining that *these* scientists are real people takes a great deal more mental gymnastics than in the case of Miranda. Such brain experiments on unwilling and talented children seem revolting to us for a reason—they are! Being part of a secret organization can't explain why scientists would do such a thing; the ultimate cause has to be more sinister and more motivating.

Sadly, we're all aware that humans can do horrible things to other humans. Nazi "scientists" did unspeakable things to people in concentration camps. The factors that can goad a person into such ghastly behavior have been studied by psychologists; one of the key elements seems to be a mental dehumanization of the victims. Some of this is evident in the opening scene of the *Serenity* movie, where River is treated more like a piece of lab equipment than as a person. But that's not the main issue; the main issue is *why* anyone would set down this particular dehumanizing road to begin with. In River's case, the only logic that would come to such a conclusion is not a human logic, but rather a Corporate one. River's brain "experiments" have Blue Sun written all over them. Sure, developing these ultimate fighters might have been a response to the Miranda debacle and the creation of the Reavers, but it's still the response one might expect of a faceless Corporation, not human beings.

Between the experiments on River and the Pax on Miranda, the *Firefly* universe portrays scientists as easily manipulated by government and Corporate interests—and maybe they are. Scientists are people, after all, and they can be manipulated right along with everyone else. But if we don't like the future portrayed in this body of science fiction, we should take a close look at what is happening around us in real life. The only way to stop these trends is to recognize them for what they are. In recent years, scientists have been speaking out about these types of government and Corporate abuses, but quite a few scientists still don't think it's their "place" to discuss political issues. The general public is getting more involved as well, although that front is hobbled by a general misunderstanding of what good science is all about, and why it is crucially important to our society.

Are we going to end up in the kind of evil-scientist future shown in *Firefly* and *Serenity*? The show's creators have done an admirable job of showing us the dangers that are brewing in our world today—from both government and Corporate control. But of course *Firefly* and *Serenity* are just science fiction; it's up to us to make sure that such a future doesn't actually come to pass.

Ken Wharton is a physics professor at San Jose State University. He is also the author of the science fiction novel *Divine Intervention*, along with a handful of short stories. For his fiction, Ken has been a finalist for the John W. Campbell award for best new writer, the Philip K. Dick award, and the Nebula award.

When Joss Whedon put together the elements of a compelling television show (and eventually movie), it seems that he was also assembling exactly what was needed to create another tasty entree in the banquet that is Firefly. *Bridges explains the world of MMOGs, and how* Firefly *is coming back to the table yet again.*

The Virtual 'Verse

COREY BRIDGES

On December 7, 2006, the news shot worldwide via the Internet: *Firefly* was not dead.

Again.

Was it another movie? Nope. A new TV series? Nuh-uh. More comic books? Not so much. It was to be (drumroll) an MMORPG.

If you're scratching your head and muttering, "MMO-whosawhatsis?" here's the deal: MMORPG stands for "massively multiplayer online role-playing game." Called MMO or MMOG for short, this genre of game is the most compelling kind of video game to be developed in years, and it's shaking that industry to its foundations. An MMOG lets millions of people meet (and socialize, fight, cooperate, or do practically whatever they want) in a computer-generated virtual world. If you've heard of *World of Warcraft* or *Runescape*, that's what we're talking about. As compelling as single-player games can be, MMOGs are orders of magnitude more rich and interesting, mostly because it's real people you're working with or against on short-term quests or epic multi-month projects. You're surrounded by friends, enemies, and people whose agendas are downright unfathomable. It's not uncommon for people to put in twenty hours a week playing these games, and play the same game for years at a stretch. Real world relationships have been made and unmade around these games. It's a remarkable phenomenon, and it may well be the future of entertainment.

Proving that God(dess) enjoys irony, the announcement of this latest *Firefly* resurrection came from FOX. Specifically, 20th Century FOX Licensing & Merchandising Division announced with upstart video game company Multiverse that they were building the MMOG. *Wired Magazine* broke the story online, and it turned out to be big news. Crazy big international news for a humble video game that isn't even built yet. Why did this strike such a chord?

As a cofounder of Multiverse and a committed Browncoat—hi, hello, nice to meet you—I can share with you the inside story of why and how this all came about. And why, even if you don't play video games, this is good news.

So. Let's start by drilling down a bit on this whole MMOG thing.

Like any respectable form of life, MMOGs evolved out of the primordial MUD. That's M.U.D., as in "Multi-User Dungeon." Created by Roy Trubshaw and Richard Bartle in the late '70s, the first MUD was an online text-based adventure in a *Dungeons & Dragons*-like fantasy setting. Your interface to the game was a screen of text describing the room you were currently in, and you could type in short commands like "look north" or "kill rat." Other people would be logged in from their own terminals (usually at universities), so you could travel from virtual room to virtual room with your friends, killing monsters and looting treasure together; hacking and slashing your way, one paragraph at a time, into high adventure. Back in the day, MUD was a specific game, but now it's a generic term for any text-based multiplayer adventure, whether fantasy, sci-fi, or what-have-you. Even with the advent of graphics and MMOGs, MUDs are still around. The current crop, while still text-based, are remarkably complex, and quite emotionally and creatively satisfying for their denizens.

Through the '80s and early '90s, as the video game market grew, role-playing games become a popular genre, adding graphics but ironically losing the multiplayer aspect for a while. The Ultima series of fantasy role-playing video games was thought by many to be the pinnacle of the genre. Then, in 1997, *Ultima Online* was released. Inspired by the MUDs (and created by some of the top talent from the MUD industry), *Ultima Online* made its land of "Britannia" habitable by thousands of people at once, as the players logged in from all around the real world. It soon garnered more than 100,000 subscribers, making it the first mainstream MMOG.

The video game business is annoyingly similar to Hollywood in many ways, so the success of one fantasy-themed MMOG inspired other game companies to create, you guessed it, more fantasy MMOGs. And as with Hollywood, I suppose I can't really blame the risk-averse producers—after all, they have to justify the stratospheric budget it now takes to build an MMOG. The easiest way to do that is to point backward and say, "Look at that last success. We're gonna do just like that, but a little bit better!" So *Ultima Online* begat *Lineage*, which begat *EverQuest*, which begat *Dark Age of Camelot*, yadda yadda yadda, leading us to *World of Warcraft*, the 800-pound gorilla in this space today.

And what a rich gorilla it is. The Donald Trump of gorillas. Most MMOGs charge their players a monthly subscription to log in to their worlds. *World of Warcraft* sells the game itself for about $50, and then charges most players $15 a month to play. As of early 2007, the game had more than 8,000,000 players. That's about a billion dollars a year in recurring revenue—from one video game. Of course, it allegedly cost upwards of $50 million and six years to make *World of Warcraft*. And before the game launched, its development team had no idea how successful it'd be, so once again, at that kind of price tag, I have some sympathy for the guy who said, "Uh . . . how about we make yet another hack-and-slash fantasy game?"

Just to give you the full context, that's why our company, Multiverse, exists. We've built a network and the technological infrastructure for MMOGs, and our customers—game developers—build their games on top of that. It saves years of engineering work and millions of dollars for the development teams. And yes, the games built on Multiverse can all be radically different from one another. The whole reason why we created Multiverse is because MMOGs can be so much more than the current glut of fantasy-themed men-in-tights games. (Instead of men in tights, might we suggest Captain Tightpants?) There are entirely new gameplay elements that can be added to MMOGs. Entirely new subject matter that can be covered in these games—how about a mature sci-fi game that's not all about killing, or a social game built for young girls, or an educational game that teaches students about the works of William Shakespeare? These are all games that are being built on the Multiverse platform, because the game developers can now afford to take chances. We're betting on the proposition that if we make it economically feasible to experiment, then we'll see innovation.

Which brings us to *Firefly*.

As it happens, movie director James Cameron (*Titanic*, *Terminator*, *T2*, *Aliens*, et cetera) and his Oscar-winning producer Jon Landau are on the Multiverse board of advisors. They introduced us to FOX, who wanted to learn more about these MMOG things the hip kids are into. Multiverse CEO Bill Turpin and I were happy to meet with FOX and share our thoughts. At one point, they gave us a list of properties they own, and asked which of them would make for great MMOGs. I sort of pretended to look at the list—"Sure, sure. Great properties, fantastic. What about *Firefly*? Do you still have those rights?" Sure enough, they did, and from that point on, it wasn't about two companies searching for a way to work together. Suddenly, we all had a specific mission. Turns out FOX is full of Browncoats. (Who knew?) They loved the idea of a *Firefly* MMOG, and put major effort into getting buyoff from the powers-that-be to make it happen. There were many superstars, but the two gentlemen who had the vision to champion this from the very beginning were Elie Dekel and Luke Letizia. A huge *Firefly* fan named Adam Kline joined FOX mid-process and helped work through some remaining roadblocks, making the final deal happen.

And the deal is this: Multiverse has "optioned" the *Firefly* property, which we will give to an independent game development team, who will build the game on the Multiverse platform. Multiverse doesn't make games ourselves—we just want to choose the team who is worthy of making a *Firefly* game. A game that, we're convinced, could be the best. MMOG. Ever.

Now, why is that? What makes *Firefly* a great property to build an MMOG around? Let me count the ways.

First up, visuals. Mainstream MMOGs do well when they have a wide range of wild-looking locations and inhabitants. *Firefly* covers that nicely. The settings we've seen in just fourteen episodes include areas that could pass for the American Old West, rural China, Victorian Europe, wild mash-ups of countless cultures in crazy bazaars (such as on Persephone), and shiny high-tech sci-fi cities. And who knows what's on the planets we didn't see? Plus, let's not forget the whole spaceship thing. Grimy spaceships, sterile spaceships, cockpits, kitchens, cargo holds, space malls—even exteriors for the EVA-minded among us.

In addition to varied locales, most MMOGs offer a wide range of professions for the players to choose from. *Firefly* showed us captains, engineers, mercenaries, bounty hunters, preachers, soldiers, police, and let's not forget space hookers. (Y'know, it behooves me to say at this juncture that all these aspects are what makes the prospect of a *Firefly* MMOG exciting. I'm not saying they'll necessarily all be in the game. That's for the design and development team to determine. Me, though, I'm going on record here as wanting to play as a Companion.)

A common element of MMOGs is quests. These provide a bit of structured gameplay for players who don't want to explore the world randomly, running into happenstance adventures. The quests in MMOGs are usually pretty straightforward—take this package from here to there, kill the monsters threatening this town, and so on. But call 'em missions, and you've got the underlying structure of the show itself—a crew that smuggles goods from sellers to buyers. Most MMOGs these days tend to offer static, pre-written quests, but what if a *Firefly* game had a more dynamic universe, where the quests that are available to you are generated based on your history or the worlds around you? And what if they included their own complications? Say you've stolen some cargo from a well-guarded train, just like Niska hired you to. But then you learn—oops—that you've just taken medical supplies from a town that really needs them. What do you do? Complete the mission at the cost of your soul? Or return the goods to the town, causing Niska to be . . . very disappointed in you? Suddenly you've got bounty hunters—perhaps even other players on their own missions—looking to haul your well-meaning butt in to him. That's good gameplay.

The show is largely about consequences, and the game would do well to reflect that. Make whatever choices you want, but be warned that they stay with you. They determine how other people—whether players or non-player characters—treat you.

Like stories, MMOGs need conflict. It's a shame that there's none in the *Firefly* 'verse. No, wait—that's the one resource they *do* have in abundance. There's large conflict, whether hot wars (Alliance versus Independents, if the game is set during the Unification War) or cold (tyranny of the Alliance over the Outer Rim worlds, if the game is set contemporary to the show). And of course, there's smaller conflict, where one crew's goals are at odds with another group's. In the show, we even see conflict within one group (why does Jayne figure so prominently in most of the examples that come to mind?). In the show, the conflict can be violent, or it can be much more subtle: jockeying for social status or negotiating against someone else for economic benefit.

For game purposes, having at least a couple of those arenas of conflict—say, physical and economic—would make for very interesting play. And having that conflict pit you against real humans (as opposed to computerized opponents) could be more interesting still. By the way, games that have a player-versus-player (PVP) element can be very exciting, but can also become really overwhelming or annoying if you're not in the mood for it. Many successful MMOGs make PVP play consensual. For example, in many fantasy games, another player can't attack you unless you're in PVP mode, or unless you explicitly accept a challenge to dual. Something like that might work in the *Firefly* MMOG. It'll be a tough balancing act for the game designer; I've spoken to hundreds of Browncoats since we announced the MMOG, and they're roughly split on the contentious question of PVP.

As important as competition is, it's actually competition's flip-side—cooperation—that ultimately provides the fuel that drives MMOGs. Case in point: fantasy MMOGs usually let you form groups and guilds. A group is a temporary collection of people that you can join for a session of gameplay—sort of like a pickup basketball game, but without all that bothersome, shweaty exercise. A guild is a larger and more persistent player-created group that provides certain benefits for members—from special titles, to free items, to a private "club" of friends you can call on for special epic missions. Guilds and groups are player-run, so every one of them is different, but well-constructed MMOGs promote guilds and groups through special game features. Guilds can easily take on major out-of-game significance as they become social hubs for many players' lives. Many veteran MMOG players swear that cooperative play is the most compelling and addictive aspect of MMOGs.

I think that Browncoats will get behind that—after all, who wouldn't want to assemble their own crew to undertake missions together, to build a life for themselves around their ship? Or what about other scenarios that are only glimpsed in the show? Why not try your hand as a settler, and work with your friends to tame a land and bring your brand of civilization to some outer-rim planet? Or how about you and your cohorts create a criminal syndicate, planning and doling out nefarious tasks to your minions? The structure for gameplay is provided by the game, but the negotiating, the planning, and the implementation, that comes from other humans.

This integration of the human factor into a video game gives rise to that holy grail of gameplay: emergent behavior. Players of an MMOG usually develop not only their own customs—like don't use ALL-CAPS to talk, because it's like yelling, and no one will want to group with you—but also their own cultures. Shared experiences and citizenship (even in a synthetic land) give rise to specialized communication, in-jokes, even values and beliefs. Such culture—such *community*—rises from and in turn supports the experience of the MMOG itself.

Let's take a step back for a minute and think about that. The thing most responsible for keeping MMOGs alive is community. Now let's see . . . what else has community kept alive? Maybe a TV show that became a movie? Wait, wait, don't tell me. . . . That's right—*Police Squad*. Oh, wait—the Leslie Nielson anthology is next month. I should probably just stick with *Firefly*. The little show that could. The show that refused to stay dead. *Firefly* gave rise to the fans, and the fans returned the favor by resurrecting the show. As comics, as a movie, as a culture. And now, as a virtual world. The object lesson of *Firefly* is that community can do the impossible. Without the incredible phenomenon of the Browncoats, the FOX execs might not have signed off on the *Firefly* MMOG.

In return, I'd like the *Firefly* MMOG to integrate, support, and build on that existing community. For example, I think a great element of a *Firefly* MMOG could be "shindigs." If you've never been to a Browncoat shindig in the real world, you're missing out. Nominally, it's any gathering of Browncoats, but at the more extravagant ones, guests dress up all fancy-like, in their ball gowns or Victorian-era tuxedos or even their dusters. So far, shindigs have mostly been confined to the real world. But

I think it would be a gracious "thank you" to the Browncoat community if the *Firefly* MMOG could enable hundreds or thousands of Browncoats to log in, don their digital finery, and party the night away with their friends from all around the world.

I think shindigs give us a clue why the *Firefly* MMOG news was so well-received: people want to be there, in the 'verse. They want to tell—to live—their own stories.

Which brings us to what the *Firefly* MMOG *won't* be. *Firefly* was a TV show about specific people. A fantastically well-written, compelling crew of people, played by the most perfectly cast actors ever. We all love them and want to see more of them, but an MMOG would be an awkward medium to advance the stories of the crew members of *Serenity*. That's not what MMOGs do well yet. MMOGs are places, not narratives. Perhaps you'll be able to run into Mal and crew (or Badger, or Niska, or Saffron, for that matter) from time to time in the virtual 'verse, and get missions from them, or work with them. But when you play the MMOG, it's got to be *your* story. Your journey.

Happily, it's a fun 'verse for a journey. It's no accident that Joss Whedon built *Firefly* with the elements of a great MMOG. After all, what is storytelling, if not the process of building a virtual world? When you make a TV show, there are at least two things you need to nail: compelling characters and (especially for sci-fi) a compelling, internally consistent universe. Joss didn't just create the backgrounds of his characters, he also filled out a whole solar system of interlocking cultures, and created a 500-year backstory to explain how we got there from here. And the show gives us only a glimpse of that. The 'verse has depth and breadth yet unexplored, and *that* is where an MMOG shines.

So that's chapter one of the story of the *Firefly* MMOG. It's been great for Multiverse to get the attention, and it's good to be working with FOX, but honestly—we just wanted to play a *Firefly* MMOG, and this seemed like the best way to make that happen. We're selfish that way, but we didn't think other Browncoats would mind.

And here, since it's just us Browncoats, lean closer. I'll tell you the real secret of the *Firefly* MMOG. We want the game to be such a big damn success that studio execs will be tripping over themselves to make more TV shows or movies.

A pipe-dream? An impossibility? Pfah. We're Browncoats. We do the impossible before breakfast.

COREY BRIDGES is co-founder and executive producer of Multiverse.

An episode of television grows and evolves during the planning of it. And then again during writing and rewriting. What emerges often seems miraculous the way the product of any evolutionary process seems miraculous. The resultant structure has that kind of completeness, almost inevitability, that seems to deny any sort of gradual development. It seems to have fallen, full-formed, to Earth. The episode described here has that feeling. But it's not a miracle, it's the endpoint of a process, and as such it's worthwhile to cut into it and look at it, because it's a beautiful object, and its architecture is beautiful.

Keep in mind, however, that the structure might not tell you anything about how to create such an object, any more than looking at the body of any one dead finch teaches us how to make one ourselves. (Although you're welcome to try. Start with a bunch of feathers. . . .)

Firefly and Story Structure, Advanced

GEOFF KLOCK

Matt Fraction and Gabriel Bá's *Casanova* is one of the most striking and original comic books to emerge in the last twenty years. Ironically, the book's originality derives from its total willingness to absorb any and all possible influences for its pulp-sci-fi-meets-James-Bond insanity. In the free-form essay in the back of the third issue, Fraction discusses his planning process for *Casanova* #3: "Mission to Yerba Muerta!"—a story that jumps around three different time periods. It owes a lot, he says, to his "favourite episode of the late, lamented FIREFLY":

> There's an episode called OUT OF GAS. In it, a thing on the titular spaceship our intrepid heroes travel on breaks, leaving them more or less OUT OF GAS.
>
> And it opens with our main intrepid hero bleeding to death in a de-powered, dark, and otherwise abandoned ship. Then the credits come up.

> BEST! OPEN! EVER!
>
> What follows is a story that's fractured into three timelines, each one feeding into and informing the next. It's a bit of narrative bravura, a piece of writing that's pure art for art's sake and I know that, as a novice, I learned a hell of a lot from studying it some. So we interwove between Cass' three faces in some kind of . . . retardedly obscure tribute to OUT OF GAS.[1]

That alone should make us want to take a closer look at the thing. What I want to do here is "study it some" in order to better appreciate its narrative bravura. After breaking it down into component scenes, labelled to make clear how the episode shifts between time frames, I will examine how all these transitions deftly work to make the episode a masterpiece. The typical aim of an academic essay is to help in the understanding of something essentially complex and difficult. What is so amazing about "Out of Gas" is that, though it is complex, it needs no explanation because its complexity is rendered so simply and effectively. It can be more fully appreciated, however, and that is my purpose here.

In "Out of Gas," three distinct time periods are braided together: the origin of the *Firefly* crew, the disaster the crew must deal with, and Mal left alone and wounded (which leads into the episode's ending). For easy reference I will label these time periods 1, 2, and 3, respectively. After these numbers I put together a probable chronological order (2.1, 2.2, and so on). With one exception (scene 1.1), within periods 1, 2, or 3, scenes are in chronological order. I have also marked what person, action, or place marks the transition between the distinct time periods (what is continuous in both the new and the old time period), since those transitions are the centerpiece of my essay. For reference, I have included schematics of the ship, and labelled where each scene takes place.

---

[1] The ellipsis is Fraction's.

Firefly's "Out of Gas" Act and Scene Breakdown

Teaser

(3.1) "Out of Gas" opens with shots of the empty and dark Firefly ship—the ship itself in space, the bridge, the hallway out of the bridge, the kitchen, the hallway to the engine room, the infirmary, the cargo bay. Suddenly Mal collapses on screen. *Transition: a beam of light hits his face and he hears voices, but the beam is a memory of the light that entered the ship when he first showed it to Zoe, and the voices are only memories as well.*

(1.2) Zoe is not impressed and calls the ship a death-trap. Mal tells her she has no imagination and that she should try and see past "what she [the ship] is" to "what she can be." Zoe deflates his ideals by pointing to something (off camera) dead or dying on the cargo bay floor, right where Mal is in Time 3. Mal wants to hire people to run the ship so he can be free; they walk out the inside cargo bay door. *Transition: the door in the cargo bay.*

(3.2) We return to the collapsed Mal in the darkened ship (the door in the cargo bay is behind him) and discover he is bleeding.

Act One

(3.3) In the darkened cargo bay Mal struggles to lift a piece of equipment. *Transition: the camera pans upward, through the floor, to the kitchen (located above the cargo bay); when we reach the kitchen it is Time 2.*

(2.1) We flashback to the assembled crew laughing in the kitchen. We learn that the ship will be travelling through a desolate area. It is Simon's birthday, and Kaylee has made him a cake. As he goes to blow out the candles the lights flicker. River says, "Fire," and a fire rips through the ship. The crew scrambles into action. Zoe is hurt, much of the ship is sealed off, and the fire is ejected through the cargo bay doors. *Transition: the cargo bay.*

(3.4) From the cargo bay Mal continues to carry the piece of equipment. His bloody hands reach the infirmary doors. *Transition: the infirmary.*

(2.2) We flashback to Zoe being brought into the infirmary, in shock. Mal instructs Kaylee to figure out what went wrong. Kaylee says, "She ain't movin'," and we think she is referring to Zoe until she continues, "*Serenity* ain't movin'." Kaylee leaves.

(2.3) Wash wants to stay with Zoe but Mal insists that he go to the bridge so that they can figure out how bad the situation is. Mal commands and intimidates him until he goes. *Transition: Wash.*

(1.3) We flashback to Wash inspecting the ship for the first time, as Mal attempts to hire him. Wash has a ridiculous moustache, dating him horribly (even in a story that takes place in the future). Zoe, his future wife, insists that some unidentifiable thing about him bothers her. In their conversation Mal mentions their "genius" mechanic; we expect to see Kaylee but it is just a ditzy-looking guy named Bester. *Transition: Zoe (who again says Wash bothers her).*

(2.4) We return to Zoe in shock in the infirmary; Simon administers an adrenalin injection. *Transition: the adrenalin injection.*

(3.5) In the infirmary Mal cries out in pain and gives himself an adrenalin shot. *Transition: the infirmary, and a flashback of Kaylee's voice.*

(2.5) Kaylee is asking if Zoe will be okay (just as we worry if Mal will be okay in Time 3). Kaylee lets Mal know that the ship is dead in the water and that they only have a few hours of oxygen left.

Act Two

(2.6) Inara checks in on the injured Zoe, who is still unconscious. In the course of their conversation Simon begins to describe the horrors of dying of suffocation.

(2.7) Shepherd Book reads his Bible and has a conversation with River who tells him he is afraid. She adds that they will not die of suffocation but of the cold.

(2.8) Mal checks to see if Wash has sent out a distress beacon. Wash tells him it is pointless, that no one will pick it up. Mal has a long-shot plan to boost the signal and disrupt the navigation of any ships that pass by. Jayne comes by and cautions them on using too much air. *Transition: the warning about air.*

(3.6) As the computer announces that oxygen is almost depleted, Mal struggles to carry the equipment down the engine room hallway. *Transition: the hallway to the engine room.*

(1.4) Mal walks the hallway to the engine room to meet with Bester, who was supposed to fix the engine. Bester is having sex with someone in the engine room. Bester tells Mal that the ship won't fly but the woman he was having sex with corrects him. It is Kaylee. She fixes it in an instant, bringing the engine to life. *Transition: the hallway of the engine room.*

(2.9) Mal looks for Kaylee, who is despondent in the engine room. She shows him that a piece of the engine has failed and tells him they need a new one. He gives her a pep talk. *Transition: the engine room.*

(3.7) Mal attempts to get the part into the engine. It falls through a hole in the floor and he shakes.

Act Three

(2.10) Mal recaps the situation for the crew: life support is failing. He tells them he wants them to leave in the short range shuttles, in opposite directions, in the hope someone will find them. He will stay behind. Wash goes to devise a way to call the shuttles back if someone answers the beacon. Inara tries to talk him out of staying behind as he heads for her ship. *Transition: Inara's shuttle.*

(1.5) In a flashback we see Mal showing Inara her short range shuttle inside Firefly. He tells her it will get her where she needs to go and bring her back home again. She tells him that he wants her, wants her on his ship, because she will grant his ship respectability. He asks her what it is she is running from. He agrees not to call her "whore" again. *Transition: Mal and Inara.*

(2.11) On the bridge of the ship, Inara tells Mal that he should come on her shuttle, that no one has to die alone. Mal tells her everyone dies alone.

(2.12) Wash explains that if a ship makes contact, all Mal has to do is hit a button to recall the ships.

(2.13) Jayne tells Mal to lock the doors behind him to conserve air. Everyone boards the shuttles and launches, leaving him alone. Mal locks the doors of each room—cargo bay, both kitchen doors—and waits on the bridge for someone to signal.

(2.14) Eventually someone does signal, but Mal must negotiate with the other captain to get him to board the ship and help. Mal says he will not open the door unless he sees the part he needs. When they do board, Mal has air to breathe, but the newcomers have come with guns to rob him.

Act Four

(2.15) The salvagers investigate the ship. *Transition: Mal at gunpoint, hands in the air.*

(1.6) We flashback to Jayne robbing Mal and Zoe at gunpoint (their hands are in the air). Mal offers Jayne money to turn on his partners and join the Firefly's crew and he accepts. *Transition: Mal at gunpoint, hands in the air.*

(2.16) The head salvager shoots Mal (hands in the air) in the stomach and tells him they are taking his ship. Mal pulls a gun and demands the part he needs. At gunpoint he forces them to leave, but then collapses on the floor from his wound, into the shot from the teaser. We again get shots of the rooms on the ship, with blood stains to show where Mal has been: cargo bay, infirmary, and finally the engine room. *Transition: the engine room.*

(3.8) In the engine room, Mal retrieves the part he dropped and gets it into the engine, starting it. He struggles through the ship toward Wash's button—we get shots of the hallway out of the engine room, the kitchen, the hallway to the bridge, and the bridge—where he collapses. *Transition: Mal unconscious.*

(3.9) The screen goes black as we hear lines of dialogue from earlier in the episode. Mal awakes in the medical room, where everyone is gathered and Zoe is awake. Mal never reached the button; they came back anyway, and saved his life. *Transition: a mixed voiceover from the past (from all three time periods shown in the episode).*

(1.1) A salesman is trying to interest Mal in a ship that he says will be with him the rest of his life. But Mal has spotted another ship—*Serenity*.

<See Figure A on next page>

Analysis

Any good screenwriting book—Robert McKee's *Story: Substance, Style, and the Principles of Screenwriting*, David Howard's *How to Build a Great Screenplay*, Syd Field's *Screenwriting* (and related books), Paul Joseph Gulino's *Screenwriting: The Sequence Approach*—will tell you that story structure is everything. *Firefly*'s "Out of Gas" follows the standard structure of a one-hour television drama closely: it begins with a teaser, then the story is told in four acts, essentially four mini-stories each with their own beginning, middle, and end; the end of one act propels the drama in the subsequent act. But Joss Whedon and Tim Minear are such accomplished storytellers that—like good jazz musicians playing off a standard chord progression—they are able to introduce and play with the massive complication of moving freely between three distinct time periods: Mal's journey alone through the ship, the story of how

Figure A

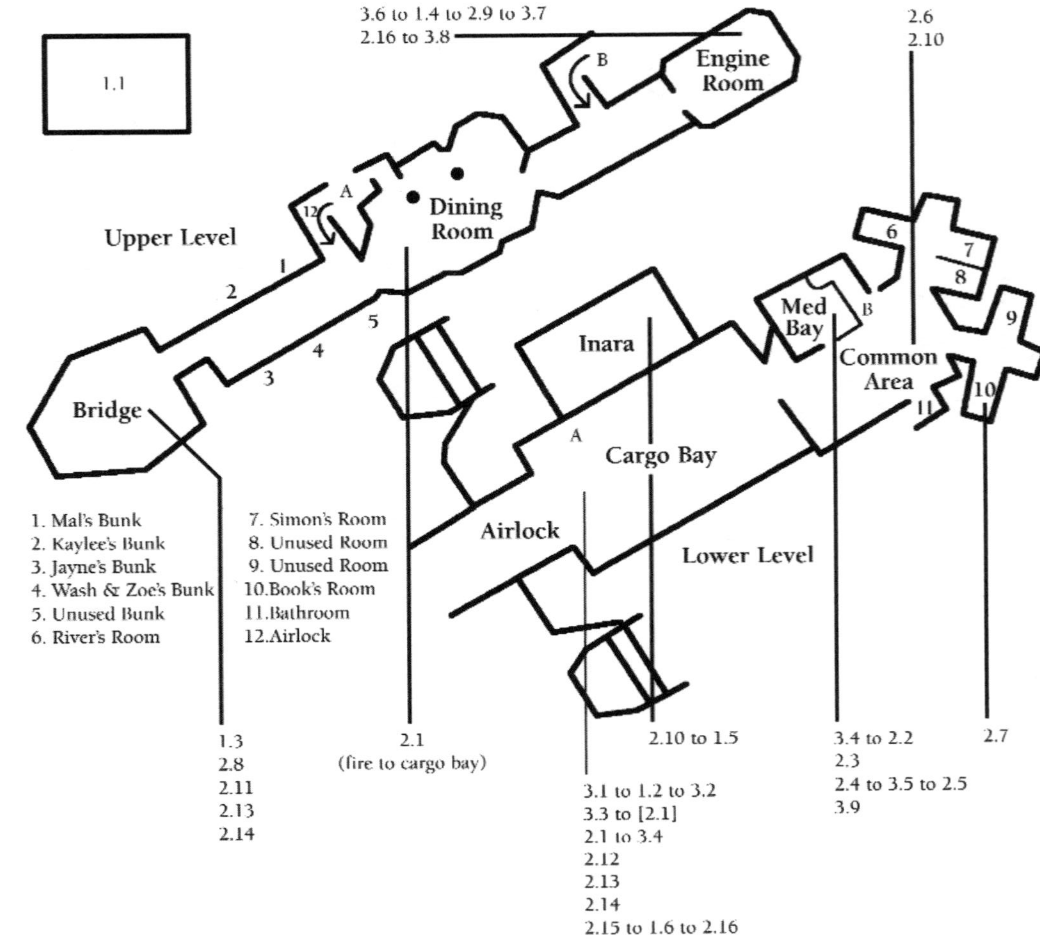

Figure adapted from http://www.fireflywiki.org/img/serenity-map.jpg

Mal got in that position, and the story of how Mal found the ship and gathered his crew.

Though it is not emphasized in the episode at all, the three time periods resonate with River's psychic abilities. Just as River is able to read minds, just as she is able to know what is happening before anyone else in the crew knows (she says, "Fire," just before there is one), we are able to watch two of the time periods knowing more than the characters we are watching. When Zoe points to a spot on the floor and notes that something seems to be dying there, we know that, in the future, Mal will be dying on that exact spot. When Zoe tells Mal that something about Wash bothers her we know they will eventually be happily married and that Wash will get rid of that horrible moustache. Minear uses the structure to create a complex emotional tone: Zoe making fun of Mal is complicated by a dark knowledge that he will be badly wounded in the spot she points to; Zoe's worries about Wash, we know, will dissolve. For this reason, River is hardly in the episode at all—her psychic abilities would needlessly complicate an episode already quite difficult. On a more pedestrian level the flashback structure allows the audience to quickly grasp what is going on in many of the scenes where exposition would be difficult if not impossible—Zoe getting the adrenalin shot in Time 2 instantly explains what Mal needs the needle for in Time 3; Kaylee explaining to Mal about the part that has failed in Time 2 explains what he is doing in the engine room in Time 3.

Lost is structured around flashbacks not unlike the flashbacks in "Out of Gas"—we experience the main characters in two different time periods and are often asked to compare. But *Lost*'s flashbacks are unified by theme—in both the present narrative and in the flashback we get to see John Locke overcoming physical limitations, for instance. *Firefly*'s, on the other hand, are unified by *space*, specifically the space of the ship. Each Time 1 flashback shows a member of the Firefly's crew that did not join the ship in the pilot seeing the ship for the first time—Zoe, Wash, Kaylee, Inara, Jayne, and finally Mal himself. If structure is everything the screenwriting guides insist it is, it is doubly important in "Out of Gas" because the structure of the episode is held together by the structure of the ship.

The space of the ship provides the anchor for the time—the ship itself holds all three times together. We know the structure of the ship is massively important to how the episode works since we are given "tours" of the ship no less than three times: the episode opens with a shot of each room, empty and dark (3.1); we see each room as Mal closes the doors behind him to conserve air (2.13); and we see all the rooms again as Mal attempts to get from the engine to the bridge to hit the button that will recall the crew (3.8). The initial "objective" tour—a tour the director is giving us without a character to follow—traces the ship from the bridge to the cargo bay. The second two tours follow Mal on the same path in the opposite direction with opposite results. The first time Mal heads off to the bridge with every expectation that that is where he will die (though he is saved by the transmission); the second time he goes to the bridge to recall his crew and save their lives (but he collapses).

The ship anchors the structure of the episode and reinforces its theme, which is how the ship is the emotional hub of the show. Mal describes to Zoe how it means freedom for him and his crew; Zoe meets her husband on the ship; Kaylee feels a deep emotional wound when the ship breaks down; Inara is running from something and this ship is her refuge; even Jayne is not unmoved, as he turns on his original crew for the promise of his own room on the ship. The final scene of the episode is Mal first laying his eyes on the ship. The flashbacks point directly to the total importance of the ship, and again a contrast with *Lost* is very helpful here. Because the concept of *Lost* demands that all the events of the show take place on an island in a very narrow time frame,[2] *Lost*'s flashbacks are the only opportunity to play on a wider stage: flashbacks allow the creators to tell stories in L.A., Australia, Korea, and Scotland. The flashback's in "Out of Gas" could allow Minear to tell stories all over the universe, but every single one is centred on the same ship that the primary story, as part of its concept, cannot leave.

Film narratives string together individual scenes, and normally we have no trouble understanding how one scene connects to the next, especially if the scenes are chronological. Even when jumping from a plot to a sub-plot, we often instinctively understand that the plot is taking place at about the

[2] At the time of this writing only six episodes of season three of *Lost* have aired. The one exception to the sentence above is in the season two finale, in which we see, for a moment, Desmond's love, Penelope, communicating with a ship in an icy landscape.

same time as the sub-plot. Occasionally, however, the audience may need a clear and concrete point of transition to carry us from one scene to the next. One way to transition smoothly from one scene to the next is to focus on a single object that will be in both scenes: the most famous transition in film history is in Stanley Kubrick's *2001: A Space Odyssey*—the ape throws a bone in the air and we transition to a bone-shaped orbiting nuclear missile platform in space. The gap in time is closed by the object—a human tool appears in both scenes. "Out of Gas" has such a complex structure that each transition from one time period to another must be handled with care, so that the episode is as clear as possible.

Though occasionally we transition from one time period to the next by focusing on the same character in both periods, most of the transitions in "Out of Gas" use the ship itself as the anchor between the past and present. Mal dying in the cargo bay becomes Mal showing Zoe the cargo bay for the first time; Zoe's adrenalin shot in the infirmary takes us to Mal in the infirmary, giving himself an adrenalin shot.

Act two has a particularly complex use of a single space to transition among three time periods. In act two the engine room and the hallway to the engine room serve as the points of transition no less than three times in a row—the four key scenes are a wounded Mal attempting to get the piece to the engine room (3.6), Mal meeting Kaylee for the first time in the engine room (1.4), Mal attempting to comfort Kaylee in the engine room (2.9), and Mal dropping the piece in the engine room (3.7). The transitions are tricky because of the direction Mal is travelling when they occur. The first transition (between 3.6 and 1.4) uses Mal heading to install the new part to go back to when Mal entered the engine room and met Kaylee for the first time. The second transition, however, goes from Mal *leaving* the engine room (having just hired Kaylee) to him going in the opposite direction (in Time 2) to comfort Kaylee. Then we transition to Mal in the engine room, dropping the piece. The importance of the failure of the engine is doubled in the structure of the episode as Mal can not get away from this room; in these scenes he is a bit like Bill Murray in *Groundhog Day*, forced to revisit the same place over and over until he gets it right (and like "Out of Gas" *Groundhog Day* involves time being distorted). It is thus important that Mal has hired, at first, the wrong mechanic—he is going to have to try again until he gets it right.

While the ship is the focus of the episode, every part of the ship is not given equal weight. With the exception of the scene where Zoe first meets Wash on the bridge, the bridge, the hallway from the bridge to the dining room, the dining room, the common area in front of the infirmary, and Book's room are not part of the deep flashbacks of Time 1 and a few only show up briefly in Time 3 as Mal attempts to get to the button on the bridge. Inara's shuttle only transitions once from Time 2 to Time 1. The medical bay is the point of several transitions but only between Time 2 and Time 3. There are only two points on the ship which transition among all three time periods: the cargo bay and the engine room. The engine room is obviously the most important room in the episode because the engine failure guides the entire episode. The cargo bay is the second major point of transition because it is the entrance and exit of the ship, the thematic center of the flashbacks about how the crew first joined.

The only other point where all three time periods transition is in Mal's head—in 3.1 and 3.9 we experience the rush of Mal's memories as voiceovers. Both of these transitions give us an audio glimpse of the final scene (1.1): we hear the salesman say "She's a real beauty, ain't she?" in both. In the second voiceover—moments before we transition to 1.1—we hear lines from all three time periods as Mal's memories reach from the episode's final chronological point to its earliest chronological point, and pick up key lines from in between, finally interrupted by Mal's overhearing Wash saying something unimportant to Zoe:

> SALESMAN: Real beauty, ain't she? (1.1)
> KAYLEE: *Serenity*'s not moving. (2.2)
> WASH: When your miracle gets here pound this button once. . . . (2.12)
> INARA: Mal, come with us. (2.11)
> MAL: Everybody dies alone. (2.11)
> WASH: I'll run up there and scrape off a piece. (3.9)

In each of these mashed-up memory voiceovers we are being prepared, in an extraordinarily subtle effect, for the final scene of the episode, in which the salesman will say "Real beauty, ain't she?" Because we have heard the line twice before—even though we did not know what it meant—it will feel especially important and familiar. As we recall the line, Whedon and Minear will achieve a small emotional burst to end the episode on, an effect they will playfully undercut as they reveal it is a description of a ship Mal will be completely uninterested in.

Most of the time period transitions not centered around the physical structure of the ship (and they are few) are centered on people, but, interestingly, only in romantic pairs. Wash and Zoe (husband and wife) each act as a point of transition: Mal yelling at Wash in the infirmary transitions to Mal introducing Zoe to Wash on the bridge; Zoe being bothered by Wash in the hallway out of the bridge transitions to Zoe crashing in the infirmary. Mal and Inara's chilly first meeting in her shuttle transitions to Inara trying to talk Mal out of staying behind with the ship, a hint of the intimacy we feel they will eventually have. It is important that the transitions not centered on the ship itself are centered on romantic relationships because they set up the final transition to the last scene, Mal first seeing the ship. Seeing this final transition in the context of the other three "personal" transitions emphasizes that this final scene is a love-at-first-sight scene. The only flashback that does not take place on the ship itself—the only scene in the episode that does not take place on the ship itself—is Mal seeing the ship from afar and falling in love with it.

"Out of Gas" tells a science fiction love story, but rather than a man and a woman against the world and time, "Out of Gas" shows us love among a rag-tag "family" of outsiders, and the love between a man and a ship, the symbol of his freedom. Whedon and Minear's unique story structure, in scrambling its three time periods, shows how the love of the characters is the thing that holds the story, and the show, together.

Geoff Klock is the author of *How to Read Superhero Comics and Why* (Continuum 2002) and the upcoming *Imaginary Biographies: Misreading the Lives of the Poets* (Continuum 2007), based off his doctoral thesis at Balliol College, Oxford. The first book applies Harold Bloom's poetics of influence to comic books; the second argues that the bizarre portrayal of historical writers in nineteenth and twentieth-century poetry constitutes a genre (and will be followed by a companion book on film). His blog—*Remarkable: Short Appreciations of Poetry, Comics, Film, Television, and Music*—can be found at geoffklock.blogspot.com. He lives in New York City.

REFERENCES

Fraction, Matt and Gabriel Bá. *Casanova* #3. Berkeley: Image Comics, 2006.

A bias against space Westerns strikes me as being as strange, and as unfounded, as a prejudice against left-handed congressmen. Like people, works of fiction are individual, and to condemn them in arbitrary categories is to completely miss that. Since I had no idea this particular bias existed, I was interested to hear more. Bethke does an excellent job of laying out the history and reasoning behind this surprisingly pervasive prejudice.

Cut 'Em Off at the Horsehead Nebula!

BRUCE BETHKE

So we're sitting in the rec room, watching *Serenity* on the big screen with the surround sound cranked. Only we can never simply *watch* a movie: there's just one degree of separation between us and the folks who did *Mystery Science Theater 3000*, and I'm afraid that all too often, it's audible.

For example, right now Larry the Astronomer is in hog heaven, trying to work out the celestial mechanics of the *Firefly* universe in his head. ("Maybe if we start with a couple of super-Jovian worlds orbiting the blue-white primary in a Sirius-type binary system, and most of these so-called worlds are actually terraformed moons. . . .") But John the Screenwriter is having some trouble understanding why I'm so excited about a movie based on a TV series that was canceled halfway through the first season. I briefly consider dragging out the DVD boxed set and forcing him to watch at least the two-hour series premiere, but there's not enough time for that, so I settle for, "John, think of this as the anti-Trek."

That's a good opening gambit. We've long since agreed that Star Trek's Federation is some kind of intrusive and heavily militarized police state. Now we only argue over whether it's a socialist or fascist utopia.

"*Firefly*," I continue, "is set some five centuries in the future, and six years after the end of a failed war for independence against the Alliance:

the oppressive central government. Now, Mal here—"

John interrupts. "—is Han Solo with an actual backstory. I get that. He's Rick Blaine with a spaceship instead of a nightclub. He's a classic lost paladin; an embittered losing-side war vet with a junk freighter, struggling to eke out a living on the fringes of civilization and the law. But underneath that rough exterior he's still got his honor, his pride, and that sense of justice that forces him to get involved and become a big damn hero, from time to time. I *get* that about him. I *like* him. And the blond guy—"

"Wash."

"He's a classic comic-relief sidekick, who gets to have all the emotional reactions the paladin can never show. Now, this tough chick—"

"Zoe."

"She served with Mal in the war, didn't she? Because she's got the whole calls-him-'sir'-even-when-she-doesn't-say-it-out-loud thing going, which is done very nicely. I also think it's really nice to see a woman in the role of the engine room grease-monkey, because she reminds me of my first wife and her intimate relationship with her Jaguar XJ6.

"But the doctor—Simon?—there's obviously some bad blood between him and Mal, so I'd have to guess he has a little black bag full of patent medicines that save the day on a regular basis and make him worth putting up with, while his sister, Buffy—"

"River."

"—is obviously the ninety-pound pixie who can toss around men three times her size when she gets mad, and I suspect she's the focus of the entire plot. But the one character here I'm really having trouble getting a fix on is *him*." John points at the screen.

"Jayne?"

"Yeah, him. I mean, clearly, he's big and tough, none too bright, obsessed with weapons, and probably worth his weight in gold in a fight. But *Jane*? What kind of name is that? Is this like 'A Boy Named Sue'? Is that why he's so surly?"

"No," I say. "J-A-Y-N-"

"Oh," John says, as understanding dawns. "*Jayne*. As in, John Wayne. Okay, I get it now. So how soon do we meet the PTP and the HHG?"

It's my turn to be confused. "The what?"

"The Preacher with a Troubled Past and the Hooker with a Heart of Gold.

They must be in this story. It just wouldn't be the same without them."

I start to tell John about Shepherd Book and Inara, but then decide to keep him in the dark a little longer. "What makes you say that?"

"Because," he says, "you're wrong, Bruce. This is not the anti-Trek.

"This is *Stagecoach in Space*."

You must understand: in the world of science fiction, there is no deadlier insult than to call something "a Western set in space." As a science fiction writer you're permitted to lift freely from any other period in history and any other body of world folklore *except* the American Old West. Authors have made entire careers out of recycling Asian, African, and Amerindian folk tales in the guise of science fiction stories, and the whole genre of fantasy can fairly be described as one endless series of Christianity-free repackagings of Celtic, Nordic, and Germanic fairy tales and heroic myths. Even the most successful science fiction franchise of all time, Star Wars, has been described quite accurately as being simply an anthology of Japanese samurai stories (most notably *The Tale of Heike*), gussied up in science fiction drag and trotted out onstage to near-unanimous critical acclaim and worldwide commercial success.

But put your hero on horseback without also giving him a sword or a lance—give him a Winchester laser rifle, a Colt proton blaster, or a broad-brimmed Stetson hat to protect his skin from the searing UV radiation of the local blue-white main sequence star—write a story that in any way reflects the actual experience and well-documented history of the American Civil War and the subsequent exploration and settling of the lands between the Mississippi River and the Pacific coast—and sooner or later some fool critic will accuse you of "calling the jackrabbit a *smeerp*" and "writing a Western set in space," and after that there's nothing left to do but build up a thick skin, because the law frowns on calling out fool critics and gunning them down in the street. There is even a special pejorative term reserved for a science fiction story that has been identified *ex post facto* as being a latent Western: it's called a *Bat Durston*.

Why?

Why, in a genre that routinely pays tribute to space pioneers, is there this special antipathy for the Western? Why, in a form where the space colony revolt is a standard summer-stock set-piece, is the American Civil

War and its aftermath strictly off-limits? Why, with all of human history and all of known literature to draw on for source material, is this one particular historical period and one body of folklore so rigorously forbidden?

Why, in science fiction's critical/literary/academic/pretentious circles, is Jonathan Swift's *Gulliver's Travels* considered an important antecedent to modern speculative fiction, while Mark Twain's *A Connecticut Yankee in King Arthur's Court* is not?

To understand the answer to this question, we must travel back to the beginning. . . .

No, not back to Verne and Wells. If you were to hop into your Wayback Machine and travel back in time to discuss science fiction with Jules Verne and H. G. Wells, you'd overshoot your temporal destination and they wouldn't know what you were talking about anyway. Jules Verne considered himself simply an adventure story writer, and while he's best remembered today for *20,000 Leagues Under the Sea*, he also wrote mysteries and satires, and it was the stage performance rights for *Around the World in 80 Days* that made him rich in his lifetime. Similarly, H. G. Wells called his early stories and novels "scientific romances," and while he did enjoy his initial success, he eventually abandoned the field in order to write what he considered more important work, now largely forgotten mainstream novels such as *Tono-Bungay* and *The History of Mr. Polly*.

No, the real history of science fiction begins, not in Europe in the late nineteenth century, but in the United States in the early twentieth, and it's mostly the story of three men: Hugo Gernsback, John W. Campbell, and H. L. Gold.

There is a curious synchronicity at work here. In 1890, the United States Census Bureau declared the American frontier officially closed, to the extent that there was no longer a discernible line of separation between settled and unsettled areas within the continental United States. In 1896, the frontier of the imagination might be considered to have officially opened, with the launch of the first pulp fiction magazine, *Argosy*. This magazine, and the many imitators that soon followed it, was in a direct line of descent from the dime novels and "penny-dreadfuls" that made legends of Wild Bill Hickok, Jesse James, and Billy the Kid. Every month it served up generous helpings of pure, unadulterated, escapist adventure fantasy to a mostly young, mostly male, and increasingly urbanized audience.

While some of the early pulps such as *The Shadow* and *Doc Savage* were simply dime novels issued in serialized format, others gave their readers a glorious hodge-podge of war, sports, jungle, railroad, horror, mystery, crime, pirate, and "scientific romance" stories, intermixed with the occasional factual article—and yes, they also ran plenty of Westerns. Genre lines were crossed and recrossed with gleeful abandon until they were mincemeat for the very simple reason that they didn't exist yet; Edgar Rice Burroughs's martians might be ten-feet tall, green, oviparous, and equipped with four arms each, and their horses might have eight legs, but in terms of behavior they were indistinguishable from any band of H. Rider Haggard's nomadic savages. Above all, the early pulps excelled in delivering what a later generation might call "that Indiana Jones stuff": lost cities, uncharted islands, vanished civilizations, and secret cults plotting terrible things, from which only broad-chested heroes with flashing swords or blazing guns could rescue the beautiful women.

In 1909, publisher, editor, and sometimes writer Hugo Gernsback launched *Modern Electrics* magazine, and to fill space he occasionally ran reprints of old Verne, Wells, or Edgar Allan Poe stories. Impressed by the positive response these stories drew from readers, in 1926 Gernsback launched *Amazing Stories*, the world's first magazine devoted exclusively to science fiction—or as Gernsback dubbed it, "scientifiction."[1]

The success—and bankruptcy, and reborn success—of *Amazing Stories* quickly led to a host of imitators: *Planet Stories*, *Marvel Tales*, *Wonder Stories*, *Weird Tales*, *Startling Stories*, *Astounding Stories*, *Thrilling Wonder Stories*. . . .

All these magazines tilled the same fields, bought work from the same writers, and played by the same rules as the older pulp fiction titles. While the genre of science fiction quickly became known as "that Buck Rogers stuff," for the very good reason that Captain Anthony "Buck" Rogers made his first appearance anywhere in the August 1928 issue of *Amazing Stories*, most science fiction stories continued to abound in that Indiana Jones stuff: lost treasures, hidden civilizations, mysterious plateaus where dinosaurs still roamed, and beautiful women who need-

---

[1] Gernsback's original term, oddly enough, did not catch on with the general public, so he later changed it to "science fiction." That name stuck.

ed to be rescued. Battles between spaceships were still as likely to be settled by boarding the enemy's ship and engaging in a sword-fight as by exchanging salvos of electro-cannon fire; the treacherous leader of the evil aliens might be a blue-skinned four-eyed reptiloid from Saturn but he still had an inexplicable lust for blonde Earth women; and the hero of a Murray Leinster tale might use an "interdimensional catapult" to journey to a new world, but once he got there the rest of the story could very well be a straight-ahead jungle adventure of the sort in which Edgar Rice Burroughs's Tarzan would feel perfectly at home.

And yes, every now and then, some magazines ran science fiction stories that looked an awful lot like Westerns.

All of this changed in 1938, when John W. Campbell, Jr., took over as editor of *Astounding Stories*. An accomplished and widely published author in his own right, Campbell insisted that science fiction readers were more intelligent than the readers of other forms of pulp fiction, therefore science fiction *writers* had to be more intelligent than the writers of other forms of fiction, and so the old-school pulp writers were no longer welcome at *Astounding*. Instead, Campbell concentrated his editorial energies on finding and developing new writers, who wrote stories in which the science was both credible and integral to the story, and in so doing he pretty much single-handedly defined what we now think of as modern science fiction.

Campbell reigned as the editor of *Astounding* (later renamed *Analog*) from 1938 to 1971, and the roll call of writers he discovered and famous stories he published during those years reads like a combined Who's Who and Hall of Fame of science fiction. Robert Heinlein, Arthur C. Clarke, Lester del Rey, A. E. van Vogt, L. Ron Hubbard, Theodore Sturgeon—the list goes on and on. And while Campbell was not the first to publish Isaac Asimov (*Amazing* gets that honor, for a story Campbell rejected), he did buy the majority of Asimov's early work, including the series of short stories that were later collected and reissued as Asimov's legendary novels, *Foundation* and *I, Robot*.

Rather less well-remembered now are the names of the 1930s pulp writers whose careers effectively ended because Campbell refused to buy any more fiction from them, as well as the names of the "slick" magazine writers whose stories he rejected on the grounds that only authors who wrote science fiction exclusively were qualified to write science fiction.[2] What we do know is that Campbell was famous for writing excoriating rejection letters, and he saved his worst verbal eviscerations for those writers he thought were trying to pass off conventional pulp stories as science fiction—especially *Westerns*.[3]

While science fiction and mystery magazines prospered in the 1940s, the rest of the pulp adventure field fell on hard times. Not only did wartime paper shortages and economic dislocations put many titles out of business, but by the end of the decade, *Terra* was running terribly short of *incognita*. There were no longer any uncharted islands in the Pacific Ocean; farewell, Skull Island and the sons of Kong. The air routes through the Himalayas were thoroughly mapped; goodbye, Shangri-La and *Lost Horizon*. There were no noble savages or ancient civilizations waiting to be discovered in the jungles of the Congo, no more mysterious cities hidden high in the mountains of South America, and getting to Mars was beginning to look like it would take considerably more effort than cobbling together a spaceship in the backyard from a discarded atomic motor and some government surplus parts. Not only that, but once you got there, the prospects for finding any beautiful half-naked Martian women who needed to be rescued began to seem pretty darn slim.

With *terra incognita* gone, then, and *astra incognita* looking increasingly unreachable, many science fiction writers began to turn to *psyche incognita*. In 1950 Horace (H. L.) Gold launched the last of the Golden Age pulps, *Galaxy Science Fiction*, with the deliberate intention of deemphasizing technology and concentrating on serious sociological and psychological stories. Unfortunately Gold also suffered from severe agoraphobia, and many writers quickly realized that they could sell to *Galaxy* by writing fiction that catered to Gold's illness, hence the large number of "domed city," "underground city," and "the whole world is just one big city" stories that dominated printed science fiction well into the 1970s. For our purposes, though, this vast body of phobic fiction is merely an unfortunate side-effect of Gold's tenure as editor. His real, lasting, and profoundly irritating contribution came in the form of these paragraphs:

---

[2] Tell that to Michael Crichton or Margaret Atwood.

[3] Strangely enough, while we have plenty of examples of the former, history does not record one single example of Campbell rejecting an Arthur C. Clarke story because it was "just another locked-room mystery set in space" or of his rejecting an Isaac Asimov robot story because it was "just another rewrite of 'The Golem of Prague'."

> Jets blasting, Bat Durston came screeching down through the atmosphere of Bbllzznaj, a tiny planet seven billion light years from Sol. He cut out his super-hyper-drive for the landing . . . and at that point, a tall, lean spaceman stepped out of the tail assembly, proton gun-blaster in a space-tanned hand.
>
> "Get back from those controls, Bat Durston," the tall stranger lipped thinly. "You don't know it, but this is your last space trip."

That's right. While it was Hugo Gernsback who named it science fiction and declared it to be a genre apart, and John W. Campbell who rejected the idea of there being any possible crossover between science fiction and other forms of fiction, it was H. L. Gold who gave that rejection its enduring name. Bat Durston first appeared in the pages of *Galaxy*—but not in an actual story. "Bat Durston, Space Marshal" was a full-page *advertisement*, which appeared under the headline "YOU'LL NEVER FIND IT IN GALAXY!" and ran repeatedly throughout the 1950s and 1960s. The rest of the ad copy went on to ridicule the idea of "a Western transplanted to some alien and impossible planet" and extol the virtues of *Galaxy* as being a magazine that published only stories "by people who know and love science fiction"—by which Gold meant authors who would never be caught dead crossing genre lines. Ergo, to answer the question we asked at the beginning of this essay: *Why*?

Because for more than fifty years now, the members of science fiction's critical/literary/academic/pretentious circles have adhered to Campbell's conceit that science fiction is somehow innately superior to all other forms of adventure fiction, by repeatedly and ritualistically beating the stuffings out of H. L. Gold's straw man.

The ironic part is, for a genre that routinely deals in stories of space exploration and colonization, the history and folklore of the American West offers a vast wealth of fascinating source materials and proven paradigms, just waiting to be rediscovered and used. It was the experience of the American West—or more accurately, the succession of "wests" that began on the Atlantic seaboard in the early seventeenth century and ended somewhere near Yuma in the late nineteenth century—that formed the uniquely American character and made the Americans a different people from their European ancestors. Even those writers who are the first and loudest to cry "Bat Durston!" routinely imbue their fictional creations with the character traits that were forged in the crucible of the American West: self-reliance, stoicism, a distrust of distant government, and a certain handiness with firearms. Moreover, it was the frontier experience that produced a uniquely American idea, and one that, however unconsciously, seems to permeate nearly all science fiction written today: that it's possible to go somewhere new, meet new people, discard the unpleasant parts of your own culture, and by blending together create a new and *better* culture.

The opening of the American West was a unique event in human history. Almost everywhere else in the world, a frontier was the heavily fortified border between two competing and roughly equivalent political powers, reinforced by centuries of distrust and cultural differences. For an unhappy Frenchman, for example, it would be madness to pack up the family and move out to the frontier, because all he would do then is end up in Germany. Only on the North American continent did the frontier—the *West*—come to symbolize freedom and the chance to escape from your past and start over. Certainly there were risks in going west—if it was easy, everyone would be doing it—but along with physical mobility came social mobility, and the environment, while often hostile, was not invariably lethal. Only in the American West was it possible to start out with little more than gumption and a few smarts, and by the grace of God and the strength of your own two hands, reinvent yourself in the image of your choice. (And with a little extra luck, get rich doing it, too!) Only in the West was *what you did* of more immediate importance than *where you came from.*[4]

Equally underappreciated, it seems, is the uniqueness in history of the American Civil War. Americans—and American science fiction writers, especially—have a strangely romantic view of rebellion. In most of the rest of human history, revolutions and civil wars are traditionally followed by the Wholesale Mass-Slaughter of the Losers, as the winners consolidate their power by the crude expedient of exterminating every-

[4] Irish and Chinese excluded, of course.

one who might conceivably oppose them in the future. Only in America did the West offer a continent-sized safety valve, where even former Confederates unhappy with the way the War of Northern Aggression turned out could find a chance to begin again.

And it is these overtly *Western* themes—no matter how vocally we may try to deny their origin—that recur time and time again in the literature of science fiction.

I suppose it was inevitable that science fiction should try to cut itself off from its pulp roots. Rejection of that which came before seems programmed into our genes. Sons argue with fathers; daughters clash with mothers; Mark Twain loathed James Fennimore Cooper. After all, science fiction as we know it today is primarily the creation of a group of young men who lived in New York in the 1930s, who called themselves *The Futurians* and thought that taking the train down to Philadelphia was a grand adventure, and who honestly believed there was absolutely nothing of interest west of New Jersey—and come to think of it, New Jersey was suspect, too.

But the conceits and prejudices of John W. Campbell have dominated science fiction for nearly seventy years now, so perhaps it's time to think about finally stepping out of his shadow. An important part of the frontier saga has always been the story of the clash between the old order, struggling to maintain control, and the new, people yearning to write their own definition of freedom.

John W. Campbell, Jr., died in 1971. Every year the World Science Fiction Society honors his legacy by giving out The John W. Campbell Award for Best New Writer, in the same ceremony in which they also honor Hugo Gernsback's legacy by giving out a bevy of Hugo Awards for various achievements in science fiction. On a different night, the Science Fiction Writers of America (SFWA) presents a battery of Nebula Awards, as peer recognition of distinguished writing.

In 2006, Joss Whedon's *Serenity* won both the Nebula Award for Best Screenplay and the Hugo Award for Best Dramatic Presentation.[5] As a

[5] Being a somewhat experienced writer, Joss Whedon was ineligible for the Campbell Award.

voting member of SFWA, it grieves me to admit that yes, I did hear some behind-the-curtains grumbling from the old guard about the fact that the Nebula was going to "a damned Bat Durston."

But I say, look. The real American frontier closed in the nineteenth century. It's now the twenty-first century. It is long past time to declare the history and folklore of the American West open for literary exploration and settlement. Bat Durston lies in a lonely unmarked grave somewhere on the windswept prairie of Bbllzznaj, where the six-legged megacoyotes howl at night, and as for me, I would rather ship out on a beat-up old Firefly than enlist in Starfleet any day of the week and twice on Sunday. It's no accident that the second most successful science fiction franchise of all time begins with these words, even though the stories rarely lived up to the promise: "Space, the final frontier. . . ."

Or as Mal Reynolds might put it, "The pulp wars are long done. We're all just writers, now."

BRUCE BETHKE was a regular contributor to *Amazing Stories* in the 1980s and 1990s, as well as to a wide variety of other magazines. A critically acclaimed and award-winning science fiction novelist, he takes strangely perverse pride in knowing that he once managed to convince the editor of *Isaac Asimov's Science Fiction Magazine* that his unabashed swashbuckling pirate story was in fact a science fiction story.

Bethke can be contacted through his Web site, http://www.BruceBethke.com.

As a Buffy *writer, I'm sometimes asked how much research we did into traditional demon myths to provide us with our villains. The answer is "almost none." We needed our monsters' properties, propensities, strengths, and weaknesses to reflect what would resonate with our characters. We needed not to research them, but to design them. In other words, we couldn't just take a monster off the rack. Something similar occurred with* Firefly. *Joss needed a war. And he needed it made-to-order. The American Civil War almost fit. Vaughn talks here about the interesting alterations.*

The Bonnie Brown Flag

EVELYN VAUGHN

Need stock villains for some escapist entertainment? You can never go wrong with Nazis. Middle Eastern terrorists also work, but then there's the messy issue of clarifying that their religion doesn't make them bad, just their zealous killing-of-people. Gang members as bad guys bring up that sticky socio-economic causal argument, and serial killers . . . well, there just aren't enough of them to provide unlimited antagonists, the implication of many television series (*cough**Criminal Minds**cough*) to the contrary.

Nope, Nazis probably remain the easiest solution, from their pseudo-historic presentation in the Indiana Jones films ("I hate those guys") to the thin disguise of the Star Wars series (c'mon—Storm Troopers?).

But before, during, and after we had Nazis, we had stereotypical southerners. Think Ku Klux Klan—unfortunately real but, at least since *Birth of a Nation*, generally considered less than admirable. Think of the Georgia mountain men/rapists in 1972's *Deliverance*. Think Simon Legree, the villain of *Uncle Tom's Cabin*, Harriet Beecher Stowe's classic novel which helped start the Civil War.

I'm guessing Johnny Reb, and versions thereof, rank in the top ten of the bad-guy list—to everyone but southerners, anyway, and we're understandably biased. In a black-and-white (no pun intended) simplification of the American Civil War, the common read is this: The mean old southerners wanted to own slaves, the noble northerners outlawed slavery, and the good abolitionist guys won.

As with most of history, there's a kernel of truth there and a cob full of truth being left out. Maybe that's just as well. Slavery's such an ugly issue, it stains all matter of discussion, to the point where attempts to objectively study Southern motivations *beyond* the preservation of slavery become almost impossible. And yes, slavery was bad. Really, really bad. But just because you had slave owners fighting for the right to have slaves in the Civil War, that doesn't mean nothing else was at stake—and it doesn't mean the destruction of the South wasn't in itself a tragedy, and shouldn't be treated that way.

Which leads us to one of the gazillion and two reasons I love the world of *Firefly* and *Serenity*. Joss Whedon doesn't rest with the stock or the simplistic, and he sure as hell doesn't overlook the tragedy. The conflict between the Alliance and the Independents allows us, at long last, to consider the devastation that was the American Civil War as someone from the South, the half most drastically affected, must have seen it. And in a great piece of synchronicity, the devastation of the American Civil War is then able to add depth and poignancy to the world of *Firefly* and *Serenity*.

How?

By editing out the messy aspect of slavery, in order to explore the sheer enormity of a conflict that continues to affect our world to this day.

The Civil War Parallel

While it's not quite as obvious as the idea that *Firefly/Serenity* is a "space Western," I'm not making any huge leaps by stating that the world of the Browncoats has some basis in the aftermath of the American Civil War. It's common knowledge that Joss Whedon came up with the idea of *Firefly* after reading Michael Shaara's 1975 Pulitzer Prize-winning novel *The Killer Angels*, about the Battle of Gettysburg. But how did he use that model?

Some of the parallels are downright obvious—consider that hoop-skirted "layer cake" Kaylee wears to a dress party in the episode entitled "Shindig," or Mal's comment to pugilistic Unification-Day celebrants:

"I'm thinking we'll rise again" ("The Train Job"). But the similarities go far deeper than a few allusions to southern fashion and rallying cries.

The words "Union" and "Alliance" are synonyms, and both reflect governments that demand a central control: "Unite all the planets under one rule so that everybody can be interfered with or ignored equally" (Mal, "The Train Job"). Both governments, the historical and the Whedonesque, are referred to as the "Feds." And the Alliance seems to have more money, greater military strength, and better technology, a point similarly made about the Union by Rhett Butler in that other Pulitzer Prize-winning novel about the South, Margaret Mitchell's *Gone with the Wind*:

> "Have any one of you gentlemen ever thought that there's not a cannon factory south of the Mason-Dixon line? Or how few iron foundries there are in the South? Or woolen mills or cotton factories or tanneries? [The Yankees have] the factories, the foundries, the shipyards, the iron and coal mines—all the things we haven't got. . . . They'd lick us in a month" (113).

Of course, the Confederates to whom Rhett is speaking refuse to believe such heresy. And Rhett himself, after the fall of Atlanta and with the war nearly lost, finds himself joining the cause:

> "Why?" he laughed jauntily. "Because, perhaps, of the betraying sentimentality that lurks in all of us southerners. Perhaps—perhaps because I am ashamed [of not joining earlier]" (382).

Which—the sentimentality, not the shame—comes surprisingly close to Mal's poignant clarification when he was accused of naming his ship after a battle he was on the "wrong side" of: "May have been the losing side. Still not convinced it was the wrong one" ("Bushwhacked").

The Independents seem to have wanted something a lot like the states' rights that the Confederacy demanded. As the teacher puts it in *Serenity*:

> The central planets formed the Alliance, so that everyone can enjoy the comfort and enlightenment of true civilization. That's why we fought the War for Unification.

Presumably, there would be no war unless the outer planets refused the Alliance's "comfort and enlightenment." In that same vein, the American Civil War has also been termed, in the South, "The War for Southern Independence" (and "The War of Northern Aggression," implying that the Union was the meddlesome side). One of the more popular songs for the Rebel troops at the time, "The Bonnie Blue Flag," puts into words what motivated these men:

> We are a band of brothers, and native to the soil,
> Fighting for the property we gained by honest toil;
> And when our rights were threatened, the cry rose near and far—
> "Hurrah for the Bonnie Blue Flag that bears a single star!"

The chorus begins: "Hurrah! Hurrah! / For southern rights, hurrah!" Clearly the fight was cast to many of its soldiers as a rebellion against insidious government control. That particular conflict, especially when removed from issues of slavery, has great lasting power—it reappears every time we debate issues from seatbelt laws to legalized marijuana. As young River Tam explains, in response to her teacher's whitewash about "true civilization" in *Serenity*:

> We meddle. . . . People don't like to be meddled with. We tell them what to do, what to think. Don't run. Don't walk. We're in their homes, and in their heads, and we haven't the right. We're meddlesome.

And River's family was on the side of the Alliance . . . at least, if the flashbacks to her even younger play-acting are any indication: "We got outflanked by the Independents squad, and we're never going to make it back to our platoon" ("Safe"). That would be right before the imaginary Independents attacked the imaginary Alliance troops, featuring young River and young Simon, with dinosaurs.

The Alliance/Independence split isn't the only parallel between *Firefly/Serenity* and the American Confederacy. Remember how often the show is called a space Western? What some people prefer not to recognize about the Western genre, whether in episodes of *Gunsmoke* or *The*

Lone Ranger, is that the majority of its archetypes hail from the Old South, the *losing* side of the Civil War, as surely as do Mal and Zoe. Consider the most prominent figure of any Western: the cowboy. Cowboys rarely hail from Massachusetts, Vermont, or New York (as the Pace picante sauce commercial used to put it: "New York City? Get a rope!"). Cowboys come mainly from Texas. And in the War for Southern Independence, Texas was the sixth state to secede (point of trivia, it's also the only state which can legally do so again). After the war, a bankrupt Texas found itself with a wealth of wild cattle and nowhere to sell them. This necessitated what would become classic cattle drives to the railheads, first in New Orleans (really!) and later in Kansas . . . known as "Bleeding Kansas" immediately before the war because of the violence that erupted over whether it would be a free or pro-slavery state. The classic Old West hookers in Kansas cow towns like Dodge City often took fake names such as "Dixie" or "Belle" specifically to appeal to the Confederate background of the Texas cowboys who were their best clients. The outlaws—and what's a good Western without an outlaw or two?—were often Confederates as well, most notably Jesse and Frank James of the James-Younger gang.

Cowboys. Outlaws. Hookers with hearts of gold. Sound familiar?

If *Firefly* really is a space Western (and . . . duh), then it's also, at least loosely, about space-southerners.

With one enormously notable difference.

The Elephant

You'll run into a lot of metaphorical elephants if you read about the Old West. "Seeing the elephant" was slang for facing the newness and thrill of the frontier and, in the case of soldiers, for seeing battle for the first time. Think of an elephant as big and exciting and kind of frightening, as well as rare for the time and place, and the symbol makes moderate sense.

This is not, however, the metaphorical elephant I want to talk about. Instead, I mean "the elephant in the room," something obvious that we could easily try to ignore—but without ever wholly succeeding. Even if nobody mentions it, you can't ignore an elephant in a small room. And the elephant in any comparison of *Firefly/Serenity* to the American Civil

War is the issue of slavery.

You may have guessed by now that I'm a southerner, by birth if not blood. Both of my parents were Yankees, but I've only lived six of my forty-three years north of the Mason-Dixon Line. As the popular bumper sticker says, "I Wasn't Born in Texas, but I Got Here as Fast as I Could."

Because of my geography, I've known perfectly nice southerners who are honestly bewildered that a symbol of their family's valorous past—the Confederate Stars and Bars—is now met with accusations of racism. I even have some sympathy for them. For what it's worth, I also have sympathy for the people who do see the Confederate flag as a symbol of racism. Go ahead and remove said flag from public buildings, by all means. *Times change.* The swastika used to be a perfectly nice Hindi good-luck symbol, but the Nazis took it over, and now it's outlawed in Germany: I don't have a problem with that, either. Yes, the Confederate flag used to be a symbol of states rights (I know, "including the right to own slaves"—I'm getting to that), but enough white supremacists have co-opted it that its original symbolism, itself perhaps naïve, is now hopelessly stained . . . assuming you believe its original symbolism had any purity in the first place.

To explain, if not excuse, such naivety, let me at least note: the majority of soldiers in the Confederacy were *not* slave owners. Feel free to ignore the suspiciously low statements by pro-Confederacy groups that "less than 5 percent of Confederate soldiers owned slaves," because really . . . bias, much? But even the suspiciously *heavy* estimates, one of which suggests that almost one third of Confederate families owned slaves, leave over two thirds of the soldiers who did not. The obvious conclusion? *Not everyone who fought for the south was risking his life merely to own slaves.* They may well have been mistaken. They may well have been misled. But at least credit those two-thirds with less villainous, if more naïve, motives: the fight for states' rights.

As I said at the start of this essay, it's an argument that gets overwhelmed with subjectivity, almost every time. And why wouldn't it? I mean . . . *slavery.*

As easy as it is in this day and age to see Nazis as evil, so it's easy to see slavery as evil. And herein lies the glory of Joss Whedon's *Firefly* parallel to the Civil War. The number one difference . . . well actually, the number one difference between the world of *Firefly* and the world of the War Between the States is the setting. Mal and Zoe's war was about planets, not states, and was fought with spaceships. But the number two difference?

The War for Independence, in the world of *Firefly*, had nothing to do with slavery.

And how do we know this for sure?

Because *Firefly* is brave enough to mention the elephant in the room.

The episode "Shindig," in particular, faces the elephant of slavery. Our first introduction to the subject was a conversation going on in a bar, as Jayne played pool with some lowlifes:

> JAYNE: Made money, huh?
> POOL PLAYER: Border planets need labor. Terraforming crews got a prodigious death rate.
> MAL: Labor? You mean, uh, slaves.
> POOL PLAYER: Well, it wasn't volunteers for damn sure.
> MAL: That why you didn't have to lay in more rations?
> POOL PLAYER: I didn't hear no complaints.

Lest we somehow missed the fact that the pool player wasn't meant to be admired, Mal picked his pocket, later noting, "They earned that with the sweat of their slave-trading brows."

Upper-class society, in "Shindig," also reflects remnants of the antebellum South. Consider the opening title card from the movie version of *Gone with the Wind*, which states that once:

> There was a land of Cavaliers and Cotton Fields called the Old South. Here in this pretty world, Gallantry took its last bow. Here was the last ever to be seen of Knights and their Ladies Fair, of Master and of Slave. Look for it only in books, for it is no more than a dream remembered, a Civilization gone with the wind.

Apparently, we can also look for this world, with its pretense at honor and its underbelly of entitlement, on the planet Persephone. Here is where Kaylee found the hoop-skirted layer cake of a dress that she believed to be so beautiful. Here is where we saw a duel over a clearly corrupted version of "honor." Here we have a glistening chandelier and pillars worthy of Tara's front porch. And here we have slaves. When Kaylee attended a glittering party in her layer-cake dress, she was treated exactly like the space equivalent of poor white trash by a clique of pampered society "ladies," at which point an older gentleman came to her rescue, targeting the ringleader of the group:

> Why, Banning Miller. What a vision you are in your fine dress. It must have taken a dozen slaves a dozen days to get you into that getup. Of course, your daddy tells me it takes the space of a schoolboy's wink to get you out of it again.

In case you couldn't tell by the kindly gentleman's comment, Banning Miller wasn't presented as any more of a role model than the pool-playing slave trader we met before. This establishes two important points. One is that in the world of *Firefly* slavery is still a bad thing, for the same reasons it has always been a bad thing despite the rationalizations of every society that ever embraced it. But the second and more important point?

Slavery still remains legal in the world where the Alliance won the war.

Clearly, the Independents were in no way fighting a pro-slavery war. Nor, considering that Mal doesn't make any blatant Alliance = slavery comments, does it seem that they were fighting an anti-slavery war. The issue of slavery remains peripheral to the independence (or lack thereof) of the outer planets.

Safe in Space

In other words, Joss Whedon has given us a world in which we can explore the tragedies of the Civil War, or a war very similar to it, without the cloud of slavery hanging over our protagonists.

We are able to see tragedy in the characters of Mal and Zoe, forever colored by their experience in the war, largely because our own culture's experience with the war affects our viewing. From the way they eat apples by cutting them first (in case they hide grenades) to their hard-won cynicism, Mal and Zoe have been changed by giving everything they had to a side that, no matter how valiant their cause, *lost*. Their story is that of the southern Confederates, but because of *Firefly*'s alternate Civil War setting, the purity of their story is no longer, as it is in Margaret Mitchell's portrayal of the South in *Gone with the Wind*, naïve. We are safe to see the vulnerability behind their resulting hardness:

> ZOE: It's just . . . in a time of war, we woulda never left a man stranded.
>
> MAL: Maybe that's why we lost. (*Serenity*)

Like Confederates, Mal and Zoe have had to re-integrate with people who do not share their experiences, or even were on the other side. Consider it: Inara, Simon, and River are shown to have supported unification. Shepherd Book, while his past remains a mystery, has an ident-card that got him VIP treatment at an Alliance base in "Safe"—treatment similar to that which the top-secret operative gets in *Serenity*. Jayne stated flat out that he wasn't in the war ("The Train Job"), and Wash's resentment of Mal and Zoe's anecdotes (in "War Stories") seemed to indicate that he, too, was on the outside of the conflict. So our protagonists, as combatants in a losing campaign, are also very much alone with their history and their lingering resentment:

> THE OPERATIVE: Our Mr. Reynolds was a sergeant, 57th Overlanders. Volunteer. Fought at *Serenity* 'til the very last. This man is an issue. This man hates us.

This is a fairly universal experience for soldiers, and a huge one for soldiers in the American Civil War—and for the entire country, afterward.

I repeat: *For the entire country*. As with slavery, our minds often veer away from the absolute devastation of this terrible war. *970,000 Americans died*, more than in all other American wars combined. Half the country—the South—was left ruined, economically damaged in a way that would not begin to heal until the mid-1900s. Lives were lost on both sides. Limbs were lost (usually amputated without anesthesia) on both sides. "Brother fought against brother" is not just a phrase from history books—*think about it*!

But many of us don't. We can't. It's just too big and awful, and for sheer safety, our minds veer away. Instead, we dismiss it. Those who suffered the most, adding lost fortunes and Radical Reconstruction to the mix, were the Confederates, after all, the pro-slavery bad guys. To feel sympathetically about them is akin to feeling pro-slavery yourself. And so even southerners, those of us who are willing to pack the Stars and Bars flag away in museums and to look to the future, sometimes repress our thoughts on the most world-changing event of its century.

But do you know what happens when people repress things? Especially experiences that, repressed or not, continue to echo through our culture like a post-hypnotic suggestion planted in River Tam's brain?

Pop psychology would tell us that, like said post-hypnotic suggestions, repressed knowledge and emotions just show up elsewhere, often in self-destructive ways. And self-destructive ways, for half of our huge American culture, could be majorly problematic.

But wait! This isn't yet another way in which Confederates make apt bad guys. It is, instead, another piece of the brilliance that is *Firefly* and *Serenity*.

By showing the pain suffered by the Confederacy, through the characters of Mal and Zoe—and by removing the issue of slavery from the mix—Whedon makes it safe to see our lost soldiers as fallen heroes. Something like the Battle of Gettysburg, the bloodiest battle of the American Civil War, is so huge that to stand, silent, at the historic site is overwhelming. We cannot fit our minds around the reality of it—three days of fighting, almost 10,000 men killed, almost 30,000 men wounded. But to fictionalize it?

> THE OPERATIVE: Serenity Valley. Bloodiest battle of the entire war. The Independents held the valley for seven weeks, two of them after their high command had surrendered. Sixty-eight percent casualty rate. (*Serenity*)

To fictionalize it somehow makes it more real, because it's *safe enough* to be real.

And what's truly fascinating is, because of *Firefly*'s obvious parallel to the Civil War, not all of that reality comes from the mind of Joss Whedon, either.

Interactive Literature

There's a theory of literary criticism which became popular around the 1970s called Reader Response Analysis. The basic idea is that literature doesn't exist in a vacuum—it is modified by its audience, each and every time a reader (or viewer) experiences it. At the risk of sounding way too lit-professorish: Each time a new reader comes to a text, a new version of that text is created.

The same can be—and is—said of works of drama. An easy way to test this theory is to find your favorite TV series from childhood, one that you haven't seen for at least a decade. Rent the DVDs or, if it's not out yet, catch some episodes on TV Land. I dare you! *H. R. Pufnstuf*. *Land of the Lost*. *ThunderCats*. Watch a few episodes and then ask yourself: Is this as good as I remember?

The answer? Probably not. But did the television series itself change? Again: probably not. So what did change? YOU! Your reader (viewer) response changed because you're a different person than you were as a child.

So what the heck does this have to do with *Firefly*? Everything! Once you recognize the interactive nature of literature, you can also start noticing the creators who use that interactivity to their advantage. Any writers who've ever used archetypes to give their characters an extra, subconscious punch, or who've ever turned a stock character on her head (like Whedon's Buffy) get the power of this.

In using a world similar to that of the American Civil War, *Firefly* and *Serenity* become the *mutual creation* of any viewer with even a passing understanding of that war.

History gives us a familiarity with Mal, Inara, Simon, and the others that makes us co-creators and so amplifies our experience of them.

On one level, we know what to expect—that's what we bring to the "reading." But then . . . then, because of that deeper starting point of recognition, the show's characterization is able to take us farther than we ever expected.

We know Mal is a Confederate cowboy, complete with the gun on his hip and the rugged individualism in his attitude. He even admitted to "Saffron," in the episode "Our Mrs. Reynolds," that his mother owned a cattle ranch. Mal's also an outlaw—consider "The Train Job," the cattle rustling in "Shindig" and "Safe," and the bank robbery in *Serenity*. All this, the writers bring to us. But what do we bring to the story?

We bring the fact that we've known Mal in other incarnations before now. Our knowledge of the standard Western protagonist keeps us aware, without having to be told, that Mal is indeed a decent, stand-up guy, as surely as Shane (from *Shane*), the Ringo Kid (from *Stagecoach*), or even Kid Curry and Hannibal Heyes of *Alias Smith and Jones*—any number of "heroes" that are also outlaws, current or former. Lines like "I don't murder children" (*Serenity*) or "I never back down from a fight" ("Shindig") just validate what we already trust, deep in our heart, because we already know Mal just that well . . . even if they're often followed by a twist, such as Inara protesting that Mal backs down from fights all the time, and Mal admitting, "Well, yeah. But I'm not backing down from this one."

We get all that because *Firefly* is a space Western. But what we bring to the story from our knowledge of real history is even more powerful. As famous as all those film and television outlaws are, they don't carry the same weight as Jesse and Frank James, Doc Holliday, or Butch Cassidy and the Sundance Kid. Because while the James brothers in particular were fictionalized in movies from *My Darling Clementine* (1946) to *Jesse James Meets Frankenstein's Daughter* (1966) to *The Long Riders* (1980), these outlaws *were not fictional*. They were real bank robbers, real train robbers . . . real innovators in both areas, in fact. We know that none of them were cold-hearted killers, and generally targeted government or big businesses (like Mr. E. Harriman, of the Union Pacific Railroad). We know they were often protected by the townspeople with whom they traded and lived because of their Robin Hood tendencies. With this knowledge, we're not surprised when our Western outlaws have fun with their crime:

> FRANK JAMES: I just need a distraction.
> JESSE JAMES: A distraction? Well, why the hell didn't you just say so?
> BOB YOUNGER: He's smiling!
> COLE YOUNGER: That's never a good thing. (*American Outlaws*, 2001)

And we need no explanation at all for why Mal, too, has fun with *his* crime:

> MAL: Hell, this job I would pull for free.
> ZOE: Can I have your share?
> MAL: No.
> ZOE: If you die, can I have your share? ("The Train Job")

We also knew that Mal would return the stolen medicine to the ailing townsfolk of Paradiso, on "The Train Job," even before he did (or, if the "trivia" on TV.com is correct, before Joss Whedon knew it—did FOX really make him add that part in?). We knew he'd help the troubled prostitutes in "Heart of Gold" and his old army buddy in "The Message." And it's not just because he's a "white hat," but because he's a man who fought a war, who sacrificed everything, for an ideal—an ideal that, unlike that of the young James brothers before their life of crime, had nothing to do with slavery.

Thus we can be wholly involved in statements like, "I aim to misbehave" (*Serenity*)—both the surface truth of it and all the self-awareness it implies about how he often misbehaves but how this time it's serious misbehavior. Why? Because with the knowledge we bring to the show, we are equally aware. And because we can come to that self-awareness guilt-free.

We can do the same thing with Inara. We bring to her character not only an existing knowledge of the standard whitewashed, fictionalized Western prostitute—like Amanda Blake's Miss Kitty of *Gunsmoke* or Joanne Dru's Tess Millay in *Red River* or Claire Trevor's Dallas in *Stagecoach*, prostitutes that always have a heart of gold. But we also bring to her our awareness of just what a civilizing force women—even prostitutes—were on the post-Civil-War frontier. We bring as well a remembrance of what true ladies, steel magnolias, the Confederate belles once were (does anyone else see a resemblance to Vivien Leigh's Scarlet O'Hara in Morena Baccarin's Inara?). All of that audience involvement gives Joss Whedon an even stronger foundation from which to provide his Whedonesque twists, in this case the fact that a "Companion"—like a southern belle—is in fact a more respectable position than that of anyone on the ship except perhaps the Shepherd. But the echoes of southern belle in Inara are, like the rest of the series, completely separate from the stain of slavery.

Other characters tap into the strength and familiarity of this alternate universe Reconstruction, letting us contribute to their reality—some more directly than others. Shepherd Book is the necessary reverend . . . one who, in as many movies as not, turned out to be a good-natured troublemaker in disguise (which made hints of Book's darker past seem downright appropriate) but who, in real life, did as much as women to bring civility to the frontier. Simon is the fish-out-of-water educated Yankee, but in this case, one without the moral superiority of having fought to free the slaves. Jayne is the double-crossing bad guy and yet, thanks in part to Whedon's writing and in part to Adam Baldwin's acting, he too surpasses his basic "Western" traits to transcend *Firefly/Serenity*'s root genre and become someone both wholly original and familiar enough to emotionally engage his audience.

In the end, *transcendence* is the perfect word for what Joss Whedon's *Firefly/Serenity* manages by presenting a similar world to the post-Civil War South but removing the issue of slavery. Just as the Reavers allow the show to give us the barbarism that settlers believed of Native Americans without the messy history of reservations and broken treaties, so does the War for Independence give the world of *Firefly/Serenity* added power. We viewers can bring a great deal of understanding—from both fictional and historical sources—to the stories. And at last, we can face the tragedy of the Confederate soldier without the accompanying vilification.

As Mal himself puts it, in *Serenity*: "Half of writing history is hiding the truth." But for this essay's purpose, he's only half right. Instead of hiding the truth, the world of *Firefly* gives us an alternative truth, less weighed down by the horror of slavery. It gives us a way to enjoy everything that is archetypal about the classic Western without having to repress our awareness of its historical shadow side.

That strengthens the world and characters of *Firefly/Serenity*. And it strengthens us.

No villains necessary.

Rita award-winning author EVELYN VAUGHN (who writes her Western historical romances as Yvonne Jocks) has published seventeen novels and a dozen fantasy short stories. She also teaches Literature and Creative Writing for Tarrant County College, in Texas. When neither writing nor teaching . . . oh, who are we kidding? She's almost always writing and teaching. And watching TV (being an addict). It helps her rest up from the writing. And the teaching.

She loves to talk about her writing (and TV), whether that's attractive or not. Check out her Web site at www.evelynvaughn.com

REFERENCES

Mitchell, Margaret. *Gone with the Wind.* New York: Warner Books, 1993.

As a movie, Serenity *is a part of the media. It is also, to a large degree, about the media. Clifton makes an eloquent, and elegant, case for* Serenity *as a call to arms, where the arms in question are critical thinking and healthy skepticism. Two of my favorites.*

Signal to Noise
Media and Subversion in *Serenity*

Jacob Clifton

The first moment of the film *Serenity* contains a powerful clue to the film's contents and themes: the logo for Universal Pictures, familiar to any filmgoer as a mainstay stretching back more than fifty years, being subtly drawn into the film itself. *For more about NBC-Universal and its subsidiaries, press "Universal." For more about its parent company, General Electric, press "GE." For a list of Universal Pictures releases, press "Movies." For information on Universal's competitors, press "Other Studios."* The logo's starry background becomes the Black, putting the Universal globe itself in the context of the show and film's 'verse itself. You could almost see it as a sly dig at the necessary use of Hollywood money in a venture that ultimately interrogates the Hollywood system itself; more cynically the studio's complacence about the film could be compared to Phillip Morris's sponsorship of thetruth.com. Earth's iconic blue and green surface becomes Earth-That-Was in the monologue that follows, explaining the history of the show's world in terms of the Alliance's propaganda: "Ruled by an interplanetary parliament, the Alliance was a beacon of civilization. The savage outer planets were not so enlightened, and refused Alliance control. The war was devastating. But the Alliance's victory over the Independents ensured a safer universe." *For more about the Battle of Serenity, press "Alliance*

Victories." For information on the Browncoats and their most prominent at-large ex-members, press "Marauders of the Outer Rim." For more about the Alliance, and ways you can join the mission to bring civilization to the known 'verse, press "Academy." For information on opportunities within the Alliance Ministry of Truth, press "Blue Sun."

It is no accident that the Alliance refers to itself as a "beacon"; its first duty, to itself and its culture, is transmission: of the rules, of "civilization," and—if the Alliance scientists had their way on Miranda—of true mind control. *For information on lost and non-terraformable planets, press "Outer Rim Non-Inhabitables." For more on the Reavers, press "Mythology and Legends of the Outer Rim."* By equating the studio with Earth-That-Was, and combining it with what we, as viewers, know to be a biased account, the film begins with a statement and admission of self-consciousness: an acknowledgement of itself as media output, echoed in everything that follows.

Serenity is a story about media, about the abuses of media that are possible, and more than probable in the current day, and the way that those media can be used to subvert and question the very ways in which they are used to control the population, both within the story and without. *For more about media use and subversion, press "Dada and Detournement," "Marshall McLuhan," or "FOX News."* It's a polemical film with a clear message and a hearty liberal (or Libertarian) bent, but its politics take place on a level above today's partisan complaints about "media manipulation." *For more information on media manipulation in Hollywood, choose "The Gay Agenda," "The Jewish Mafia," "Other Crackpot Conspiracy Theories," "Air America," "Rush Limbaugh," or "The Age of the Punditocracy."* The film looks instead at the properties and possibilities for media use by both the governing body and the individual, and the critique it offers favors self-determination and awareness over passivity and unthinking consumption: ideals that transcend political divisions.

In other words, *Serenity* is a movie that doesn't concern itself with political motives so much as it does with political procedure and the uneasy bedfellows it often makes with seemingly soft entertainment, seemingly unbiased journalism. The world described above is the same as that which the film's audience sees around them: a clean, happy, safe world in which everyone feels safeguarded and complacent. There's no reason to look closer, there's no sign or gap into which one might fall that would lead to closer interrogation. *Serenity* doesn't point fingers at the politically unaware any more than it does at the machinations of politics and industry for doing what they do best. It takes place in a primarily amoral universe, in which personal choice is the only sturdy ethic, and for which there are no objective bases for comparison: heroes and champions do what they must, because of what they've seen. The people of the Core Planets aren't to be decried for their ignorance, but that ignorance must be acknowledged . . . before it is destroyed. The only binary division with which the show *Firefly*, or the film *Serenity*, busy themselves is that between innocence and experience, ignorance and knowledge, secrecy and transparency: and it unequivocally privileges the latter, in each case. *For more about innocence and paradise lost, see "The Myth of Eve," also named "Zoë."*

More knowledge is always better, innocence is unsustainable without infantilization (or worse), and transparency is the key to the film's political ideals. Anything beyond the facts, and the right to make decisions based upon them, is noise in the system, meant to obscure and control. In an anarchic or nihilist story-setting, we'd see government itself as the noise in the system; here the only true signal—the truth inside the noise, the motivation for the crew's political action—exists to shore up a failing, "noisy" political structure, righting its course in the name of freedom.

But the story of *Serenity* hasn't started yet; we are still in the prologue. A short conversation among schoolchildren, questioning the basis of these assumptions, becomes River Tam's fever dream during her abuse in the Academy—and we are again asked to look at the world of the film as a media construct, as this sequence too is betrayed. Her rescue by her brother Simon, and thus everything previous to the moment of their escape, is revealed to be a surveillance video being watched by the Operative. *For more information on self-created belief systems like the Operative's, or Malcolm Reynolds's, choose "Bushido," "Stockholm Syndrome," "Atheistic Sour Grapes," "Existential Black Marketing," or "Post-Traumatic Stress Disorder."* We learn the truth that we, as viewers, have been seeking since the show's first episode: why the Alliance is so interested in recapturing River. Her secret is the secret of the Alliance itself, gained by telepathy—a kind of interpersonal media exchange—which we learn later is the Pax experiments on Miranda that created the Reavers.

Again we see this idea of secrets as sickness, in the comparison of River's severe mental illness to the Alliance's hidden rot; both River's true, magnificent intellect and the beauty of what the Alliance has accomplished are obscured by layers of lies and (it's said) psychosis. Her secret is most plainly illustrated as a blockage to normal functioning, and as above, so below: the same secret, and the human error behind it, has created the Reavers, every bit as wild and uncomprehending as River in her worse moments. (The linguistic difference, it's been noted, between "River" and "Reaver" is negligible at best: they are siblings, children of the Alliance, connected every bit as closely as Simon and River herself, by blood and by the Alliance's paternalistic meddling.) In this way, as another weapon of the Alliance gone wrong, we see that River is her own secret: the information poisoning her, for which she is being chased, indicts both Miranda and the Academy itself. River herself describes the shape of a feedback loop—no wonder she's so hard to understand! In acting as both the transmitter and the message, both the truth and the lie hiding the truth, she confuses the signal even further. Not even the government that created her can be sure what she'll do next. *For more information on telepathy and psionics as specialized media and/or political hot potatoes, please press "Joan Vinge," "Psi-Corps," "Dark Phoenix," or "The Dead Zone."*

The fact that we finally learn the nature of River's secret during the most complex and graceful jumps from context to context of the opening is not unimportant: River's journey, and her cathartic release of this secret's burden ("buried beneath layers of psychosis," it's said), are accomplished in a similar movement through layers of lies and media, like peeling an onion. *For more on the cathartic release of denied and/or repressed secrets, please press "Wilhelm Reich," or "Carl Jung." For more on psychotic onions as a therapeutic model, please press "Inanna's Descent Into the Underworld," "The Myth of Orpheus," "Buffy the Vampire Slayer: 'Spiral'," "Grant Morrison's The Invisibles," "Wonderfalls," "Good Will Hunting," or even "The Prince of Tides." If you'd like to learn about other incidents of cathartic release, population awakening, and political empowerment, and if you would like to cry some tears of joy, please press "V for Vendetta," or "Buffy the Vampire Slayer: 'Chosen'."*

We are presented at first with baseline River, weird and uncanny, familiar from the show. At the Maidenhead, thanks to the Alliance's subliminally coded advertisement, we will be given a new level of violence—and a new level of understanding, as the first clue in the story's unraveling is presented: River's violence itself, and Miranda. On Miranda, through *another* recording, we'll learn the secret of the Reavers, and River will cough out the virus that's plagued her since the moment recorded at the beginning of the film, returning to sanity. (She'll still be weird, but she was weird well before the Alliance found her.) Finally, Mal and the *Serenity* will take this information to the skies in order to bring down the existing system and create a new world, without all the Pax and lies and secrets that caused the disease in the first place.

Also note the way that the story begins by moving from monologue to seminar discussion to dream to rescue to recorded account, in a way that would be impossible if we were not watching a movie, a media product: parts of what we've just seen would have been hidden from the Operative. That was a story constructed just for us, in order to sell us on the film's central conflict: before the politics, before the media theory, there's a violent man looking for a girl, and there's her brother that saved her. This is the first emotional hook we're given, as viewers new to the *Firefly* 'verse.

Free of the competing layers of propaganda and storytelling devices (for now), we are given our reintroduction to *Serenity*'s crew (in a continuous, luxurious tracking-shot, itself self-conscious as a well-known filmic technique, further twisted by the single concealed break halfway through). *For more about continuous tracking shots, please press "Hitchcock," "Altman," or "Welles."* A typical mission reacquaints viewers with the crew of *Serenity* and their means and philosophy—and provides the audience with their first close Reaver encounter, as well as a reacknowledgment of River's stranger behaviors and physical feats—and soon enough we're on our way to Beaumonde, to meet Fanty and Mingo in a bar called the Maidenhead. Given that we've already established the importance of one maiden's head in particular, and what it contains, the significance is apparent; the word's obvious primary meaning, that of the hymen, a symbol of innocence, also comes into play throughout.

In a story about the revelation of information and the loss of innocence, which itself privileges the experience of its world-weary crew over the stupor and complacency of the Core Planets, the bar's name is a multilayered sign that the revelations have begun. *The word "virgin" is derived from Latin* virgo, virginis; *the roots of this word lie in vir, meaning man or husband, and genere, meaning "created (for)." For more about the virginal literary character Miranda, including information on her father Prospero, who controlled the thoughts and minds of everyone on his island until finally being shown the error of his ways, please press "The Tempest."* In the Maidenhead, the world changes: not just for River, who is able to access the word "Miranda" along with her most violent tendencies; not just for Simon, who premieres River's "safeword"; not just for the crew, who are forced once more to reevaluate Simon and River's place among them; but for the audience itself: no more secrets. This movie will, at the least, explain what all the River fuss was about!

For all practical purposes, the vid screen in the Maidenhead is our first real look at media in the 'verse: repetitive, *kawaii*, sing-song, and uncomfortably close to our own present-day advertisements and disguised-advertisements. Across the whole *Firefly* series, media entertainment was rare, to the point of being almost nonexistent. "Cortexes" were presented as primarily communication devices, and mentioned most often in connection with Simon and River's schooling: more innocence, more received information. Of course, this media entertainment contains a coded message for River, designed to send her berserk and drive her out of hiding, which is what it does, alerting both the watching Alliance—and those that watch the watchers—to her position. It's only the Alliance's safeword, uttered by Simon, that blocks the threat River becomes: "*Eto kuram na smekh*!" means "enough to make the hens laugh." Colloquially, it implies the kind of accusation and ridicule that brought everyone's attention to the Emperor's New Clothes, or rather the lack of them—and as we'll see, that moment of doubt, the kind of strength required to laugh in the face of power, is an unimaginably strong weapon. *For more about this quaint tale from Earth-That-Was, please press "Hans Christian Andersen."*

In all River's nightmares, in her suicidal requests to Simon that he never use the safeword again, we see a continuing image: that of people, children, lying down, to go to sleep. This is an internal image of a real, tangible physical event: River's secret itself. As a metaphor for both the people of Miranda and the people of the Core Planets, it's incredibly useful, but in terms of the developing media story here, it's also important to note that River is only "put to sleep" with the safeword once, and that it terrifies her. With her secret buried so deep, her fate tied so strongly to the Miranda victims (both the sleepers and the Reavers; she's an index of both), it's no wonder that she fears lying down and sleeping against her will so strongly. We would do well to emulate her.

The incident in the Maidenhead brings us to the character in the film most intimately tied to media and its use and abuses: Mr. Universe. Mr. Universe introduces the central media theme of the film for the first time explicitly: "There is no news. There's the truth of the signal: what I see. And there's the puppet theater the Parliament jesters foist on the somnambulant public." It doesn't get any clearer than that: Mr. Universe takes the noise and signal of the entire system, and condenses it into truth. "Can't stop the signal, Mal. Everything goes somewhere, and I go everywhere."

(To step sideways for a moment, to a slightly different but no less political 'verse, consider Buffy's Faith, and her reflex self-declaration: "Five by five," a reference to signal quality. It's the measure of a given signal's strength [from one to five] and clarity [from one to five]: a way of stating the ratio of signal to noise in the system. Optimal strength, optimal quality, are not possible unless steps are taken to eradicate the noise from the system. There are psychological, political, philosophical—even theological—antecedents; from classic analysis to revolution, to deconstruction and Gnosticism: only in this space-cowboy 'verse could the technological be so closely tied to Faith's emotional ideal.)

Names are, as usual in a Whedon story, central: Mr. Universe takes the "five-by-five," "everything goes somewhere" concept to the highest possible level. He is open, though his media technology, to all the received wisdom and media that the Alliance can provide. Only by maintaining an internal state of simultaneous awareness and discernment can he possibly filter out the noise and perceive the signal. It's this self-aware and self-empowering state toward which the rest of the movie—and the characters, most obviously River—will work itself, and which is most profoundly a state of political awareness. Mr. Universe is able to acknowledge the entirety of the system—both signal and noise—in order to discern a higher clarity: he sees meanings in the patterns, spikes, blips, and anomalies that a more casual (or complacent) viewer would disregard. The lesson that we, and the crew of the *Serenity*, learn from Mr. Universe is to listen to the universe herself—the signal *and* the noise—and how to tell the difference.

By discerning the clarity within the signal itself, and questioning—or flouting, or exposing, or disrupting—the noise of the Alliance's propaganda, *Serenity* becomes a beacon of reconstruction: a transmitter of the true signal, of freedom and clarity. In fact, what Mal, River, and Mr. Universe design—chaotically, to be sure, and without ever agreeing on it aloud—is a feedback system: by reintroducing the clarified signal to the system, *louder than everything else*, the complacency and openness to control that defines most denizens of the post-war 'verse becomes in itself a political weapon. Just as the Operative requires only a sit-down viewing of the Miranda tape to lose his complacence, we're left with the feeling that *Serenity*'s crew can change the world simply by putting the right truth in the right place. If the Core Planets are Muzak, and Miranda the sound of tombs and beasts, *Serenity*'s pure rock and roll. With *Serenity*'s help, the Alliance and Rim can begin to readjust for their political and scientific excesses, rebuild in the wake of their violence, and return to Mr. Universe's natural five-by-five state.

On Miranda, the sequence of events involving media in the first half of the film—the nested scenes that introduce us to the characters, the subliminal commercial in the Maidenhead—are one by one reversed, each time through the power of transparency and open secrets; peace is restored and innocence is destroyed, in equal measure, by the sharing of secrets. Evidence of the results of the Pax experiments—or to my mind, the experience of sharing in this proof with her new family—releases River from her burden.

Pax is revealed as a new prototype form of population control, a chemical pumped into the air processors on Miranda that caused almost everyone exposed to "just lay down." As it's described, first for the *Serenity*'s crew and later for the Operative: "The G-23 Paxilon Hydrochlorate . . . was supposed to calm the population, weed out aggression. Well, it works. The people here stopped fighting. And then they stopped everything else. They stopped going to work, they stopped breeding, talking, eating. There's a million people here, and they all just let themselves die."

The remaining tenth of a percent reacted less passively: "Their aggressor response increased beyond madness," we're told, and they became Reavers, butchering and abusing the survivors before taking to the skies. Certainly a population under the sedation described could conceivably do one or the other, perhaps to exclusion: either to rage or to lie down and die, but certainly not to live, at least as fully as we might desire.

As a metaphor for the unquestioning consumption of media, it's not entirely off-base. The comparisons to our own media culture, sci-fi luminous though they may be, are clear: setting aside high- and low-culture boundaries, the truth remains that any media product, consumed unthinkingly, leads toward either stupor or mob thinking. The repression of societal elements such as violence or sexuality forces those elements to find their way into the expressions of culture, creating a warped mirror effect in which the difference between life onscreen and life out here is either dissonant or frighteningly isometric. We are defined by the stories we tell, and by the stories we hear: stories are the way a culture defines itself. A media culture under the grip of industry, government, or any other paternalistic influence designs its own downfall, expressed in the lives of its constituency. Citizens of a culture that doesn't change, or move, don't fall down together. They fall apart.

If Pax is censorship or simply journalistic bias, nine-tenths of us will sleep and one-tenth will rage . . . unless somebody speaks up, reminds us that the culture is us, and we are the culture. That the Emperor wears no clothes, and that we are, in turn, the Emperor: if consumption is "voting with dollars," then media culture is the true representative government, and it's in our best interest to vote well, and alertly. In the *Firefly* 'verse, it's River who provides the way out: by expressing and sharing the secret, by clearing the signal of its noise, she's in effect reduced its deleterious effects to a minimum, leaving only strength and psychic power. Five by five.

After River's freakout in the Maidenhead, the crew peels its own onion, so to speak, being led down the rabbit hole into the genesis of the Reavers, and a new calling: "This is what they feared she knew. And they were right to fear. Because there's a whole universe of folk who are gonna know it, too. They're gonna see it. Somebody has to speak for these people." This is the moment the signal is first picked up for transmission; this is the moment that River's sickness reverses itself and becomes the key to redemption for every person on *Serenity*'s crew. Led by Mal, the crew returns to Mr. Universe's base to transmit the truth they've found, only to encounter both the Operative and Reavers—both sides of the Pax equation, the sleeping and the raging wakeful—blocking the way.

As a newly empowered and uncrazy River fights off her Reaver brothers to save what's left of *Serenity*'s crew, Mal is able to transmit the signal to a most unlikely receiver: the Operative, a man described earlier by Inara as ". . . A believer: intelligent, methodical, and devout in his belief that killing River is the right thing to do." He is defined by this belief, and by this mission: his name marks him only as a tool of the establishment, with no signal inside the noise. Compare the Operative to Mal, for a moment: He is a hollow man, a believer, a swallower of the message. No amount of intelligence or method can balance the damage of unthinking consumption; intelligence only increases that consumption's potential impact.

We are shown the Operative's dedication to duty and the rules that Mal regularly flouts during his introduction in the film's opening roller-coaster ride: he's a man of honor, like Mal, but one who fully supports the Alliance and its aims, in the belief that he is cleaving to the right. When Mal forces him to watch the Miranda tape—"your greatest wish, a world without sin"—he is taking the Operative's innocence, just as our own was taken, with River's, in the Maidenhead. Deprived of the noise on which he's built his life, confronted with a signal whose clarity is nearly blinding, the Operative seems to lose all spirit: to lie down like the people of Miranda, and give up. But the battered crew of *Serenity*, the survivors and the newly sane, have gained the strength and power of a true calling: the transmission of the signal, the awakening of the known 'verse to freedom.

Whereas the truth about Miranda—the Pax video—is what ceased River's suffering, here it is the thing that causes the Operative to lose all sense of self: the Operative is opposed to River not only in method and perceptual paradigm, but finally in his placement within the system. Asked by the facts to consider the larger picture, and his place in it, he finds that he has been too long complacent, a carrier of the noise, and he is destroyed. The purification which was River's redemption has an equal but opposite effect on the Operative. The removal of the Alliance's influence left her with the universe as it truly is, whereas left without the infallible Alliance's help to comprehend the system, the Operative finds he has nothing left.

It's no coincidence that "River" takes over the pilot's console from "Wash" after his death, nor that their final flight in the film is through rain and into the sun. By taking on this alchemical work after Mr. Universe passes on, the crew of the *Serenity* become alchemists in their own right, breaking down destructive patterns (Mal and Inara) and unnecessary barriers (Simon and Kaylee) in order to attain a higher degree of functionality as a working group. We see again this idea of the signal, of that clarity that can't be stopped by adversity, or authority, or even death, in Zoe's and the crew's strength and determination to carry on after so much is lost.

River, once the living embodiment of the system's noise, now the signal's avatar, pilots the Firefly in tandem with Mal, his faith in himself and his mission reborn; Mal has a clear war and a clear goal, for the first time since the Battle of Serenity. "Independent," a word and concept which nearly laid down and died after the war ended, is itself reborn, in holy disobedience: framed in light, Mal heads into the future he himself declared, before Miranda: "I aim to misbehave."

If *Serenity* is a polemical parable, it's also a didactic one, and a cautionary tale. As media proliferate and recombine, as the lines are blurred between our computers and telephones and television—even our science fiction blockbusters—it becomes easier for us all to sit still: for our people, like those of Miranda, to lie down and never get up again. There's an incentive for both the political and industrial quarters to accomplish this kind of unthinking consumption on all levels; in a 'verse of governmental and sociological systems held accountable by no one other than the people whose lives they structure and vice versa, which is to say an amoral universe in which things happen according to laws and algorithms, supply and demand, the market cannot be indicted on the merits. It's not enough to rail against capitalism, or government spending, for doing what they do best, which is to grow and to consume, in their turn. Politics and commerce both have as their unit of measure the human head, *per capita*; every minute that passes marks the creation of a new way to co-opt consumption, to lead the public mind to the next programmed step, to create an environment better and better suited to consumption. Even education has its place within these twinned systems, as any Academy-trained youngster can tell you. Best to be skeptical from start to finish.

The only solution is for us, as individuals, to think carefully and analytically about our entertainment, our news and media, without resting in the moral vindication that identifying these systems and decrying them can provide. It is not enough to simply swallow the highest level of entertainment, to sternly force ourselves to listen to NPR and watch PBS, and think that in so doing we can somehow change the world. That's just another kind of spectacle in which we're invited to take part. It's not the media that need changing, it's not the entertainment that has the power to change things: it's the viewers.

The burden remains on the individual to challenge and interrogate these data, in order to keep from falling under the Blue Sun's spell—but stories like *Serenity*, taking place in the area of media itself, are a necessary way of waking us up to these possibilities, and to our personal responsibilities. The mission of *Serenity*, its call to awareness and discernment, is ultimately a signal meant for us all, and in paying attention to its warnings and exhortations, we join in its mission ourselves. By taking the step beyond simply enjoying the story as entertainment, as we are urged, by taking its message more deeply into our lives, by doubting and questioning and "misbehaving," by keeping and spreading vigilance and awareness of our entertainment and its meanings, by preserving just a single moment of doubt before giving in to what we're hearing, if that's all it takes. By keeping our eyes open to propaganda and manipulation in all its forms, by taking in the transmission and retelling it anew, we perform our part of the alchemy: we join in the signal, and ensure it never stops.

JACOB CLIFTON is a staff writer for the Web site Television Without Pity, writing weekly columns about television topics and series of interest (currently: *The Apprentice*, *Doctor Who*, *Battlestar Galactica*, and *American Idol*). Excerpts of his writing have been used as readings for graduate and undergraduate classes in women's studies, media studies, and psychology. Other media credits include appearances on *E! True Hollywood Story*, commentary on media topics for *MTV News*, and several national newspapers and radio shows. Jacob lives and writes in Austin, Texas, and is currently editing his novels *Red Settlement* and *Serious Vanity* for publication.